THE SOFT CITY

THE SOFT CITY

SEX FOR BUSINESS AND PLEASURE IN NEW YORK CITY

terry williams

COLUMBIA UNIVERSITY PRESS
New York

Columbia University Press
Publishers Since 1893
New York   Chichester, West Sussex
cup.columbia.edu
Copyright © 2022 Columbia University Press

Disclaimer: All names have been changed in the interest of privacy.
All writers of field notes are anonymized. Consent to use notes in the text
has been given and permissions granted.

Library of Congress Cataloging-in-Publication Data
Names: Williams, Terry M. (Terry Moses), 1948- author.
Title: The soft city : sex for business and pleasure in New York City / Terry Williams.
Description: New York : Columbia University Press, [2022] | Includes bibliographical
references and index.
Identifiers: LCCN 2021046704 (print) | LCCN 2021046705 (ebook) | ISBN 9780231177948
(hardback) | ISBN 9780231177955 (trade paperback) | ISBN 9780231555012 (ebook)
Subjects: LCSH: Sex-oriented businesses—New York (State)—New York. |
Sex—New York (State)—New York.
Classification: LCC HQ146.N7 W55 2022 (print) | LCC HQ146.N7 (ebook) |
DDC 306.7409747—dc23/eng/20211006
LC record available at https://lccn.loc.gov/2021046704
LC ebook record available at https://lccn.loc.gov/2021046705

Cover design: Julia Kushnirsky
Cover photograph: GettyImages / Ted Thai

Contents

THE SOFT CITY

Introduction

I arrived in New York City in 1964 after traveling across the country by Greyhound bus, from the dirt roads and pine trees of Mississippi, over the rolling hills of Tennessee, through the flatlands of North Carolina, past the marble sculptures of Washington, DC, and, a few hours later, into Manhattan. As we drove through Times Square, I saw through my window the throngs of people, bright lights, and sights and sounds of the big city, which I was visiting for the first time. Where were all these people going, and where did they all come from? I would later recall how naive these questions were but, also, how Times Square would eventually become a central part of my intellectual life.

A decade later, Professor William Kornblum at the Graduate Center of the City University of New York was teaching ethnography, a brand of Chicago School sociology that was just right for engagement with the city, whose heart was Times Square. But by 1974, this was a different Times Square. I had taken an interest in sociology, particularly its ethnographic method of going out into the world, because it fit with my life at the time: adventuring, hearing and telling stories, writing notes, and discovering new worlds. I had a negative opinion of the discipline of sociology at that time and wanted to go beyond what I felt was merely academic voyeurism and into an honest engagement with the different people I met and larger worlds I encountered. I became enthralled with the darker, seedier sides of Times Square and other parts of the city and the alternative cultures that fed them and into them. I lived at night and slept by day, got up at sunset, roaming the city from Harlem to Greenwich Village.

I remember hanging out with a university colleague at a bar on West Forty-Third Street. On the surface it looked like any other bar, but after a few minutes, nuances of the "pimp" and "ho" game became apparent to my trained eye. I had learned how to "see" the hierarchy of the pimp game. For example, the women would avoid eye contact with the pimps they didn't belong to, in other words, not looking at any pimp other than the one who "controlled" them. This act of looking astray, called "reckless eyeballing" by the pimps, was a "chargeable offense" in their world. If a woman was caught "peeping" at another pimp, she would have to pay whatever fee the offended pimp requested.

At other times, rather than exploring with a colleague, I would find a "street sponsor" for my ventures. This was a person who would inform me about a new happening in a forbidden area; point me to the leader of "bottle gangs"; show me the haunts of cisgender and transvestite prostitutes, such as those who lived in the salt mines along the West Side Highway; or tease me with the latest street slang. But even more frequently I went alone to those areas of the city. I would find myself following some lead into the Meatpacking District, which was flooded with streetwalkers, hidden alleyways, and transfer trucks rocking from the action in the back. Other times I would sit in a dark corner at some dank after-hours club in Yorkville, engaging in conversation with strippers after they completed their shows. On occasion I would take a book to indicate to people that I was a student, but most of the time I didn't need to do, because people took me for who I was. It was these folk, the people of the night, the habitués of the half-world between night and day, that twilight time of forbidden tastes in a city of desire, who made the whole enterprise memorable. They invited me in, provided information, and did and said the most intriguing things.

Learning, for me, involves doing. And by engaging emerges a new way of perceiving—who, what, where, and how—the city. The night was the new frontier, and the people of the night became my raison d'être. Those who occupy the night include sewer workers doing electrical repairs, plumbers in Grand Central Terminal, truckers at Hunts Point, and the "san" (garbage) men. Then there those who live by night because there is no other place or time for them: the transvestite prostitutes, the gay men and women, the "weenie whackers" at sex clubs all live at night out of a kind of mutual necessity, and not always because they desire to do so. Some people must live at night because to show their faces in the day would be shameful. I'm reminded of disfigured indigents, people with Tourette syndrome, homeless people, and others haunted by the stigma cast upon them by daytime citizens. And then there are those who live at night because of a driving urge fed by obsession, an addiction to excitement, pleasure seekers who belong to the night world of pleasure, of vice, forbidden sex, crime, and toxicomania.

Night has its own hierarchy, one distinct and apart from the day. The night becomes a ritual, a way to focus attention, a situation where total absorption can take place. I wanted to know what went on inside, behind the drawn curtains, the iron cages, the brick walls, the dungeons underground, the rooftops, the all-gender toilets. These fringe worlds of "misfits," "whores," "toxic maniacs," and "outcasts" are arguably the flipside of our everyday neighbors, the postman, the banker, the judge, the secretary, and they had become my obsession, one of the reasons for my life in the city. Perhaps I was just curious, but I believe I was also driven by a need to see who I was and what I was made of. Since starting this work in the mid-1970s, I have been underground in the stench of the sewers, in drug spots and freak dens, in crack houses, in tunnels and abandoned buildings and five levels below Grand Central Terminal, and in many other rialtos in the city. And after peering in houses of prostitution and other places of ill repute, shaking hands with murderers and millionaires, playing cards with rapists, and shooting dice with con men, I still wanted to find out more. The need to discover the city's unknowns—or its little-knowns—became my addiction. What makes it possible to do this decade after decade is that the Soft City is always changing. It is full of expendable people: military veterans living in park hovels, opioid/heroin shooters in public toilets, and teenagers in tunnel lofts, and the former expendables would later become abandoned in nursing homes and hospice centers. It wasn't difficult to find what I wanted as a researcher in the city. In that search I have seen whole communities lost and forgotten, such as the South Bronx or the Lower East Side in the 1980s, when real estate values crashed and landlords torched building after building for insurance money. The only winners were real estate companies, slum land owners, and other unscrupulous investors. Yet throughout these many years of research, there was always something about that first experience, fresh off the bus, of discovering the existence of a different dimension of the city—the Soft City—that I could relive time and time again.

In 1991, after completing a Yale University visiting professorship, I accepted an assistant professorship at the New School for Social Research in New York City. After three years I started teaching a series of courses under the rubric of Seminars of Engagement.[1] The New School at the time was located between Fourteenth and Thirteenth Streets on Fifth Avenue, in what had been a department store building. That building has since been demolished, replaced by a modern structure, often photographed by gawking tourists. In a third-floor classroom I sat with students who had decided to join my seminar, to work together to unravel the dialectic between interpretation and experience. Ask people how they know what they know, and they inevitably respond first by saying they know through books, lectures, and media, but eventually they get around to identifying lived experience as one of the ways of knowing and even of validating the knowledge they have obtained otherwise.

Sociologists tend to overdo the distinction between qualitative and quantitative research, but, in fact, especially in comprehensive community studies, both are equally valuable. More to the point, "the numbers" have often gained us entry into social milieus that we could not have otherwise entered. The ability to conduct quantitative research has often been the key to enabling continued ethnographic research. Field research among street populations, of course, does not present the same difficulties of entry as does field research among people of wealth and power.

Shortly after joining the New School I began to experience locations like the West Village as having a more socially tolerant community. At the same time, I realized the city at large was a terrain of desire, and much of that desire was being consummated at various public venues in the Village. I began to construct maps, pinpointing establishments and locales catering to sex-related behaviors: sex-video bookstores, topless bars, gay baths, spas, burlesque houses, transvestite and heterosexual strips and strolls, lesbian clubs. I also collected more impressionistic accounts. I chose locations where people went because they wanted to be there. This distinction would lead to an observation: there is a specific difference between the kinds of sex I recorded—which was public—and the kinds of sex that were considered private. For the latter kind, I had to meet owners, discover locations, and learn the specific times I could visit. All these venues only opened after midnight, and many were very expensive to get into. Public sex provided a more accessible angle for engaging with the Soft City materializing before my eyes.

New York City is a logical place to explore sex. The city has always been in the vanguard of sexual openness and diversity. It was a center of the suffragette movement and later women's liberation. It is home to one of the largest gay populations in the world and the now-landmarked Stonewall Inn, where the modern gay rights movement began. Despite the annoying presence of Mickey Mouse, it still houses the most famous of all red-light districts, Times Square. For foreign visitors and many Americans, New York is the quintessential American city. All over the world New York City holds a special place in the minds of many people as a bastion of diversity and personal freedom. Times Square has changed and is changing—while the grittiness, the hustling hucksters dressed as cartoon characters, the pickpockets, and the dealers of one kind or another are still there, most of the sex shops are gone.

At the same time, moral attitudes often rooted in fear act as barriers to insulate people from the Soft City, since many see it as a place with threatening, challenging behavior. The Soft City is therefore not always centrally located, and it is, in fact, moveable, floating through warehouse and meatpacking areas,[2] near the waterfront, adjacent to central business districts, near ports of call, on the wrong side of the tracks, opposite cheap hotels, in regions of anonymity, in slums, in underground pockets, bordering legitimate theater areas, or flourishing in vice districts and busy rialtos. Times Square, the area formed by intersection of Seventh Avenue, Forty-Second Street, and Broadway, is both a hub of the Soft City and the heart of Manhattan, through which millions of people pass daily.

I learned the Soft City has its own coded language, and because much of what happens in it cannot be publicized in the media, it has its own grapevine to let people know what is happening when and where. Thus a kind of cognitive mapping and identifying must take place in the mind of the visitor, the tourist, the voyeur. Such maps help us make decisions about what we do and where we do it. Some cognitive maps express our predilection for personal safety, others for pursuits of a dangerous nature. This cognitive mapping is essentially our mental comprehension of a place, a collection of locations that we recall when we wish to find and satisfy desire. The compilation of a cognitive map is something we do through trial and error as we observe the world around us.

This book covers a wide range of time in the city's relationship to public sex. Some of the first notes were written by William Kornblum and our late colleague Vernon Boggs, who composed them as a graduate student working in Times Square and Greenwich Village, a collaborative process that began in 1974. This book also draws on hundreds of notes written by me and a host of others made over the course of four decades and from four locations in the greater metropolitan area of New York: at the City University of New York (1983-1987), at Yale University

(1989–1990), at Columbia University (1987–1988), and during most of my tenure at the New School for Social Research (1991–). Much of what appears on the printed page is field notes by students that capture—as best as is possible—initial encounters with the Soft City. The themes of these notes concern bars, street life, and sex in the city, and they describe what's going on in the streets of Times Square, Harlem, Greenwich Village, and other locations, revealing the intensity of street life, the hustle and bustle, the energy, craziness, and sexuality of the city.

At the synchronic level, the number of field notes and the fact that many of my contacts observed the same venues—gay, lesbian, straight, cisgender, sadomasochistic, fetish—at the same time allows for an exceptional observation of the variety of what I'm calling the Soft City; the limits placed upon the ethnographer's observation by his or her positionality fade away as one reads not one, not two, but five or sometimes more accounts of the same event.

Sometimes the variation is minimal, but often, as apprentice ethnographers of various genders, ethnicities, sexual orientations, ages, and national origins jot down their observations, the notes command the immediate interest of the reader: one event, bound by space and time, becomes multitextured. In that sense, the series of ethnographic notes, indeed the body of notes, is a witness to both the positivist, scientific dimension of ethnography and its interpretative, literary quality. The observations converge at one level and diverge at another; both the event and the observer are clearly demonstrated to entail both an objective "thing" and become saturated with meaning, and hence open to interpretation.

New York City has changed in crucial ways during the decades covered by the notes: many neighborhoods have gentrified, including in Harlem, Williamsburg, parts of the Bronx, and Queens, and the city has seen a sharp decrease in crime.[3] Perhaps unsurprisingly, both changes were accompanied by striking transformations brought by the mayors Rudolph Giuliani (1994–2001) and Michael Bloomberg (2001–2013), whose administrations produced new policies aimed at regulating sex in public spaces.[4] Changes in sex policy resulted from a 1994 Department of City Planning study that led to the 1995 Zoning Ordinance, or "five-hundred-feet rule," permitting no sexual establishment to be within five hundred feet of a school, church, park, or another sex-related business.[5] Similarly, under Giuliani, a 1998 Operation Policy and Procedure Notice issued by the city's Department of Buildings included the so-called 60-40 rule, where no more than 40 percent of the material sold in any sex shop/store can be sex related. As a result, not only has the city changed, but so have our attitudes and our ways of viewing sex. Our understanding of the role of sex in the public sphere—particularly, changes in the meaning of "sexual contact"—has changed as well. This change is no more evident than in the development of Forty-Second Street, where a kind of Disneyfication ended the agglomeration of sex shops and venues located right next door to one another.

It is important to note that the purpose of this text is not to romanticize the sex-club industry. I recognize the seedy and shady aspects of the business, from money laundering, to the exploitation of minors, to violence. The Soft City is not just the sex-club industry but an amalgam of many venues, all facets of the expression of sexual desire. I am aware of the licentious nature of some of the material put forward. I realize, too, that some readers will have strong personal reactions and will be offended, angered, irritated, and uncomfortable with the text. *Soft City* focuses on people who openly and freely experiment with their sexuality and with where and how they do so. It is not just about sexual professionals or people living terrifying lives of sexual and economic servitude. And just because something is uncomfortable does not mean we should ignore it. Some might see this as urban degradation, but I see it as that extreme moment when "the city awaits the imprint of an identity," for good, bad, or indifference. I see it as that rare moment that invites the voyeur, the stranger, the visitor, the resident, the other, to come in and play and be molded by "when the city goes soft." In the soft part of the city, once you've decided who you are, "the city will assume a fixed form around you."[6]

chapter 1
Soft City Encounters

The term "Soft City" was first coined in 1974 by Jonathan Raban in his groundbreaking portrait of London. Written nearly five decades ago, Raban's empirical gaze brings the reader on an interactive journey of discovery into the world of sex and the city, and it is in Raban's ethnographic method that this book finds its center. The Soft City is an invisible part of the city by day and a lively, excitingly risqué section by night. Its invisibility depends in part on venue, place, and function. It is "soft" because you won't find it outlined on any geographical maps or tour guides of the city. It is also a nomadic community, always moving and changing. It doesn't matter whether the physical place called the Soft City really exists or not: the people who visit, work, and live there believe it does.

After observing the city for forty years, both as visitor and resident, I have seen these soft parts of the city ebb and flow. They develop customs and institutions, standards of life, sentiments, and interests. Portions dim but then are relit by new generations of folk, who reinvigorate old areas with massive nomadic movements of desire sweeping across the metropolitan terrain. In many ways, the physical individuality of these soft areas of the city is reemphasized by the cultural individuality of the folk that inhabit and pass through these spaces. Although I can't map the boundaries of such a city, even now, after years of research, I believe in an alternative to the Hard City of urban planning and development.

What are the characteristics of the Soft City? This chapter develops an analysis of the emergence and spread of a collective sex scene, with particular attention to the structural forces and historical contexts emerging in sex clubs. "In addition, the theatrical metaphor of the word 'scene' reflects an emergent urban social-psychological orientation—that of the person as 'actor,' self consciously presenting herself in front of audiences," writes Erving Goffman. The field notes excerpted in this chapter address this social posture—the self-conscious actor—that occupies scenes, the actor who in everyday life manages impressions of self in full view of others as audiences.

Traditionally, "public places" refer to any regions in a community freely accessible to members of that community. "Private places" refer to regions where only members or invitees gather—the traditional concern for public order begins at the point where private gatherings intrude upon neighbors.[1] The entertainment zones of the city are both public and private. They present an opportunity to invite speculation into the coordinates of the Soft City. I want to address sex clubs first, since they occupy a strange status as both public and private, unvisited and revisited. The idea of expressiveness in social worlds, where people act and participate in these worlds for immediate results rather than later gratification, will take precedence in the observations that follow. In sex venues, such acts are voluntary, elitist, and available to a specific, limited, in-crowd public.

Is the private now public? Bloggers, for instance, suggest this is the case as they abet the blurring of the public/private distinction. What was once the private diary is now public. The sharing of information about oneself in a blog is an act of being private in public. This "genre" is now somewhat derisively being called the What-I-Had-for-Breakfast blog. Ultimately, the question is this: Are people just expressing themselves? Could Van Gennep's concept of the rites of passage be one way to explain behavior in sex clubs, since there is no latency period during which men and women cool out their sexual appetites? These questions and others become part of the narrative notes discussed in what follows, beginning with specific areas where sex clubs once proliferated.

WILLIAMS FIELD NOTES: MEATPACKING DISTRICT DESCRIPTION (1994–2000)

This area is now mostly covered with fancy shops, including Diane Von Furstenberg, Stella McCartney, Hugo Boss, Jeffrey's, and Armani. Some of these stores were damaged during recent riots. Historically a spot where meat marketing flourished for the city, this area used to be called the "Meatpacking District"; live cattle, chickens, hogs, and other animal produce were slaughtered on the premises. The area runs along West Fourteenth on Belgian block-paved streets past

Gansevoort Street to the Hudson River, an area roughly bordered to the west by the West Side Highway next to Tenth Avenue, to the north by perhaps Seventeenth or Eighteenth Street, to the east by Ninth Avenue, and to the south by Horatio Street.

I [Williams] can still see vestiges of the old meat market here. Marcelleria, at 52 Gansevoort Street, is one of the few remaining markets, and sitting across from the West Side Highway, immediately in view of the Hudson River, is Interstate Foods, a red-bricked building with signage reading "provisions, poultry, meats." But today, most trucks bringing meats to freezers, factories, and distributers head to Hunts Point in the Bronx.

Visually, this specific area resembles an erstwhile industrial zone, one not yet entirely spruced up. Luxury developers have taken over, and few grocery or convenience stores are found; residences in the condominiums, co-ops, and loft-type, high-rent apartments above street level abound, and there are many restaurants in the neighborhood. What is missing now are the sex houses, transvestite spots, dance clubs, and Michelle Dell's iconic Hogs & Heifers bar. One of my favorite restaurants, Markt Café, closed years ago; it is now an Apple store. Some of the newest restaurants include Valbella, Dos Caminos, Santina, and Bagatelle.

This area is surrounded by several residential neighborhoods, which have slowly encroached on its borders; the High Line, an old elevated railway line that has been converted into a public park, brings in additional tourist traffic. Private spots like the Soho Hotel and the Chelsea Hotel, slightly farther to the north, have been increasingly taken over by gentrified residents. Sex shops, newcomers to the area, have moved into some of those locales but have increasingly moved out altogether, mostly to Brooklyn and Harlem.

The Meatpacking District is now designated as historic and has been granted Landmark Protection since 2003; it is still a heavily gay neighborhood in Greenwich Village. But the West Village and WesBeth to the south remain more populous spots in Manhattan. The area of the far West Village just bordering the Meatpacking District is perhaps still populated by professionals, predominantly gay and lesbian singles and couples with kids, working in various artistic fields.[2]

In this next section I present the notes of some exemplary flaneur types, ethnographers who bring the notion of "being there" to the fore. We begin with Susan, twenty-four, nicely dressed, scholarly; her main interest is in constructing field notes. She is a fine writer, and her notes here are well placed.

CONTACT: SUSAN, MEAT MARKET "STROLL," SATURDAY (1994–1995)

10 p.m. This first "official" expedition to do field work observation in the meat market was particularly interesting to me because I [Susan] happen to live within a few blocks of this neighborhood—on Hudson St. at W12th St. This is three blocks below 14th Street, one block east of 9th Avenue. By standards of distance measured in a suburban or rural area, my block would probably be considered part of the meat market area, since it is literally within two blocks of it, but in Manhattan, neighborhoods can change within one block or one street. My block is more reminiscent of the residential, quaint Village style (the family-oriented version rather than the more heavily gay one) and seems to be if not a world away from the underground we are going to observe, at least half a world away.

I have lived on Hudson St. for two years now and am familiar with the area of the meat market. I dine occasionally in several of its restaurants (Florent—Gansevoort St. and Rio Mar—13th St., both of which I visited before living in the area), and yet I rarely find myself walking within or through the area. It is directly north and west of my block, but I am much more likely to go either south, east, or directly west—when I go north I always go east first and then north.

All of the grocery stores, cleaners, and magazine/newspaper shops and most of the restaurants I frequent are in those areas. I have often seen prostitutes on the corners around 9th Avenue and 14th St., if taking a taxi home on late weekend nights (several friends live on the Upper West Side, so the most convenient route home is directly down 9th Ave.) but have never investigated any deeper. Before going out (with Xavier and Shanti), I looked through an article that I had on the meat market area, as well as at the "Top Hat Erotica" listing of sex clubs and bars given to us by Michelle.

I knew there was a lot of "action" in my neighborhood, but I had no idea how many clubs there were. Just within the few blocks of the meat market alone (not counting all the gay and lesbian bars, clubs, etc. in the main part of the West Village) there are at least seven S&M clubs (some gay which allow women, some male only, and some heterosexual): Hellfire—9th Ave. near 14th St.; Jackie 60—Washington St.; J's Hangout—9th Ave. near 14th St.; the Cooler—14th St.; Hogs & Heifers—Washington St. and 13th St.; the Vault—10th Ave. at 14th St.; and Manhole—9th Ave. near 14th St.

Some of them are more obvious than others from the exterior, but none of them have more than a simple sign outside stating the name and perhaps a bouncer positioned outside. Most of them are industrial-looking buildings with windowless steel-door entrances that do not give any indication of what might be inside—anyone going there has to know where they are going and have a general idea of what they're going to find inside.

These are not places one just happens upon and goes into, with the exception of Hogs & Heifers, which is a corner bar and is very visible, with windows opening to the street and music blaring. (Although despite this, the neighborhood is one that few people would just happen to be wandering through, so most of the customers would seem to be regulars or those who go there intentionally). Although, after initial investigation, [Hogs & Heifers] does not seem to be S&M oriented at all.

We did not go into any of the clubs because we decided that even for the more mainstream ones, like the Vault or the Cooler, we looked much too "touristic" that night (in our jeans and earmuffs)—we decided to go back to the Vault another time when we were at least a little more appropriately dressed.

We hung out by 9th Avenue and 14th St. for a little while, but there was not much prostitute action. Perhaps it was too early or just too cold. We saw only three or four prostitutes—two of them were obviously transvestites, the others I don't know. . . . They didn't seem to be having much luck, at least during the time we were there. After walking around the neighborhood and checking out places on my list (from the exterior), we went over to 10th Avenue and walked south along the West Side Highway to Christopher St. We walked on the east side of the highway, not on the west side next to the piers, so I don't know if there was anything going on over there. There was an adult video store at the corner of Christopher and the highway and we went in to see if they had the Rick Savage: Streets of New York series.

They did, but for sale only, not for rental. They had a lot of other videos as well (heterosexual, homosexual, S&M, and lesbian) and sex toys, or accessories. They also had a room in the back with video viewing booths where you saw

100 seconds of video for $.25 and could choose from around 25 videos. We watched *Puerto Rican Blowout* for a few minutes, which was not particularly interesting. What was different here from Show World Center was that when you chose a "channel" the video would start from the beginning, including all credits, etc., so it took a few minutes just to get into the video.

At SWC the videos are "loops" which run continuously and have no credits—they go straight to the action so the viewer is not forced to spend quite as much money. What was interesting to me about this "field experience" was in terms of understandings of the space of the city and its neighborhoods, or non-neighborhoods. In this case I became a "tourist" literally in my own back-yard. Geographical proximity, or being physically located in a particular geo-graphical neighborhood, does not necessarily allow entry into a socio-cultural space or "neighborhood."

This is a kind of neighborhood, or (S&M) community, which is concen-trated in a specific geographical area (in a way which might make it appear to resemble a more traditional neighborhood) but which cognitively and in terms of individuals' participation in it as a group is not based on its geographical space. It comprises a social or cultural community. (Also, there are other S&M clubs in the city, but there seems to be a high concentration in this spe-cific area.)

Not only does geographical proximity not necessarily allow entry into this social community, but it also does not necessarily allow or impart any knowledge of such an area to a cultural outsider. Even after having lived within three blocks of this area for two years and having visited it occasion-ally for other purposes prior to this time, I was virtually unaware of the content and extent of this cultural community coexisting within my geo-graphical community.

It was invisible to me because I was not looking for it—and the nature of such an underground community (its closed, windowless doors, with simple signs, etc.), it seems, is that one needs to be specifically looking for it and already know of its existence prior to entry. Once I knew what to look for, the external signs became obvious, although the internal reality is still vir-tually unknown to me. The façade of these places does not reveal their con-tent, or interior, because that content is not explicitly condoned by the vast majority of society, although some or perhaps many of its members may in fact participate in mainstream society most of the time. And I suspect that this hidden, and illicit, aspect of these S&M clubs and this community is for many participants part of its appeal.

It is also interesting to [compare the Meatpacking District to] the characteristic of the (mainly) heterosexual, non-S&M sex world of the Times Square area, which makes no attempt to hide its external and obvious presence. In fact, [Times Square] goes to the opposite extreme to scream out its presence. It therefore attracts individuals who are specifically looking for its services, as well as those who happen to be passing by and even tourists staying in the area. Another interesting comparison to a community such as the Times Square one is that most of those establishments are in a sense passive, or one-sided, ones—there are employees who "perform" for customers, but there is little interaction between the two parties (in fact, such interaction is often specifically prohibited).

These performers are paid to entertain guests. In my limited knowledge, I understand that the S&M clubs of the meat market are places where people go either as singles or couples specifically to interact with each other (of course there may be some voyeurs there as well)—to engage in mutually desired interaction.

During protracted ethnographic research, the field worker will find certain locations where they feel most comfortable; in a setting they get to know, one with special ambience, the field worker encounters people they wish they could know more intimately. Susan brings this wistfulness to our attention in her account of the local neighborhood.

Podophilia, more commonly known as foot fetishism, is considered to be among the paraphilic disorders, meaning that the clinically diagnosed fetishist is characterized by the inability to orgasm by traditional foreplay or intercourse and relies on or needs the feet to reach climax.[3] Feet have an inherent symbolic dimension of dominance and submission. The submissive party kneels at the feet, massaging and kissing them, while the dominant party stomps, treads, and tramples. Yet despite the dichotomy, foot fetishism and fetishists are diverse. Sarana is a young woman who brings wit and eloquence to her notes about her experience

1.1 The Vault Fetish Party. New York City.

as a foot model at foot-fetish parties in New York City; she gives us a sense of what it is like to pass beyond the borders of the Soft City.

CONTACT: SARANA, FIELD NOTES (1999)

I [Sarana] attended foot-fetish parties in New York City for my personal research. A girlfriend of mine from college used to be a "foot model" and had her feet worshipped during paid sessions. I contacted her when I decided to explore this world for my own edification. She explained to me that no women attended these parties as guests, even as foot fetishists. I had to be a foot model if I wanted to get in.

I realized that if I was to do this, I would have to be completely detached from my body. I knew that physical objectification would be worse at these parties, since there would be many men and I would be standing, vulnerable in my lingerie, hoping they would choose me. This appalled and excited me at the same time. While I was doing this for research reasons, the thought of getting chosen based strictly on my sexuality, and being paid such a large amount of money for something as harmless as feet worship, was empowering.

A man chooses one (or more) girls to have private sessions with in one of the smaller rooms off of the hallway. "Ken" led me to these rooms. There were about five rooms (and two small bathrooms) extending from the hallway. In each of these rooms were smaller "curtain rooms" set up. Black curtains were hung from the ceiling and walls to make tiny, cube-like spaces for the actual sessions. Some "curtain rooms" contained a chair, others a couch, and all of them had a roll of paper towels and rubbing alcohol (for sanitary purposes, Ken explained). Ken also informed me how the party works: men subscribe to his emails for twenty dollars per month, which let them know when the parties are.

Most girls were in thongs, bras, and high heels. That was it! Thankfully I saw a few in the type of outfit that I had brought . . . a short black skirt, black bra, and a black, lace tank top to wear over it. I also had just gotten a pedicure (red polish) to match my open-toed red heels. I was set! As I changed, I overheard some of the girls' conversations. It seemed like everyone knew each other from previous parties. No one said anything to me or even acknowledged that I was there. After I changed, I noticed that the girls were congregating in the large, main room. I got a little nervous as I left the safety of the changing room. "Here goes nothing," I thought to myself. By this time it was about seven, and some guys were beginning to filter in. They all gathered in the same large room.

Some of the girls went up to talk to them, obviously knowing them from previous parties. I felt really awkward and strange standing by myself, in skimpy clothing, and wished that they served cocktails at this party. I decided to go and sit on one of the couches on the periphery of the room. As I sat down, I wondered how I was going to get any guys to have a session with me. Would they just come up to me and start talking? I also decided that I wanted to make up a fake identity. I decided on the name Ashley (the first one that came into my head) and concocted a story about recently moving to New York City from California and doing this for extra money while I looked for a job. Obviously, all of this was completely untrue.

Half of the time I was sitting on a chair and he was on the floor massaging and licking my feet. He would then switch positions and sit on the chair next to me and masturbate. At the end of our sessions, he grabbed a piece of paper towel and came into it. He was extremely appreciative, thanking me and apologizing if he had made me uncomfortable in any way. He said that he wanted to do sessions with me every time he came.

He gave me his cell number and asked me to text him if I was going to be at future parties because he would only come if I attended. He even tipped me an extra forty dollars at the end. As he pulled up his pants, he told me that he had a special request. He asked if it was possible for me to wear thigh-high stockings at the next party, explaining that he has a major "stocking fetish" and that he thinks nothing is sexier than a woman in thigh-highs and heels. So from then on, I texted him whenever I knew I would be at a party. He showed up every time and only had sessions with me. I wore the stockings he requested, and sometimes our sessions would last for up to an hour and a half. He was never disrespectful and never made me feel uncomfortable by making inappropriate demands.

He was forty years old, married, and Asian. That is all I ever found out about him. He had a trampling fetish and was more interested in me walking and stepping on him than actually touching or licking my feet. When he first asked me to walk on him, I agreed, although I really had no clue what I was doing. I took my high-heeled stilettos off (naturally) for fear that I would hurt him. However, he asked me if I would keep them on and walk on him with them on my feet. Surprised, I asked him if he was sure, and he said that was what he enjoyed. So during our sessions I would walk back and forth from his face to his penis while he lay on the floor. I felt really uncomfortable walking on his face with my pointy-heeled stilettos, but that was what he wanted. He even had me walk all over his penis and balls (they were not exposed, but I still could not believe he got pleasure from this).

I thought back to our class discussion on S/M because that is essentially what this was, just with a foot twist. We discussed how masochists get pleasure from pushing their bodies to the pain limit and how it is an adrenaline rush. After I trampled him, Ken would always sit up and masturbate until he came. It was as if he needed that pain before he could experience the release of pleasure. It amazes me that the majority of my regular customers had fetishes other than the simple, run-of-the-mill foot fetish. I never would have thought that a foot-fetish party could have had so many other sexual elements to it. While the majority of men were there for the girls' feet, a surprising number were there for other reasons, whether it be tickling fantasies, S/M activity, trampling, "golden showers," actual sex, or recruitment for other sexual-themed parties.

Sarana's field notes are an entry point. The path she travels in her mind before and during her job as a model offers some tools for how to rethink power and sex work as a whole. She starts by worrying whether she will be physically objectified if she becomes a model but finishes by feeling empowered by the money that customers will pay merely to worship her feet. Here we have a perfect expression of the power that the desired object exercises over the one who desires it.

Sarana is objectified, but that objectification also empowers her, because she is exercising some kind of power over the customer. This reminds me of how desire and objectification are viewed by Dwight McBride, regarding race in the gay marketplace:

It means articulating painful lessons learned about your value—or lack thereof—in the dominant logics that fuel that same marketplace. It means speaking about the ways in which the variables that constitute value in this marketplace—those variables of race, gender, affect ("butch"/"femme"), body type (muscle queen, gym bunny, swimmer's build, fat, slim), age, penis size, style (leather, preppy, corporate, pseudo alternative, A&F all American, boy, bear, homo thug)—all work to construct and constitute what we come to accept, and in some cases to celebrate, as our value. To speak about the gay marketplace of desire and the terms under which it produces value means having to speak about related issues around which we are taught to observe and endure a code of silence or shame.[4]

A final vignette is by Valerie, a loquacious, smart, terrific writer, twenty-four at the time of her experience. She admitted to knowing the area where the venue is located quite well. Like Sarana, she describes a sense of the social space existing at the precipice of the Soft City and captures what it means to be physically present but still distanced as an observer. She describes the social dynamics and the complexities of relationships necessarily based on transactional objectification, dynamics that reside in the background of all of the Soft City's sexualized encounters. Behavior that would be completely intolerable under normal circumstances is permissible, but what is permitted isn't necessarily desired. Even in the Soft City, boundaries need to be communicated.

CONTACT: VALERIE, THE VAULT, BEING GAZED UPON (SPRING 1995)

11:15 p.m.–1:30 a.m. I have an overwhelming sense of some kind of sheer desperation. If women are often the object of "the gaze," if I often feel on the streets (and elsewhere) of New York a heavy gaze upon me, these men at the Vault seem so desperately to want to be the object of such a gaze—someone, anyone's gaze. Milling, milling restlessly about, constantly moving through the space, hungry for attention, satisfaction—but what kind of satisfaction? Fondling themselves distractedly seems to part of the expected activity here. Many of them seem simply to want to be observed; those men are more stationary, and I saw more of them in the beginning of the evening. They would post themselves in a room, and when someone entered they would drop their pants, either posing themselves for maximum exposure or simply touching themselves.

But the majority [of the men] seem to want something more, and their movement is constant in search of that. How can I observe when I'm trying to avoid any kind of eye contact that might establish a connection? Those dozens of men milling past, I can feel the strength of their sheer will trying to exert a pull, a magnetic influence on my gaze—pulling it toward them—as if it were a real, material thing itself. I feel it necessary to fight against that. A strange kind of role reversal. Often enough, on the streets of New York, I feel myself the object of unwanted, violent (what I consider nonsexual in its violence) attention. But here, it is these men who openly want themselves to be the object of attention. At the same time that I feel the need to avoid contact with them, I feel a certain sadness that here I become the possessor of power—a power which I neither want taken away from me outside this space nor want to gain inside it.

The Vault: my destination. What do I know about it? I've read that it is a multilevel heterosexual S&M club located in the meat market, about four or five blocks from where I live on 14th Street and the West Side Highway. I have mentioned to many of my friends that I will be going there. Many of them are nonacademics and find it amusing, somewhat interesting, or a little strange—but the majority of them have heard of the Vault, and some know people who have gone there. A few agreed to come with me. Even the owner of the clothing company I work for knows of this place. It has underground, controversial connotations, but simultaneously it is known in more mainstream, "fashionable" New York culture.

We arrive at 11:00 p.m. to meet the rest of my group. We wait on the street outside, probably conspicuously, with the others. After about fifteen minutes we are ready to go in. We are told that we are not allowed to carry weapons, cameras, or mace and are half-heartedly searched before entering. The normal entry fee is $35. The entrance is down a flight of stairs from the street, into a basement space. I feel a sense of disappointment, or anticlimax, after having mentally "prepared" myself for some kind of scene I imagined we would enter. The room we enter is fairly small and is practically empty, except for our group of a dozen. It is square, with columns in the center and a square bar placed at the center of the wall opposite the entrance. It is painted black, the lights are slightly dimmed, and there are black lights, which cause anything white to glow. Music is playing, but not too loudly. Along the wall to the right of the entrance is a table and beyond that a coat-check room.

A large woman, wearing a black cotton Lycra unitard with the bodice cut out, exposing her large chest, is standing in the coat-check room. Along the wall to the left of the entrance are padded banquettes divided every four or five feet. In the center of the room are a few objects I don't pay much attention to at the moment but later see are some kind of wooden "rack" (a wooden frame with manacles toward the top). At the far left are signs for a men's and a women's room. There are about ten other people in the room aside from ourselves. We stand and talk with each other for fifteen minutes or so, and I wonder when something might happen. Of course, it is early for many people to be at a New York club on a Saturday night.

My friends have gone walking around and come back, having found other rooms where apparently more people are. They tell us to go and simply sit in these other rooms. I walk over with my friends to that side of the room and discover that there is another medium-sized room (with some kind of seat or bench placed in the center of it) and a smaller, long and narrow room off the side of that room. The smaller room has a metal cage (bars sectioning off a square area approximately six feet by four feet) against the wall opposite its entry and a long padded bench or banquette against the same wall for the rest of the length of the room—perhaps fifteen feet. This room is approximately eight feet wide by fifteen to twenty feet long. The wall opposite the one with the bench is completely mirrored. A video game console stands against the mirrored wall at the far end of the room.

As we walk into this room, a man is standing next to the metal cage with his foot raised on a stool or something. He has removed his pants and seems to be making sure that he is exposing himself to our view. We file past him and go sit on the bench at the far end of the room. The three of us sit down and begin to talk with another mate sitting to the other side of him. A man comes and sits on the bench next to me, pulls out his penis, and starts "playing with himself." I can sense him repeatedly looking in my direction, wanting me to look at him. I suspect that he wants me to observe his actions so that my eyes can provide the satisfaction he does not seem to be able to get. But I cannot and really do not want to grant him this. With the opposite wall mirrored, I have to work hard not to look at him and to find another place to look—I look everywhere except at him or his hands. Finally, perhaps realizing the exertion of sheer will was not going to be enough to get me to look at him, he speaks to me—"Is this the first time you've come here?"

With this I can no longer "deny" his presence beside me. A connection is made, which, out in the "real" world, I might respond to or might completely ignore, depending on the situation. But here, this reaction does not seem possible—I have not only chosen to come to this place, have paid for the privilege of doing so, but am also meant to be doing fieldwork. As a result, I cannot pretend disinterest or simply dismiss him as some pervert (which is the reaction I had when something similar occurred on a New York subway car). I am here to do "fieldwork," to observe objectively the behavior going on around me. But "simple observation" is not possible and perhaps for the simple fact of existing, observation and the observer (in this case myself) cannot be detached from the experience—unless perhaps the observer is enclosed and hidden from the view of those being observed, in which case the observer is actually removed from the situation and the experience, or action, itself. Thus the "participant observation" of anthropology is not only a desired part of gaining knowledge; it is an essential and inescapable part of that knowledge—it is the experience itself through which knowledge is gained. That process is thus necessarily a "personalized" one. The reactions, the information or insights gained, are obviously an intimate part of the experience as well as the life and worldview of the observer.

I turn, look into his eyes, and politely respond to his question—"No, I haven't been here before." I immediately look away and have still succeeded in ignoring his hands. He speaks again in a perfectly nonchalant, polite manner and tells me that the place becomes much more active by 1:00 a.m. and that there would be a lot more to look at then. I, again, look at him, smile to acknowledge this information, and look away. We sit a few moments more, then get up to leave through another door at this end of the room.

I am here to observe human behavior, to try and learn something about human nature, about the culture in which I live, and in particular at this moment, about the subculture congregating in this particular club. But in this case observation and participation, quite literally, mean that I become a sexual voyeur—observation of the act, in fact, constitutes participation in the act. What does this mean I'm participating in? Are the observations invalid or insufficient for meaningful analysis if I am not actually participating? Or am

I actually observing (and therefore participating) since I am seeing what is going on, without trying to openly stare at anyone?

While I want to observe and know everything that is going on, I find that I do not necessarily want to be a participant in those activities. I am not interested in making moral or value judgments, and I suspend as much as possible my own personal ideas regarding appropriate behavior, since I do not want to judge the behavior but rather explore what its significance might be and why it exists. But the process of divorcing oneself from oneself becomes more difficult the closer one gets to deeply ingrained beliefs and mores.

To do the work I am here to do means I should not get up and walk away. I should stay and talk to this man (who in any case has been pleasant, seems genuine, and obviously poses no physical threat to myself), to try to discover his motivations for coming here and illicit his observations of his own experiences. But to do so means that I engage in his sexual act. It is much easier to do fieldwork (to make observations) at someplace like Show World Center because there is no expectation by the customers that I might participate in any of the activities with them. In the video booths I can watch the videos, observe people going in and out. In the live shows I can watch the performers and observe the customers watching those performers—I can make dispassionate and detached observations of activity going on around and in front of me and can "participate" to a certain extent by going to the place (entering into that "world") and physically placing myself in the audience in the position of the viewer to get a vague idea of what their experience might be. But at the Vault, observing in this manner, I suppose I can observe superficial behavior, but what am I really learning about the experience of these people from their point of view? Why they are there. What they are expecting to find or experience. What kind of satisfaction they get from the experience.

I have lived in Manhattan for thirteen years, and although I am still amazed every day by something I see or experience in the city, I have nonetheless simultaneously developed the blasé (perhaps protective) attitude typical of New Yorkers, which only comes out in me in certain instances. At the Vault I find this tendency surfacing—to remain cool, detached, and unaffected no matter what I see. I suppose this is also an aspect of trying to be an "objective," "scientific" observer. I refuse to be phased by the fact that the man sitting next to me is "jerking off" (or really to even acknowledge to him that I notice he is), and I carry on a polite, superficial verbal exchange with him, the tone of which is not unlike a conversation one might have with the person next to oneself in the supermarket checkout line. And in reality, being a New Yorker, I'm not actually shocked—definitely surprised and, yes, interested, but not shocked.

We sit for fifteen or twenty minutes in another area and then decide to go upstairs, where I have heard only couples are allowed. Up two flights of industrial metal stairs is a heavy-looking door with a sign outside reading something like: "No fellatio, no anal intercourse, only male-female couples, etc." Again, we wonder what we're going to find on the other side of the door. We open it only to find a large room with a bar to the left, some small tables, and a "stage" area with a small video screen on the wall to the right (behind the stage) where porn films are playing. There are two or three other couples sitting at the small tables talking. We sit down and talk for a while. Anna and a friend come up later, and we stay for perhaps thirty to forty-five minutes. The music playing is a very annoying, continuous, and repetitive beat. It is one track that plays over and over the entire time we are in this room. At the bar there are also a few trays of (unappetizing-looking) food laid out. Nothing seems to be happening here so we decide to go back downstairs.

It is now close to 12:45 or 1:00 a.m. There are many more people downstairs, and everyone is moving about. In the center of the larger of the two smaller rooms is some kind of bench. There is a brown leather seat, which resembles a bicycle seat, and a backrest on the same horizontal plane as the seat, about three or four feet above the floor. A man is reclining on this seat and backrest with his back to the floor. He is naked and wears only some silver metal chains around his wrists. The coat-check woman is standing next to him, speaking to him and rubbing his chest while he is touching his penis. Neither of them seems to be very excited about, or sexually aroused by, what they are doing, and it seems more like they're just chatting. Many of the customers are watching them. I do not know if the two "performing" are paid by the club to do so or not—it seems very likely, but I did not ask. After about fifteen minutes the man gets up, puts his clothes back on, and they both leave the room.

In a corner of the same room is a video screen where S&M porn films are playing. There is also a couch against one wall where a group of people are sitting. There are a few women and about three or four men. One of the men starts kissing and touching one of the women. I cannot see exactly what is going on because all of a sudden everyone in the near vicinity surges toward them to watch. I move a little to the side and continue to observe all the other people walking through the room. I have the sensation of constant movement. Few people are standing still, as we are. Most of the people seem to constantly be circulating, moving through the space. Most of the customers seem to be white males, ranging from late teens to fifty or sixty years old (although the majority seems to be in their late twenties to mid-thirties). The ratio of men to women seems to be roughly eighty/twenty (or perhaps seventy/thirty).

I start to notice that nearly all of the men are walking around with their flies unzipped, touching themselves or just letting their penises hang out. They continue to walk through the rooms in this manner, seeking something. Being one of the relatively few women there, I feel a sensation of their desire to be observed, to be looked at. Most do not approach or actually say anything to me, but they do not need to—the strength of their wish is heavy and intense in the air. This is the single strongest sense I have the entire evening—this heavy pull of their will to look at them as they pass—which as I am trying to observe what is going on, I am simultaneously trying to avoid. This is no easy task, because there is almost no place left to look. More surges of movement happen from time to time. Every time there seems to be any kind of activity between two or more people everyone around them surges forward to watch.

Sound in the Vault seems to have a strange character—one I do not expect in this environment. In most discos or clubs the music is so loud that it seems to fill every space and to seep in between not only empty physical space but also around the spaces between people's movements and actions. Voices are completely drowned out across any distance greater than that between mouth and ear nearly connected.

At the Vault it seems more like being at a party in someone's basement where the music is coming from the next room. I can easily hear voices, footsteps, and the other background noises produced by human activity that normally disappear in a club environment. As a result it seems that everyone walks around hushed—removing their clothes, touching themselves, walking around, and looking around—they almost seem embarrassed by the noise they make and speak very little. This is a physical and cultural space where "standard" social norms of acceptable or appropriate behavior (sanctioned behavior) have been suspended or altered. Upon crossing its threshold the rules are changed. Outside it is considered clinically "perverse," or "sick," to get sexual pleasure from pain, from self-exposure, from voyeurism (or even from a stranger). It is unacceptable for a man or woman to expose their sexualized body parts in public. But inside this space it is conveyed that those rules do not apply and are invalid. Somehow a new, and quite different, set of rules (because there are still rules—chaos does not reign) has been devised and been communicated to and agreed upon by the participants. There is still a code of behavior, but this code is very different from the accepted norm. At about 1:30 my friends and I decide to leave. We go out, and they walk me to my door five blocks away. It has been a very interesting evening, and I cannot stop thinking about what I have seen and the sensations felt.

Valerie emphasizes a crucial aspect of the situation: when others respond to our expression of human sexuality by gazing at us, they validate our feeling to be desired, to be the object that arouses others. This sense of positionality vis-à-vis desire will be important to keep in mind as we move through the various scenes that make up the Soft City.

chapter 2
Topless and Bottomless Bars

When I started in this business we were just whores; now they call us "sex workers."
Who said there ain't been progress in this city?

—Former streetwalker

Before Rudolph Giuliani became New York City's mayor, Times Square was the beating heart of the Soft City in Manhattan. The iconic Show World Center sat cheek-by-jowl with the Port Authority bus terminal. Thousands of visiting tourists could easily observe and participate in the area's street life, with hustlers, bottle gangs, dippers (pickpockets), and three-card monte players popping up everywhere. The flaneur and the tourist became indistinguishable, as they merged with the teeming crowds entering and leaving the many peep shows and sex shops. As a sociologist, one way to interpret behavior in and around sex venues and strip clubs is to view it as similar to behavior in public drinking establishments. They all provide voluntary, "timeout," unserious behavioral settings.

I interviewed many women working in the Times Square area about how they use their erotic capital to advantage. They told me stories of themselves as voyeurs, sex workers, and sex objects; they also had access and bore witness to a predominantly male world. They depicted in vivid terms the exploitative side of the sex industry. Yet this view is only one of many in effect here. I will discuss some of those views as I move to the next set of notes. The best fruit is always at the end of the branch.

Strip clubs and bars are social spaces, ones offering play, sexual acts, drinking, and drug use. The fact that unseriousness is an important feature of these

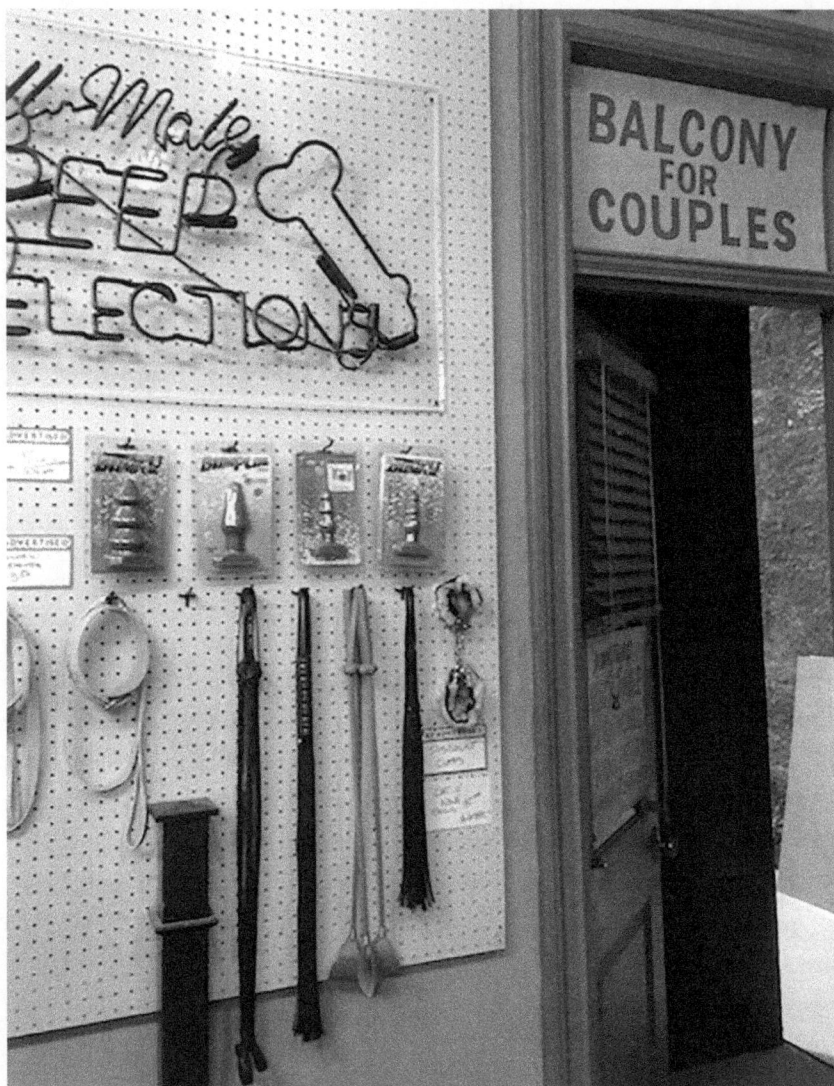

2.1 Show World Center. Times Square.

spaces suggests that the play involves boundaries. These settings are controlled temporally and spatially within the context both of house rules (for example, no sexual intercourse and no public ejaculation) and of external and official rules (for example, state ordinances prohibiting the sale of alcohol on the premises).

In this section, we hear the voices of three different women visiting three different clubs from three different eras. I begin with notes I took in the 1980s, and I include a composite sketch of the women employed in the Soft City area, excluding the "prostitute," and I discuss the perceptions of the men they serve or entertain. The information was collected from conversations with women as they passed in and out of a local hangout. They are Latinx, white, Black, short, tall, young, old, educated, and from all socioeconomic backgrounds and areas of the country.

Even though no one category is broad enough to describe adequately the female employees of the Times Square area, there are commonalities. Generally, they view their participation in the sex industry as a job, just as a telephone operator or secretary would view hers, and all have the "entrepreneurial spirit," the desire to make money by using their wits. All have aspirations that go beyond working in a particular peep show, massage parlor, or emporium. In other words, employment in the sex industry is a job, not a lifestyle. The topless bar has become hip, fashionable, cool, and looked upon as a creative way to make fast money.

WILLIAMS FIELD NOTES: TIMES SQUARE (1980s)

Historically, female pedestrians for the most part avoided the street corridor in many locations in the city. In fact, males outnumber females by at least three to one; at night, the ratio exceeds seven to one in places like Times Square. The incidence of verbal abuse, the prominent display of pornography, and the general "tackiness" of the area made it unpleasant for many females. Women used to scurry across Forty-Second Street toward work or home, eyes averted, past the maze of drug peddlers and hustlers. Few stop to purchase any of the peddlers' wares or to browse in the numerous bookstores. Yet the Times Square area is not "man's country." Women are an integral part of the area's economy: they are employed in the peep shows, massage parlors, and emporiums located in the area—and, of course, as doctors, lawyers, accountants, and other high-level professionals.

Nina, a tall, slim, dark-haired sex worker in her mid-twenties, offered the following account. Quick to disabuse me of the notion that she was somehow defective, she described herself as a "nice Jewish girl" from Long Island. Nina gave me one of my key entrees into the stripper's world, although she took pains to let me know she was more than just a sex worker. She had spent a year in college but found it boring and decided to drop out. She came to New York City to find a good-paying job and independence. Instead she found a variety of low-paying receptionist and waitress jobs. Finally, she answered an ad for a topless dancer in Midtown. She has been dancing for five years and considers it a good job because she's able to support herself and her boyfriend as well as pursue her interest in art. Topless dancing provides a lucrative income in a city that has become prohibitively expensive. Most of her $700-a-week income comes from tips.

When I appeared surprised that the "nice Jewish girl" from Long Island could appear topless in front of strangers, she pointed out that "it beats being felt up by every guy in the office. The customers look, but they don't touch, unless I want them to." She is able to protect herself from intrusion because the rules are laid down by management, whereas a low-level straight job invites sexual harassment. After a performance, if a customer wants to take her upstairs to the lounge, where he can talk to her for long as he wants—and can afford. He must buy a seventy-five-dollar bottle of champagne for each fifteen minutes and can have no physical contact with the dancer (though exceptions are made, for a fee).

The dancer receives 30 percent of the total champagne sales. As a result, her income is largely dependent on her ability to charm the customers. It also helps if the dancer is able to consume large quantities of champagne without becoming inebriated. Women who can't hold their liquor cannot work as long and thus are not able to make as much money. These are usually neophyte dancers; veterans can drink as long as the customers can talk and still get up to dance the next set. "Girls interested in making money learn how to drink," Nina explains.

I suggested alcoholism must be a problem among some women, but she maintained that "most girls I know, including myself, only drink on the job." Her best friend, Ruth, from the Dominican Republic, has been working as a dancer for twenty years and has made enough money to bring her entire family to the United States. She admitted that "Ruth drinks too much, but it hasn't impaired her ability to make money. Alcoholism may be an unfortunate occupational hazard, but everything has its price, and the working conditions aren't that bad, once a girl learns to get along with the manager of the club."

The manager at her last job accused her of pocketing seventy-five dollars from a champagne sale. She simply moved to her current job and now has no difficulties. She's never had a female manager and believes that it wouldn't work: "most of the girls are too strong-willed to take directions from another girl." Even though some managers are "creeps," they seldom hassle the dancers, since they "want them to keep dancing and drinking champagne, so they can continue to reap the benefits."

She works from 6 p.m. until 2 a.m., six days a week. Hours vary from club to club; the women with the most seniority have the best hours. She gets to her apartment in Queens by about 3 a.m. and may sleep until noon. Her days are spent shopping, visiting friends, going to her painting class at the Arts Student League, and hanging out with her boyfriend. She spends money fixing up her apartment, buys her clothes at Saks and Bloomingdales, takes an occasional vacation to Florida, and "cops the best cocaine around." Her neighbors and other acquaintances believe that she is a housewife, since she is at home during the day. She feels no need to discuss her occupation, because some people "wouldn't understand." One day she plans to have her own art show to launch her career as an artist. In the meantime, "topless dancing beats sitting around in an office typing all day."

Her favorite customers are European businessmen in town for a few days on expense accounts. They are between twenty-five and forty-five, and most of them have heard about Forty-Second Street before they enter the topless bar or emporium. Often they will stay three or four hours, watching the same woman dance, eventually offering to take her upstairs. Nina believes that the Times Square area is as well known as the Village to tourists coming to New York from Europe. "We make them feel right at home as they come through the door because we know they have a lot of money to spend." These guys need a warm, friendly atmosphere in which to unwind after a busy day on Wall Street or Sixth Avenue. A topless bar or emporium provides them with entertainment and a haven in a city that can appear menacing and cold. The bars are close to their hotels—a short cab ride or walk—and they can come in and relax. "Many of these guys would not pass up a visit to their favorite bar or hangout when they're in New York. They spend their money and enjoy themselves."

I asked Nina whether most men spend large sums of money. She found European businessmen to be the biggest spenders but that American businessmen made up the majority of the customers (and were soft touches). Nina considered the junior executive in his early thirties, the older middle-class "tunnel trick" who comes to Times Square to get away from the "wife and kiddies," the assorted college students, the regular guys from New York, and the single men coming to the club by themselves to be not just "lounge trade" but the "meat and potatoes" of the business. Most of the time they just sit and watch the dancers, maybe put a

$5 or $10 bill in a garter, but this all adds up, whereas the European big spender doesn't happen every day. But all men, most men, argued Nina, no matter where they're from or how much money they spend, come to topless bars to live out their fantasies. Some masturbate as they watch the dancers, others develop attachments to some women and follow them from club to club, and most have a "pleased far-away look in their eyes." Nevertheless, the majority of the guys are "too intimi-dated to ask a girl to go out."

Nina, like most of the dancers, does not fraternize with any customers after work. Her boyfriend, Jim, an unemployed jazz musician, would get jealous, and besides, "Most of the guys are too uptight to enjoy themselves or don't really have much to offer a dancer. Of course, each girl always tells a story about the rich oil tycoon from Texas, anxious to marry her." In addition, many of the customers, especially some of the junior executives, enjoy being humiliated by the dancers. "These guys love being treated roughly." Nina theorized that many of the junior executives held jobs that were beyond their capacity and came into the bar to get "cut down to size." When she first began working as a dancer, it was difficult for her to "get into the putdowns," but as time went on, it became easier and easier. Now she enjoys hurling invectives at the customers and watching them get drunker and drunker. She explained the secret of working in any sex establishment:

> You figure out what the customer wants and then give it to him, regardless of how strange it seems. Once you know which guys want to be humiliated, you continue to humiliate them, and they come back for more. Other guys just sit and stare or, as in the case of the European businessman, come to the bars to have someone to talk with for a few hours. You must be able to decide who wants what and figure out how to give it to them.

Nina feels the regular patrons of a topless bar or other sex-industry establish-ment are not "sick" or "maladjusted" or in any way that different from other men. "They are really uptight guys who visit topless bars because they believe that's what men do." She claims that the culture portrays sex entertainment as fun and manly, and as a result, most men believe that visiting topless bars or emporiums is a male prerogative:

> A lot of young college boys come in here and ask the girls to perform at fra-ternity parties. It's not weirdos and freaks coming in here; it's usually the

square middle-class or upper-middle-class Joe. A weirdo may come once or twice, but he can't afford to come often, or he comes and wants to have sex with some dancer and that's strictly forbidden. If he's behaving strangely or talking loudly, the management will ask him to leave. The guys are well-behaved run-of-the-mill guys, coming here to let off steam.

Nina believes that the bars provide a healthy sexual outlet for upright men and thus perform a necessary social function:

> The society, through television and advertising, convinces men that they need a lot of sex and also tells them which type of woman is desirable. Often they don't get as much sex as they need, nor do they find the girl of their dreams. Coming to a topless bar allows them to live out their fantasies and thus satisfy some of their unmet needs. Wives and girlfriends are not as exciting as the women in the topless bars or emporiums. We are fantasy objects and can represent anything the customer wants. Do-gooders and hypocrites who want to close the bars and clean up the Times Square area should realize that, due to the demand, the sex industry is here to stay. Besides, to the women, it is a means of making a good living.

Since she's financially independent, Nina considers herself a feminist, yet she does not participate in feminist organizations. She believes that the women in feminist organizations believe that women in the industry are exploited by the managers and the men who come to watch them. She doesn't feel exploited by either group of men and reminded me that "everyone has a boss, and everyone is exploited in one way or another." In fact, she thinks that women in the sex industry are treated with more respect than most other women. "They are in control of the situation and have power over the men coming in to watch them. We are giving a service to a patron that can be withdrawn whenever we choose to withdraw it. It's not like working for a boss whom you have to cater to. You play the role as long as you want to. The customer doesn't make you do it; you do it because you want to continue." The exchange between a topless dancer and the men who come to see her is strictly business, according to Nina, not the one-sided relationship women have to contend with in offices. She says many men come into sex establishments to let go of the macho image and enjoy having tough, dominant women around.

Nina believes that women in the sex industry have real power over men or at least are not subjugated in the exchange. According to her, most of the women have a healthy regard for men; they are not man haters and grow to like some of the customers. Since women are in power, they find men less threatening. Nina leads one to assume that the women in the sex industry and their patrons have a relationship that could be seen as a prototype for good male-female interaction.

When I asked her whether she would allow her daughter to work in the sex industry, she gave a simple and terse "no," which, while technically answering my question, also let Nina avoid explaining why she wouldn't. When I asked her if she would allow her son to go to topless bars or emporiums, she replied, "How would you expect me to stop him from going?" It seems clear that her feelings about the sex industry are ambivalent, but they appear on the whole to be more positive than negative, based on her relationship to the men she entertains and the money she is able to make. Any attempt to identify larger themes or talk in depth about other issues, such as the exploitation of women, was viewed as a personal attack on her and not as a topic for conversation. Some things were clearly none of my business.

This attitude points to one of the most striking characteristics: a sisterhood has developed among the women who work in the industry that is rarely seen within traditional female work groups in more socially legitimate occupations. Although there is little emphasis on the dangers inherent in these occupations or on the physical demands the work makes on a dancer's body, most women realize that "the other girls are the only ones who are really going to watch your back, that you really can't depend on the manager to watch out for any funny stuff or to put you into a cab and send you home if you have had too much to drink."

The "them" and "us" mentality is the prevalent attitude among the women in the industry and extends to other women. In fact, they believe that the area's "bad rap" is caused by other women, who look down on their occupations. "They won't allow their husbands to visit bars or emporiums because of the type of women that are employed."

I met with the owner of a local bar who said he had a new stripper I could meet. Her name is Lightning Sal. I asked how she acquired the name, and in a sultry Lauren Bacall voice, she said:

The first night I stripped in a club was in Fort Worth, Texas, and lightning struck the corner end of the building. I was dancing, and the place caught fire. I was on stage and never stopped dancing . . . everybody started running but I stayed on stage and the owner came over and gave me a big hug and told me I could work in his place as long as I live. I thought it was a sign from God to keep on dancing because he didn't hit me with a bolt. So the owner started calling me "Lightning Sal." My real name is Sally.

The sociologist Catherine Hakim coined the term "erotic capital" and describes it as multifaceted. Erotic capital

combines beauty, sex appeal, liveliness, a talent for dressing well, charm and social skills, and sexual competence. It is a mixture of physical and social attractiveness. Sexuality is one part of it, a part that is easily overlooked as it applies only in intimate relationships. However, sex surveys carried out around the world show that people in affluent societies are now having sex more, with more partners, than was generally feasible before the invention of modern contraceptives.[1]

In the next section, three women used topless clubs as their strategic research sites. One was the Blue Angel club in the trendy upscale Tribeca area of Manhattan, located between the West Village and the Financial District. This is home to expansive and expensive lofts as well as chic, celebrity-owned restaurants. These women tell their stories as voyeurs, as sex workers, as sex "objects," and as regular women in a predominantly male world; they express a narrative as both ear- and eyewitnesses to the exploitative side of the sex-club industry. Jenny is a woman in search of herself and her lover; her lamentations while observing the scene offer glimpses into her innermost thoughts. Readers—another type of voyeur—will read about her "thought stripping" and how it mirrors the "clothes stripping" of onstage dancers. Her notes offer an enlightening view energized by the sheer pleasure she derives from observing women undress. Deedra, nineteen years old and from Washington State, describes her attendance and subsequent months recording notes at a popular topless strip joint. She, a former sex worker herself, decides to perform at a sex club in order to break the dichotomy between subjective and objective model so prevalent in the field of ethnography. Pearl, a twenty-three-year-old who recently moved to New York, sees the same scene entirely differently:

we wonder if the two women have not wandered into two completely different Blue Angel clubs.

CONTACT: JENNY, BLUE ANGEL (1995?)

"We walked to the Blue Angel in the rain," Jenny writes.

"I was drenched when we finally got there. I went with two male classmates, Jack and Jeff. After Jeff took us around the streets of Tribeca, insisting that Amity Street was right around here somewhere, we finally stumbled upon the black warehouse door with the single black light giving off that eerie blue illumination that we assumed must be the Blue Angel.

The Blue Angel is a strip club, as you of course know. I was telling Jack and Jeff how bummed I was that we were going to a heterosexual strip club. I envisioned hard-bodied, poofy blonde-haired bimbos wearing cheesy boas. I thought big bonehead thugs in tuxes would be patting people down at the entrance. I figured I'd see some fat Mafia man slapping strippers around if they didn't fuck the strip pole the right way. I figured I'd hate it.

The Blue Angel doesn't fit that description. There weren't even any men there at all except for four lonely-looking guys sitting at different tables. They were all white, older men in their fifties. Two of them resembled high school principals; one suave-looking Hispanic man, who was a little younger, sat near the back. Another man sat and read a newspaper through most of the dances. The other principal-looking guy sat right in front of the stage, glancing at every girl, tossing a dollar onto the stage when they would show him her pussy. I chose a table for the three of us, one right next to the stage so we wouldn't miss anything.

When we walked in, we saw this single bar to the left and a small couch room to the right draped in black curtains. The very attractive woman behind the bar asked us for $15.00 plus the $5.00 mandatory first drink admission fee. She rattled off the nonalcoholic drinks that we could choose from. I was excited because they had Coca-Cola in those little glass bottles. This was my favorite drink. In the couch room I saw the silhouette of a woman sitting on a man as if they were "hooking up." In all my naïveté I assumed they weren't really hooking up sexually. The room straight in front of us was a little larger, with romantic candlelit tables covered with velvet cloths. The room looked as if it belonged in a quaint Village cafe or Italian restaurant. I loved the decor. I noticed one man sitting on a couch just on the outskirts of the tables, against the wall to the couch room. He was sitting with two girls whom he seemed to know.

When a delivery man came in with a bag of food, one girl dressed in "baby doll" clothing, a silver tight half-shirt that read "Brat," silvery pink skirt, silver platform sneaker/shoes, silver thigh-high stockings, and pink Minnie Mouse suspenders, twirled around for the delivery man in a flirty way as if to show off her outfit. I was immediately taken by her beauty. This is very strange for me to write about, because I have never felt so much like a man in all of my life. I have never been so sure about my attraction to anyone as I was at the Blue Angel.

I feel like I have to explain my state of mind. I have never been so stressed out in all of my life as I have been for the past few weeks. I have been planning a conference for what feels like an eternity, and we were getting down to the wire. I'm sick with this weird thing (not contagious, so don't worry), and I don't handle stress too well because of it. My girlfriend dumped me a few days before this, which in some ways was a relief, but it was probably the time when I needed someone the most. I also had lost all interest in sex. I have no idea why, except that the weird illness is partially to blame; also, the stress had made me depressed, and my girlfriend and I had had "issues."

The funny thing was that right before we went to the Blue Angel, Rick Savage, the filmmaker and star of sex movies, had come to our class, and he explained so much. I was actually suffering from performance anxiety. I know it doesn't seem possible that a girl could be suffering from performance anxiety, but I was. You see, my (ex-)girlfriend is used to dating models and actresses, and I felt so inferior. I was always so worried that I couldn't compete. We had the worst sex. She was so beautiful and wonderful, and I wanted to be better than all of those people I could never compete with. I wanted it so bad that I froze. I wasn't confident and smooth; instead I was clumsy and weak. It all made sense that night, on that dreary walk to the Blue Angel; I realized that I had ruined our relationship with my own insecurity. For whatever reason, Rick Savage's words freed some part of me, and I began to feel things again. The Blue Angel didn't hurt either.

The first dancer was the most beautiful girl I had ever seen. She was the "Brat" and sauntered out behind the backstage curtain clutching a teddy bear. The funky, mellow, eerie, somehow comforting sound of Bjork began playing as she started to dance. She looked like Drew Barrymore except that she was black, and cuter. I fell in love with her. She danced so well, she actually danced to cool music, and danced in cool ways. She moved to the other stage right next to us, and it was there that she stripped. I was so embarrassed but I couldn't help but look. She was so cute. She was getting naked right in front of us, right in front of me. I just couldn't get over it. Jeff and Jack thought it was so funny. I tried hard to act disinterested. I am above these things. I'm a "feminist," goddammit. Stripping is exploiting women. I loved it.

After she was done, she put her underwear back on and walked around to the tables. Everyone gave her money. I gave a dollar (if I had it, I would have given her fifty). I asked Jack to put the dollar in her underwear for me. I wanted to touch her, and she didn't seem to mind, but I thought she'd be totally grossed out that a girl would put money down her underwear. She smiled at me, and I still can't get it through my head; that smile was not for me but for my dollar. It's so cruel.

The next dancer was also amazing. She strolled in with such confidence, saying hello to everyone. She was wearing tattered jeans and a leather jacket. She had her lip and eyebrow pierced. She talked like a dyke. She looked like my butch ex-girlfriend Susan, and Jack agreed. However, upon closer examination, she didn't look tough at all. Instead she was wearing a tight-fitting black evening gown. She had her hair slicked back. When she danced she would lean far back, exposing her pierced nipples and clit. I was giddy with elation. Fuck that, I was giddy because I was turned on. I tried to hide it, but after a while it was like, "fuck it." I still cannot believe the Blue Angel exists. Why isn't there a lesbian strip club like that? It was so calm and comforting.

They played the best music I have ever heard. All of it perfectly choreographed in a mellow funky way. All of the girls were so hot. I mean every one! The one that looked like Susan looked at me several times. I swear. Don't deflate my fantasy. I know she looked at everyone, but she even encouraged me to put the dollar in her underwear. I would've given her five hundred dollars, too.

I wanted a lap dance. I didn't think they would let me, a girl, do that, and I didn't want to make them uncomfortable. I really had a genuine crush on them, much like if I met them in a bar. I wanted to pick them up, but I also understood that this was their job.

CONTACT: DEEDRA, BLUE ANGEL (1995)

Deedra, a tall, handsome woman with a butch look, arrives with the idea of being a true participant-observer. She goes to the club with the intention of working there to get "authentic field notes" and cash:

I got there pretty frazzled and relieved that I'd actually found the place. Going down the steps into the club I got the feel of an old jazz club, hidden in a TriBeCa alley. There's a lot of excitement in going underground to get into a stripper club. Most of the people I watched coming down those stairs throughout the night all had similar expressions on their faces. They seemed to come with no sense of authority but were ready to experience whatever was in store for them.

As I paid the woman at the door, I noticed that she was about my age, height, weight, and style. It occurred to me right then that it could be me working where she was. Before I knew it I was inquiring about the job.

"Are you a dancer?" She asked me.

"Uh, I like to dance, but, you know, I've never done it before. I'm just curious."

Sizing me up, she nodded toward the stage. "Come in, see what we do, then come talk to me on your way out." So there I was, doing a whole different kind of case study than I thought I would be doing, but I wanted this to be authentic. I sat down with the rest of the class. I was late, so they had been there a while longer than me.

The dancers came out one at a time. As opposed to the other strip bars I've been to, this one was more like a variety show. Lots of themes, lots of types. Some women didn't even strip. They just came out in costume and danced around for a while, made people laugh, got some tips, and left again.

In the relaxed mood of the latest dancer's antics I went back to the bar to speak with the woman about working there. Her name, I discovered, was Lilah. From that angle I saw a whole aspect of the place that I had completely missed: the lap-dancing room. As I talked to her I couldn't really keep my eyes off the women grinding on top of the men in there. Unlike the clubs in San Francisco, where the dancers have their backs to the customers as they lap dance, these women had the men straddled, face to face. They moved up and down on the men's chests, rubbing their butt cheeks on their laps. They wore no tops, so the men could caress their breasts, but a G-string was firmly in place. Lilah laid out the job description as I observed it with my own eyes.

"So what did you think?" she asked.

"I like it, but I'm new to this, and I don't really know what to do."

She became a little concerned about me at this point and said, "Well, come back on Monday or Tuesday. Be prepared to dance. Have your costume and G-string ready. Come early to audition, and that way you'll have a chance to talk with the other girls."

"Do you have to lap dance to work here?"

"That's where you make your money."

"How much do they make?"

"It's twenty a song, plus tip."

"Thanks a lot." Kindred smile.

As I was putting on my backpack to leave, I heard the owner madam come behind the bar and exclaim to Lilah, "Did they love me? I think they loved me!" I took one last look at the lap dancing. I looked at the girls waiting to dance in the corner; they were smiling and laughing. I left. As I walked out, it gave me a thrill to think I could be leaving work for the night, sexy, happy, and a few hundred dollars richer.

The next time I went there the whole crowd of friends and staff seemed bored and disgusted with the place, and this really affected my attitude as well. I was embarrassed to admit that I had inquired about working there; I was embarrassed to admit that I enjoyed being there. Fortunately they left shortly and I was able to loosen up.

I notice one dancer in particular. She blows kisses at herself. She humps herself. She pretends to masturbate by rubbing her long, polished middle fingernail on her clitoris. What does she see? What does she feel? Just by observation it looks as if she's enjoying herself immensely. She's wearing black vinyl: top to bottom. Her hair, black and shiny like the rest of her apparel, falls loose, obscuring her face. Is this intentional? It's hard to say—not all transvestites in the club hide their faces. Some shove them proudly into the disco light, smiling big and bright. The beauty that I watch, though, seems mysterious, and she rubs herself slowly and strong. I wonder what brings her to the mirror. Is it seeing herself as a "woman"? But does she feel like a woman? (Incidentally, what does it feel like when you're a woman?) Or is the arousal that of experiencing manhood while seeing womanliness? (It occurs to me now the problem of my questions. It could be that these questions are not pressing at all. I am projecting what is intriguing to me. Indeed, I didn't talk to any transvestites/transsexuals/cross-dressers that night.)

What arouses me about this place is that people are playing with impressions. Impressions of themselves and impressions of each other. The sense that most of my questions will go unanswered, that the "essence" of the person I watch will remain hidden to me, is the overwhelming sense I get from the club all night. I romantically imagine that it is that way for everyone that is there. In retrospect, this is probably why I didn't talk to anyone but students in the class all night. Even when I was being hit on by a guy that seemed ready and vulnerable and open to share with me why he was there and hear why I was there, I shied away. Throughout the night I much preferred to dance and watch and be as nonverbal as possible. What intrigued me were the mirrors and the flashy smiles and the lights and the music.

I am afraid to go for the subtext. What are people like underneath this exterior? I am unequipped to answer this question because inherent is the assumption that Edelweiss [another sex club] is a façade. What is "fake" about makeup and cross-dressing? I don't know. Rather than pursuing this issue, I moved and danced to absorb the physical sensation of the club and avoided the emotional and intellectual dimensions. I walked out and carried with me a whirl of images, impressions, and feelings. One dancer did a traditional Chilean dance. Albeit very sexy and erotic, she didn't take off any of her clothes. I was surprised that no one looked like they had been robbed. Another woman who had an enormous Betty Boop head on did a Mae West number. Though I didn't see her face, from the folds in her skin I gathered that she was an older woman, probably in her fifties. She was heavy too. Not at all what I imagined an erotic dancer to be. A third dancer fit more of the mold that I had had in my head when she came out in a leather jacket and spike heels. She fully undressed, but no one seemed any more impressed with her than anyone else.

In fact, the crowd surprised me too. Rather than the group of drunken, middle-aged men that I had expected, the crowd was surprisingly young, and at least half of them were women. I didn't see any women that appeared to have come there on their own, except for myself, but there were many situations that appeared to be fun dates. Women all over the audience appeared to be enjoying themselves with their male companions, and more women tipped the dancers than men. There was one table that three gay men occupied. They seemed to be having a better time than anyone else. They especially enjoyed the more thematic dancers, like the Chilean woman and Betty Boop. They definitely appreciated the DJ, a young, un-shy gentleman of about twenty-three, whose job it is to sort of cheerlead the dancers. I found his "how many feminists does it take . . ." jokes annoying, but most of the crowd totally ignored him, like he was an old friend that was just being typical.[2]

CONTACT: PEARL, BLUE ANGEL (1995)

Pearl, a dark-haired, bespectacled, humorous young woman, looked and talked like the 1930s film star Myrna Loy. She tells me:

> Despite reading the list of field trips, I mistakenly thought that this was a gay men's club, and I didn't understand why I was being allowed in. I stood at the top of the steps, gazing down into the bar of the club. I could see flabby white bellies and the upper parts of polka-dot bikini bottoms. "Great," I thought, "I'm going to have to spend the night staring at skinny, flabby white men in blue polka-dot bikinis." I considered going back home. If they were fatter, I wouldn't be bothered at all.
>
> I felt even more disoriented when I got to the bottom of the steps and saw a thin-faced white woman glaring at me through the window opening. She probably wondered why I stared at her, looking so confused. Then I saw other white women in polka-dot bikinis at the bar, and a woman on stage, wearing just boots, dancing. I heard people calling her Julie. I was mumbling something like "What's this?" when the first woman said, "There's a ten-dollar cover charge, and one five-dollar drink minimum."
>
> "I usually just take the five dollars now," she made quite clear. I gave her the fifteen bucks. "Just go in and sit wherever you like. A waitress will come bring your drink." Unfortunately, alcohol was not served. I paid five dollars for nonalcoholic beer. There were two big Black men by the doorway who may have worked there.

A lone Black man sat at a table, intently watching the boring blonde on the stage (really a raised platform), "Julie," slither around in boots, daintily touching her vagina with a riding crop, then slowly touching the tip of the crop with her finger, then bringing her finger to her tongue, quickly wetting it. She repeated this gesture, which baffled me.

I sat by myself. There were only a few people beside the lone Black man. Two young women sat at a table talking. A woman sat with a man at another table. Three young college-boy types came in and sat near me. I didn't see anyone from class. I already couldn't wait to leave. I sipped my beer and then watched "Julie." It was like watching a robot. She finished her dance, approached my table, introduced herself as Julie, asked me how I was doing, and then informed me that it is customary to tip the dancers. I gave her a dollar bill, and she moved on to the next table. No one danced again for some time.

The club was filling up. More people came in: couples, groups of couples, a few individual men, some people in their twenties, but most people were thirty and above. Someone came to my table, smoking, with big blue eyes. He was skinny and young. "Yeah," I said, "You can sit there." Secretly, I dreaded conversing with this skinny little pervert. I was convinced that he was going to reveal his fantasies to me for two reasons: he appeared completely at ease in the club, and this wouldn't be the first time I'd learned things about strangers I did not want to know. After hearing his accent and seeing his soccer jersey, I thought he was Irish.

He introduced himself as Alex. I introduced myself and tried to ignore him. He was wondering about the drinks because he saw the bottle of nonalcoholic brew and wanted to know why he couldn't get any alcohol. I explained this was a nonalcoholic beverage, the only kind sold on the premises. He was thirsty and signaled the waitress for a soda. Then he started talking about himself. He was from England, here on an internship doing television editing. He just kept talking, and, as it turns out, he was so pleasant, I hardly paid any attention to the people coming into the club. In fact, a significant number of people from the "Sex and the City" course filed past me into the back of the club, where they were seated at two tables. A couple in their early forties sat at my table. They were married and had heard about the club in the paper. This was their first visit, or so they said.

In the meantime, a Black dancer started dancing to a song by Prince. The club was full now. This dancer was sticking her vagina into a white man's face as she danced. It was amusing to see how he tried to pretend nothing unusual was happening. His face was frozen, his eyes glassy, his upper body stiff. His table companions, a man and two women, simply carried on their conversation, laughing and talking, with their faces turned away from the stage.

Alex was looking for someone he'd dated the last time he came to New York. Her name was Melody, and she used to work as a coat check in a club—now closed—near this one. He could not remember Melody's last name, which I thought was strange, but he'd asked around and found out that she was employed here as a dancer. He was disappointed and sad to know this, but he wanted to see her. He hoped she would appear on stage. The women that worked there knew of her, they just didn't know where she was, and they wouldn't answer any questions about her. He couldn't remember her last name, but it was a common name, like Lee or something, he said. I believed his story thus far.

Each time the dancers came to the table, Alex tipped them, which was fine with me, except for one girl that we both thought looked like a twelve-year-old, a light-skinned Black woman with curly, copper-colored hair. I told him I'd thought about dancing because I thought it would be easy money. And I could work two nights a week, and that men wouldn't touch me, but then I talked to a friend who told me about "Champagne Rooms" and having to work five nights a week, sometimes earning very little a night. Then he told me a long story about a woman friend who started dancing to pay for college about six or seven years ago. She's now a coke addict and likes to dance nude. So I forgot about it.

The woman on stage started dancing. She was dressed like a sexy schoolgirl, in oxfords, knee-high socks, a miniskirt, a white blouse, and glasses. She stripped, and Alex decided that she no longer looked like a twelve-year-old, but I was disturbed by the child image she projected and was suddenly aware of a sweaty fat man in my peripheral vision giving off heat. I sensed alertness from him, a tension. He was staring at the dancer with rapt attention, until he noticed me staring at him. He took a sip of his drink. The dancer was one of the women sitting in the club when I first arrived. And the lone Black man presumably had a relationship with the first Black dancer, who, when she finished, sat on his lap.

Later, a DJ appeared on the side stage to announce some new acts. He tried his attempt at humor, addressing a table of men and women who identified as Persians calling them "Iraqis." He wanted to know how it was that all the "newbies" and the college crowd came to the club together, since they were all from Texas, Maryland, Florida, Massachusetts, etc. I laughed when someone answered that they were students at PS 158.

The DJ, back on stage, yelling in a screeching voice, "Do you like lesbianism? I do! I love lesbianism!" He was trying to rev up the crowd for the "lesbian" scene, doubtless just beautiful women playing with each other to turn on the men in the audience, not real lesbians performing for lesbians. Three thin, petite women slinked on stage and gymnastically began cunnilingus, stroking, and kissing. One woman grasped a bar above her head, so that the rest of her body was limp. The other women moved like wrapping vines around her and between her legs, kissing, licking, and stroking her. The audience fell quiet, possibly enthralled, possibly waiting for something a bit more stimulating than this trio. There were still some people who pretended to ignore the spectacle by looking away from the scene or by looking completely disinterested. I was becoming annoyed by the performers' hairless bodies, the pretty, clean way they played with each other, and the false air of pleasure they all seemed to share. Maybe they were just winding up, but I was bored. I decided to leave. Alex left with me. He lived very close to me, so we took a cab uptown and spent the rest of the night drinking beer and talking, which was the highlight of that evening.

I wondered, "Is this really an erotic dance club?" My preconceptions of a dark, filthy, old ballroom with cum under the tables was shattered by this relatively cheerful, funny, hip, young crowd. The walls were covered with art photos of big, voluptuous women; the waitresses and bar staff were cute, energetic, and strong. The dancers seemed to enjoy their jobs. And no one was drunk: people innocently sipped Pellegrino and watched the show. Now, at this hour, it was like a talent show with a lot of audience laughter and participation.

The owner of the club, a dark, slim woman in her forties dressed in a tight, full-length slit-up-the-side evening gown, sang three slow, dramatic songs. She was so pleased with herself and her performance and her club; she thanked people over and over for coming to the Blue Angel and making it the "success" that it is. She said, "We've gotten so much media attention lately, I hardly know what to do. I see some familiar faces and some not-so-familiar faces. Thank you."

On the way out, I noticed a cutout of a piece in the *Daily News* about Drew Barrymore going to the club and stripping after being cheered on by the audience and with her boyfriend's approval. No wonder the place looked so clean and dry and filled with quite a few seemingly disinterested couples. It was a place where people felt safe for beginning explorations of underworld sex in New York City. But I thought: What woman would honestly enjoy sitting with her man watching some sweaty woman with enormous breasts, shaved pubic hair, and spiked heels wiggle around on stage as horny men below her strained to put their fingers in her vagina and her anus, to somehow touch her while she danced? Well, from the audience here tonight, quite a few.

Leslie and Susan, two recent arrivals to New York who are both from the Midwest, are determined to write about the local topless bar scene. Leslie told me she wanted to write "ironically" about the people she'd meet in these clubs. Both Leslie and Susan offered observations of a 1960s holdover bar, Hogs & Heifers. Before it closed permanently in 2015, it was right in the middle of the Meatpacking District and a site where women—patrons, not employees—were asked to remove their bras and hang them on the back of the bar. When I visited, I noticed hundreds of bras strung above and behind the bar. It's a strange ritual reminiscent of the "bra-burning days" of the 1960s. Michele Dell, the owner of Hogs & Heifers, closed the bar in 2013 when rent skyrocketed from $14,000 a year to $65,000. The lease expired in 2014 and was purchased by a developer (Thor Equities) for $96 million dollars.

CONTACT: LESLIE, HOGS & HEIFERS (2000)

Leslie is twenty-four and curses like a sailor. She observes:

> I walked into Hogs & Heifers at the corner of Thirteenth and Washington Streets, at about 10:10 p.m., Saturday night, where approximately five of my friends were already gathered. I walked past a few small groups of people spilled out onto the sidewalk, which was surrounded by motorcycles parked

on both sides of the corner. The bar was not too crowded yet, and my group was gathered at a table toward the back, against a wall opposite the bar. The bar was along the wall on the left-hand side of the room as you walk in. The center of the room was open with wood-plank flooring, and there were a few tables with chairs on the right-hand side of the space. Beyond this large rectangular space were men's and women's toilets to the right and to the left a pool table, where a few people were playing.

The music was a mix of country rock and a little older "classic" rock. There was a predominant "look" among the male customers—long hair, at least partially unshaven faces, jeans, T-shirts, or plaid work-type shirts, many in work boots or cowboy boots—what might stereotypically be called a "redneck" look. Many of the women were wearing tight-fitting blue or black jeans with T-shirts, tank tops, or work shirts with the sleeves cut off. The decor had a lot of Americana memorabilia: an American flag, signs, license plates—there might even have been an animal's head trophy. In fact, I think there was a set of horns on which were hung hundreds (?) of women's bras.

This place, in comparison to some of the S&M clubs we'd been to in the neighborhood, is very open and public. It is clearly visible from the street; in fact, much of the activity seems to spill out onto the street (a big part of that seems to be the display of motorcycles on the sidewalk and street around its corner location), and there is no attempt to be secret or any affectation of secrecy in what it's about. This is in direct contrast to most of the other clubs in the neighborhood, with their heavy metal doors, windowless exteriors, and small (with the exception of the Vault) name signs.

We spent a little over one hour there, just watching all the patrons and listening to the music. It was a pretty lively crowd; everyone seemed to be having fun, dancing, laughing, etc. The most interesting event (to me), which recurred several times, was when the bartender (a woman) would scream out to everyone that all the women should get up on the bar and dance. She yelled that all the women there should know their "duty" (as women), which was to "dance on the bar," and that the men should also know theirs, which was to "buy the women drinks and get them drunk." She yelled that she wanted to see some "sweet white asses shaking up on the bar." That time about six women did go up and dance. Another woman yelled that anyone who thought this behavior was sexist "didn't know what it was to be a woman" and that "if they didn't know how to use, or what to do with, their womanhood they had a problem." The crowd around me mostly laughed when they heard this.

A birthday cake came out later, and everyone sang "Happy Birthday" to Steve (?), a customer at the bar. Another call was made for women to get up on the bar, and again many did. The bartender kept up a fairly regular call to the customers to either get up and dance, to show their excitement more (by yelling or clapping louder), and mostly to "buy more drinks!"

No one paid much attention to us, kind of huddled up at the corner table.

At about 11:30 it was decided that we would move on to the next location. As we were walking out the front door, one of the customers was talking to one of my friends (who is Vietnamese). When he saw all of us he made an interesting comment: "Wow, what is this? The United Nations?" I assumed he was making a reference to the fact that the crowd is ethnically a very diverse one. This seemed to kind of sum up the feeling of the place.

CONTACT: SUSAN, HOGS & HEIFERS (2000)

"I'm in the Midwest again," Susan says. She wears a hat that comes down so low it almost covers her eyes.

I shuddered as I observed the Harley Davidson motorcycles all lined up in front of the place, heard the good ol' white boys ... rock music, and watched three amazingly extroverted heifers, wearing tight pants and cut-off flannel shirts, stomping to the beat with preternatural energy and chutzpah. It wasn't the Midwest but, on some level, Hogs & Heifers was close enough for me. This was an overwhelmingly white working-class environment, and the space was a fairly small one, resembling your stereotypical "redneck" fraternity boy's room; this fraternity would consist of Harley Davidson riders and "Dead Head" followers, of course. I guess you could call this place "Hogs—and the Heifers who love them." There was an upside-down motorcycle extended from the ceiling right above the restrooms, hundreds of bras hanging above the bar (the bras were thrown into the crowd periodically), and a pool table in the back. A huge plastic green beer bottle (around five feet long) had been filled with air and was attached to the ceiling. There were four fans circulating slowly, and around each fan was a circle of black and green residue, which must have resulted from years of cigarette smoke drifting upward. In short, this place was an anal-retentive person's nightmare. My private suspicion, however, is that most hogs and heifers are not prone to being anal-retentive.

Although it was only 11:00 p.m., the crowd was wired, and the sporadic and frenzied dancing was not uninteresting: it consisted of stamping one's foot hard upon the floor in a style that had almost a country-western feel. Sometimes men would swing their women partners in country-western style, and other times they would grind their hips against each other in a decidedly sexual manner. I have to confess that rarely have I witnessed so many seemingly extroverted individuals in one room at the same time. Or so many beer guts, for that matter. Staring at their beer guts I theorized that they imbibed the lyrics of "Beer is good for you" in more ways than one. Yet there was a festive atmosphere characterizing this space, although members of our clique appeared somewhat muted. Sex clubs like the Vault or Club Edelweiss we could deal with. But had the Other ever been so entirely unappealing? And ever so white? The refreshing thing about this space was that one would have to be extremely creative to offend anyone. I mean, go ahead, burp, belch, fart—hell, do it simultaneously—who would care? I remembered an essay by the anthropologist Susan Harding that dealt with the question of the socially repugnant Other and the problem of conducting fieldwork in an arena that is viscerally disgusting to you. Indeed, something about this crowd was making me uneasy, although no one was overtly rude to me.

Soon there was a flurry of activity and the owner, yet another gregarious woman, summoned "all white asses" to dance on the bar. It's a good thing she specified "white," lest any people of color climb on the bar counter—God knows I had to contain myself. The owner's language matched her crude persona: she yelled out that if anyone found this to be sexist that they had "their heads up their asses." Up to nine "white asses" (all women) crowded on the bar counter and danced to the rock music while the crowd yelled encouragingly and cheered. Some of the women who didn't have the nerve, or perhaps the verve, looked somewhat envious as they saw the women getting off, so to speak, on the crowd getting off on them. I found it a little strange because, in this particular context, it all seemed so normal. I mean, these women were just basking in the attention, interacting with the crowd, and clearly feeling the music. The dancing wasn't especially lascivious, although certainly sexual and suggestive at times; it all seemed so innocuous and somewhat ridiculous. What was interesting was that it was the women in this context who were assertive. But these women, presumably, weren't sex workers or strippers; they were doing this because they clearly reveled in the limelight. The men seemed passive and quite content just to be entertained.

When we left, I noticed that the Lure (a gay men's club) was around the corner from Hogs & Heifers. What strange bedfellows we have here. It would almost seem that the people from Hogs & Heifers, some of whom were clearly "rednecks," would want to beat up the "fags" at the Lure. It was interesting to observe perfectly chiseled and beautiful gay men going into the Lure when we had just seen some hairy and unkempt men with bandanas, beer guts, and flannel shirts strutting their stuff.

I recall Susan appearing in my office, eating a sandwich, forms in hand, requesting permission to take an urban sociology course. She said, at the time, that this was her first year in New York and that she wanted to do "theory and practice." Her subsequent work and field experience is captured in the notes she wrote.

This section considers impressions of gazing. It moves from topless bars to the consideration of strip clubs, a different site of gazing, and spectatorship. In what follows, Susan continues to opine about her experiences at the clubs.

CONTACT: SUSAN, TIMES SQUARE CLUBS: STILETTO AND PRIVATE EYES

I had never been to any strip clubs before the Hogs & Heifers experience. However, when I read Samuel Delany's *Times Square Red, Times Square Blue*, I wanted to experience for myself the surroundings and happenings. I also wanted to test the degree of comfort I would feel. I decided to ask a straight male friend to be my escort. I went out fairly late and stayed till the early morning hours to observe the late-night clientele and other possible happenings. I was at the same time excited and nervous, chiefly because I did not know what to expect. My friend suggested we should go to the Times Square/Eighth Avenue area. That was just what I had in mind, and I readily agreed. Ken (my friend) also reminded me that I should dress low-key, preferably in black, and not too revealing. I took his advice; I clad myself in complete black and made sure that I was well covered, though I tend to wear pants most of the time anyway. For some reason, I made sure I wore my ring on the ring finger of my left hand, as if I was scared of people picking me up.

It was again a Tuesday evening. Ken and I went south along Eighth Avenue. The surroundings got progressively sleazier as we slowly approached the Times Square area. Ken told me (as I have read in Delany's book, too) that years ago this area used to be sleazier, but the ex-mayor Giuliani has since cleaned up the area and completely transformed it into a "La-La Land." But Eighth Avenue itself is still very interesting; toward the east side of the street there are theaters and restaurants, and it looks very touristy. To the west side of the street there are a series of strip clubs, pornography video stores, and a few peep show establishments.

It was past 11 p.m. when we arrived at Stiletto's. As a result, we were required to pay the $15 cover charge. In addition, there was an $8 charge for an open bar. I knew beforehand some venues would not serve alcohol, and I wondered if this establishment was one of those.

I had a complete shock when I entered the main lounge after the security discreetly checked us out. I had no idea at all what I was going to encounter in a strip club, and thus I was totally unprepared when I was greeted by a topless young woman carrying on a lap-dancing session with a man seemingly in his thirties. I was suddenly tense. I was even more uncomfortable to notice that I was the only female aside from the women staff.

The club has a front room with a stage in the middle. There was a stripper dancing slowly. The lighting is a dim blue and pink. There are mirrors surrounding the whole place, creating a visual illusion of expansion. The sitting area consists of a long, extended sofa, with a few tables around. It seems obvious that any drinking activity is not the main focus. The volume of the music is moderate and gearing toward some sexy, pop-beat style.

We picked a small table near to the stage but at a suitable level away from the lap dancing. I was still trying to adjust my mood when a very cheerful waitress approached us for drinks. As the establishment is a "nudie bar," the drink list consists of nonalcoholic drinks ranging from fruit juices to soda.

By the time the drink arrived I was already more settled down, and I began to observe the action around me.

There were about ten men in the club. Some of them were watching the stripper on stage; the others were eyeing the girls walking around, trying to get lap-dancing sessions. Ken told me he was surprised to see the general high quality of the girls. They looked young, all in their twenties, with strikingly pretty facial features and equally impressive physiques. All of them were wearing bright, very revealing clothing (dresses of varying lengths). The girls appeared to be a mixture of ethnic groups, although I noticed the absence of Asians. Perhaps the cultural traditions created discomfort for them to take up such a profession.

The girls seemed comfortable with their surroundings; they walked freely back and forth, and from time to time they solicited freely with the guests, offering lap-dancing sessions. Ken told me we were unlikely to be approached by the staff, as we looked like a couple trying to "figure out what's going on." True, the staff seemed to consider us as observers only and concentrated on the men on the other side.

During the lap-dancing sessions that I witnessed, the girls first placed a towel on the lap of the patron so as to create a barrier. This is done primarily for hygiene reasons. The patron is not allowed to touch the dancer and need to remain fully clothed. As for the dancers, they took off their dresses but kept their little mini G-strings on. A standard lap-dancing session lasts a couple of minutes, but the patrons usually buy multiple sessions.

The dancers either danced facing the patron or danced with their backs toward them. Although most of the patrons spent their time staring at the breasts of the dancers, I noticed a guest chatting amiably with one of the dancers. He seemed to be a regular. The dancer was happy to see him, and they were carrying on friendly chatter all through the lap-dancing session. But the general atmosphere is sexually charged, and everyone is focused, "down to the business."

Besides the main area, there are also back rooms for private lap-dancing sessions. The doors are opened, and the bouncers, all dressed in suits, patrolled the whole establishment continuously. There was not any big difference in the back rooms; besides the seeming "privacy," the action was very similar to what was going on in the main area. There were strippers on stage for the whole time; they were called onto the stage one by one and performed a strip session to whatever song the DJ chose.

I was cautioned not to discuss the clientele until I was outside the bar. Still, I noticed that the all-male patrons, all in their thirties and forties, seemed to come from the lower income groups. They were all dressed respectfully, though; shirts and pants is the predominant dress code. The patrons were predominantly white. A lone Asian patron right across me kept on staring at me, no doubt wondering whether I was a tourist, a curious onlooker, or actually engaging in the sex industry.

Overall, I was pretty impressed with the professional attitude of the girls. They look as if they are enjoying their work, and I did not see any exploitation going on. They seem to be very friendly with the bouncers, too. Ken told me, when we finally left the club, that this is a very high-end, classy place, and they are trying very hard to project that image by maintaining the standard of the girls and the quality of security.

We visited the Private Eyes Club about two hours later. It was already two in the morning, and I wondered how busy these clubs could be on a weeknight at this late hour. As with Stiletto before, we were required to pay a $15 cover charge. The establishment is divided into two parts: there is a full bar outside that appeared to function on its own, and then there is the paid area with a heavy black velvet drape as the "door." The bouncers at the door were very friendly and wished us a good time.

Compared to Stiletto, Private Eyes seemed a notch lower in class. This environment had more standard strip-club surroundings, Ken told me. The color theme is black, and the sofas are red. There are mirrors on the wall, also. The stage is right in the middle, with two strippers dancing at the same time. There was an electronic advertisement billboard-type strip surrounding the stage, with messages like "Bachelor Parties Available. New York's Gentleman Club. Buffet Available." There is a pole for dancing on stage. Though Ken told me that the quality of the girls seemed lower than at Stiletto, I checked them out carefully and noticed that while they still looked pretty to me, there was really a very subtle difference: perhaps the degree of elegance was lower—perhaps the girls looked more like pornography-type beauties.

There seemed to be a dress code for the girls in Private Eyes; most of them wore floor-length gowns. I also noticed that the general attitude of the strippers on stage was different from the previous establishment, as well. Here the strippers looked less enthusiastic. Maybe it was late; maybe they were tired. But they looked preoccupied, at least some of them. Since alcohol is served in this club, the bouncers patrolled around the club, making sure all the men were adhering to the rules of no touching and no public display of sexual organs.

The patrons, once again, were predominantly male, though I noticed, beside me, another female patron. She was there with a sizable group of men. I wonder if she was a hooker or something. The male patrons fell within the age group of late twenties to early forties and seemed, curiously enough, to come from a slightly higher income group than the Stiletto clientele. We noticed a familiar face not too far across us; it was one of the men we saw at Stiletto. Apparently he was strip club hopping.

There were a few lap-dancing sessions going on, pretty much in the same fashion as Stiletto. Again, towels were placed between the dancer and the patron as a barrier. Not far from us I saw a Black dancer engaging in a lap-dancing session with a Black man. The club was still pretty busy at this late hour, and there were many dancers engaging in lap dancing. Those who were not dancing freely solicit around the club, sometimes sitting at tables of patrons for chats, sometimes asking whether a patron wants a lap dance. A tall brunette by the name of Marie approached us with a very friendly smile and shook our hands.

We exchanged pleasantries, and I felt very surreal. Exchanging pleasantries with a stripper; that was certainly a very new experience for me. She was pretty and very nice, though. She said hello to me first and then concentrated on Ken. She asked if he would like a lap-dancing session. Ken told her politely, "Thank you, maybe later." I guessed if he ever wanted to do it, he would do it without my presence.

Again, I found the atmosphere sexually charged, though less so than Stiletto felt. There were more conversations going on; there were groups of men chatting, with beer in hands. They seemed to be having fun and were generally happy to enjoy lap-dancing sessions. As a straight woman, I felt better sitting in Private Eyes than in Stiletto; perhaps the atmosphere was less sexually charged, perhaps there were more girls walking around, perhaps the size of the club was bigger—and perhaps I was drinking bourbon and feeling more relaxed!

I can imagine how sleazy this Eighth Avenue/Times Square area could have been several years ago. Now there are significantly fewer establishments, and most of the surviving ones have different atmospheres. I can still sense the "prosperity" of the sex business back in the golden years. For a woman, I did feel uncomfortable visiting the venues; perhaps I felt less welcome in the establishments that are available for males predominantly.

There seemed to be an air of "why are you here at a guy's place?" attitude surrounding some of the male patrons, who cast curious looks at me. Perhaps they thought I was invading their privacy or robbing them of a place that they could enjoy sexual entertainments without the prying eyes of their girlfriends/ partners. However, the staff at the clubs was friendly, and they seemed to have no objection with girls visiting the clubs. Ken told me afterward that I was exceptionally quiet whenever I was in the clubs. I figured that since I did not want to say anything potentially offensive, and that I really did not know how to react in such establishments, I tried very hard to talk less. I also noticed that there were efforts to keep the establishments looking respectable; the dress codes of the staff and the patrons reflected a degree of such attitude.

Susan's reference to the "sleazy" atmosphere years ago is not a stray observation. The "cleaning up" of the sex industry profoundly affected the whole outlook of the enterprise, and everyone seemed to be trying their best to retain the excitement of the business while abiding by the stricter laws. I have more respect for the women working in the entertainment industry, since they reinforce the idea that it is just a choice of profession. However, sometimes the attitudes of the clientele do reflect negative images of these sex industries.[3]

chapter 3
Gender Play

---

*Honey, let me tell you something; once we come outta that hole, we all in drag
after that.*

—Judine

Many people question the validity of using binary terms such as male/
female and girl/boy to designate gender identities. "Transgender" refers
to those whose gender identities do not align with their birth-assigned
sex. In fact, to question the applicability of gender binaries, those whose gender
identities do align with social norms are now referred to as "cisgendered." *Cis* is
a Latin word meaning "on this side of." It is the opposite of *trans*, meaning "across"
or "beyond." The "trans" aspect, in contrast to the "cis," is key to our understanding because "trans" evokes the blurring, the soft focus, of gender dynamics in the
Soft City.[1]

Erving Goffman, in *The Presentation of Self in Everyday Life* (1959), noted two
types of interactions. Frontstage behaviors are visible actions available to the audience and are part of the performance. Backstage behaviors are the actions that
people engage in when no audience is present. What we witness in the following
chapter is the manifestation of the transcendence of backstage and frontstage.
In my courses, I often pose the questions: What is your gender? Do you cross-
dress? These questions often spur contacts to go out in search of answers.[2]

I chose the locations covered in this chapter in order to take the reader with
me on a series of explorations. The G. G. Barnum Room was a spot near Forty-
Fourth Street, and two local transgender scenes were Club Edelweiss and Gray
Gardens. I begin with the G. G. Barnum Room, where early on I had an unset-
tling experience in doing this work. As I look at it now, this scene raised some

3.1 Late night along West Street, Greenwich Village, under the old West Side Highway. Trans kids trying to work the streets of New York City, c. 1982.

profound questions about my own identity. Here's what I wrote in 1981: "I had never been to these places before, and I had to summon all my manliness or my manhood to keep from succumbing to the impulses of what were named negatively as 'those faggots' in drag."

I did not really consider them "faggots" at the time. I simply did not know any better; I was ignorant and repeating a word I'd heard transvestites use in the street. At the time I thought they were only pretending to be women (to make a buck) for the night or for the time they were in the clubs. At any rate, identifying as queer certainly wasn't abhorrent to me. I felt as liberal and accepting of the queer lifestyle as of any other. I simply wanted to write about the life of the transvestite as best I could. And as quickly as I could.[3]

I met several transsexuals, homosexual men, dog queens, and street prostitutes in the darkened club called the Gilded Grape, more commonly called the G. G. Barnum Room. This was where many of these individuals were performing the role of women, dressed in the most outlandish costumes: makeup, eyeshadow, wigs, high-heeled shoes, and the rest. But I was nervous and avoided eye contact. I tried hard not to touch as we passed each other. I never danced. I had to talk with some of them for my work, so I couldn't avoid all contact. I wondered out loud if I held some secret desire to be like them. I had expected before I went on the assignment that it would be exciting. But I did not think of it as some hidden desire located deep in my unconscious to be gay or a cross-dresser. It was an absurd thought. The most I'd ever done was put on lipstick one time because my former girlfriend had asked me to do it. But my mannerisms were always suspect, since I had long fingers, a tall body, and long legs. These physical features would take on more exaggerated meaning in the course of my work with the transvestites and as this world was becoming more intriguing to me.

Clearly, but mysteriously, these transvestite club scenes were having an influence on my own sense of identity, including my heterosexuality. The first two sets of notes in what follows, both my own, are followed by two informants, Bichat and Billy Joe, whom we will meet later in the chapter.

WILLIAMS FIELD NOTES: GILDED GRAPE (G. G.) BARNUM ROOM, TIMES SQUARE (1980s)

Meet Judine, a nineteen-year-old, self-described "Queen" I met in the G. G. Barnum Room while conducting my research. She is tall, thin, her hair braided in a ponytail. Her Danskin Lycra suit is tight fitted, and she's stacked like two scoops in a small cone. She cautions about the "phony faggots" on the streets. "Some of those you see out here are not true to the profession," she intimates.

> They hear how they could make money out here and they dress up. But in the daytime they change back to the straight life. The pier is full of them. Go downtown and walk along the pier and you'll see what I mean. Some of them work at Edelweiss, some at Show World. But I'm a woman twenty-four hours a day. I live my life as a woman. It doesn't matter what I do in bed. I'm still a woman.

Judine doesn't look the part herself just yet, because she hasn't learned the art of dressing up. Her makeup is ill-prepared; she looks like a kid who got caught in her mother's makeup kit. She is awkward when standing, sitting, and walking. And she is the only one I met who professed to be a woman yet maintains some part of her masculinity—a tiny mustache. I cannot tell whether this is intentional

3.2 Legendary transgender punk-glam Venus DeMars plays at the lesbian bar Meow Mix on Houston St, New York City, with her band All the Pretty Horses, c. 1992.

or hirsutism. For others, identification with women is all but total. They had not yet become transsexuals—that is, they had not had surgical operations to remove, rearrange, or reassign genitalia.

"Most of us come from gay backgrounds," Judine is saying now, her eyes sparkling.

I have always liked men and boys as long as I can remember. I have always known what I wanted to be. But that doesn't mean I'm ready to take hormone shots or have any operations. When I started putting on mother's clothes as a little boy, my father got furious. Fathers always take these things harder than mothers. My mother tolerated it, but then I started to live secretly. But when I was eighteen I decided I couldn't hide anymore and made the big announcement to my family that this was the way I intended to live.

Judine says she has no intentions of getting a sex-change operation but is saving money to get silicone implants to enlarge her breasts.

A patrol car edges by. The street is flushed with queens. Tourists pop in and out of side streets; patrons from local gay bars saunter along the sidewalk. Two young Puerto Rican boys play a portable radio and chat with Judine and her friend Glenda, a tiny South Asian cross-dresser who has worked the street for only one night. Her legs fly up and down as she gives the finger at two men staring at her. "Fuck you," she shouts as they cross the street.

When I first started out in this business [prostitution], I was young, dumb, and full of cum, and everywhere people fell in love with me. I could sing a little bit, so I met a whole lot of people. I met Bette [Midler], Diana [Ross], and Liza [Minelli] in the dungeon one night. People loved me whether I was in drag or not. You see, that's the thing—the transsexuals and transvestites I know strive so hard to be women. I feel no matter how good I look, it's got to be in my attitude. I'm not going to try and psyche my own mind out that I'm a woman. I know what I was born. I know I can live with some man and psyche him out for a while and he'll never know. But I'll know. You understand? [Smacking her lips] The majority of the time when I go out with guys, they ask me—"are you a girl or a guy?"

And I tell them right away I'm a guy. I tell 'em because I'm not looking for no shit and I don't want no hassles. Listen, I grew up on the Lower East Side, and you many not believe this but I was born on Friday the thirteenth at twelve o'clock midnight. I had a twin but he died. When my mother found out I was gay she said the best part of me rolled down my father's leg.

I stand not too far up the street from what was once a raffish brothel but is what I would now call a "one-night-stand hotel," located across the street from a construction site. One of the two Puerto Rican boys who had approached now sit on the hood of a parked cab. The driver asks him to get off, but he doesn't budge—the cab pulls off slowly down the street. A patrol car rolls up and over the loudspeaker asks the kid to get off.

The streetlights blink on and off; the hustlers, the tricksters, and the whores linger on. I'm caught in the spell of the street: the queens, the expressions, the deep eyes, the bitter smiles, the excess perfume as Judine puts on more lipstick, stops momentarily, watches the street, throwing her hands up in mock excitement. Most people see the transvestite as just one of many characters in the city, where so much is "camp" anyway. Transvestite prostitution is not common in every neighborhood of the city, but around Times Square and in Greenwich Village and the Lower East Side, it is plentiful. It is busiest in areas with large numbers of tourists and where an active gay community persists.

In the old Times Square, the location of the prostitutes and the peep shows shifted constantly, driven by the whim of developers and the current political climate. One month, for example, they may be on Forty-Fifth Street but because of construction move to Thirteenth Street.

The transformation of parts of Times Square from a sophisticated theater district or rialto into a sex-market zone was a gradual process spanning several decades. Some argue, like the sociologist William Kornblum, that

> it started back in the 1920s: when businesses based on long hours and high turnovers took the place of high-priced restaurants and hotels. These businesses catered to less "respectable" clientele, who drove out more desirable patrons. The end result was an area serving a lower-class clientele. Even the most run-down properties in the Times Square vicinity yield huge profits for their owners, who did not want to sell them.[4]

It goes without saying that only certain types of businesses can afford the high rents in and around West Forty-Second Street. Such economic forces played a major role in the evolution of Times Square as a central marketplace for commercial sex and pornography.

At the time of this writing, much transvestite traffic has shifted to the piers, specifically the Chelsea piers; others have relocated indoors. Another location for trans individuals is clustered in the salt mines along the West Side Highway facing the Hudson River.

CONTACT: BICHAT, CLUB EDELWEISS (1995)

Bichat, a twenty-two-year-old from South America, is a graceful wordsmith, poet, and inquisitive interlocutor who pays close attention to details. In this section, she describes the "institutional codes" related to social interaction in the club. While transvestites perform roles as hostesses and workers (bargirls, dancers) in these locations, introducing themselves as incarnations of different feminine stereotypes, the men of different ages, styles, and appearances playing roles as male customers strike me particularly. Some of the "trannies," as they refer to themselves, are tall and thin, others short, some fat. But all of them sell their bodies as representations of different female identities.

When I agreed to be Terry's contact person, I decided to study with the team who would examine the question Terry posed on Judith Butler regarding gender trouble. This was my first team visit to this particular club. When I finally got to the club I noticed the place [Edelweiss] was divided into three sectors. Each of these constituted a different environment, each with specific communicational codes. The first one was the bar, a typical American bar where people drink beer and have informal chats. The second area was a kind of alcove space with a circular bar with enough free space and some tables distributed all around. As soon as we entered the place, the majority of us went directly to the second area, probably because we needed each other and the atmosphere was more relaxed there. This area also provided better opportunities for having conversations with different people. I remember thinking about the local disposition of chairs and tables. Tables provide the opportunity for starting intimate conversations between customers and amphitryons [men who dress in women's clothes and women who dress in men's clothes]. They also create several small environments where people can establish their own game rules. It happened there. A different negotiation between customers and hostesses was taking place at different close environments, as if nobody were witnessing the situation.

As the time passed, our original group began to split off, but some of us were still gathered around different tables. I felt hypnotized by the atmosphere. I stayed for almost one hour, observing different histories, which seemed surrealistic to me. At one table, there was a group of about six or seven people who were celebrating a birthday or having a private party. The spectacle was really nice. It seemed to me like a tiny stage where women and men laughed and talked as if they were a family enjoying a sunny day. Near the group, there were two television sets displaying porn movies. There were also two transvestites playing games with two customers. One of them was wearing just a knit and was trying to hug the costume with her legs. The client behaved in a double role. In the beginning he started caressing her legs, but then he quit and soon afterward moved into the first bar. I thought that probably our presence as "voyeurs" contributed to his attitude. Another transvestite (a short Oriental guy) was dancing in the middle of the bar, seducing another customer (a fat and bald one).

Her movements were very seductive and soft, and I could scarcely believe that this tiny Oriental girl had originally been conceived as a tiny Oriental boy. At this point, I started asking myself about customers' motivations to come to this place. They did not conform to any one physical stereotype, and in fact, there were young men, old, fat, and a couple of them were handsome. I was wondering what kind or incentives they found to choose this place. My first temptation was to think about indirect homosexuality: men search for transvestites in order to have sex with men, dealing with their homosexuality in a hidden way. Following this theory, men approach other men using the illusion of femininity as protection. But this hypothesis was not very convincing to me. Maybe it could explain part of the phenomenon, but not the whole.

In fact, some of the transvestites were really pretty, seductive, and, though this is a loaded term, "feminine." Why could not men feel attraction to them? I spent a lot of time trying to understand transvestites' identities. To some extent, I was shocked by their open demonstrations of femininity and seduction. They also developed a mixed role between aggressiveness and passivity, a particular feature that could constitute another appeal for men. Anyway, I believe that we need more information about what motivates men to choose transvestites instead of women as partners. What kind of advantages do men find for choosing a transvestite instead of a woman?

Why do men come to this place, and how often? Could we discern a common pattern for these men? The fact that these men are willing to pay for the pleasure of interacting with men who look and act like women but are in fact men is part of the allure. What would happen if men were confronted with the option of choosing between a beautiful woman and a beautiful transvestite? Are men tired of dealing with women, and also, do they want to try new experiences? Or maybe it is because their self-esteem is too low to seek women, so they instead prefer a transvestite? What kind of conversations do they have? I remember myself thinking along the lines of these inquiries, and now as I am writing down these questions, new inquiries emerge. I would have enjoyed posing such questions to the customers at the pub, and one of my methodological dilemmas consisted of how to approach them with these issues.

A major dancing area and a third bar were located downstairs, and at some point we decided to move there. A few transvestites were dancing in front of the mirrors, and some men were standing around. Transvestites were as busy seducing each other as they were seducing the males upstairs. Mirrors helped them to play an erotic role. Dancing alone in front of a mirror has the double property of being with one's self (one's image) while—at the same time— showing a double image directed at others (the real figure and the one that is reflected).

Bichat says that in Argentina the fashion of dancing alone in front of mirrors was introduced in gay bars toward the end of the last military dictatorship in 1983. She says the same is true in Brazil, where the mirror is a goddess, capturing not only the surface of the person but the whole soul. Recall that in the 1980s, gay people were still persecuted and marginalized in much of South America.

My friends and I were standing around the dancing area. Some of them started dancing, and I wanted to create a link with the people there. At this point I felt that the collective support [that is, Bichat had come to this club with numerous classmates] was an obstacle for me to initiate a conversation either with women or men. Another person I should mention was Andrej, a Roma friend who helped me, probably without noticing that he was helping.

He started talking with a transvestite sitting next to us. After a while Andrej came over to me and said, "Bichat, this woman speaks Spanish." At that moment, I realized that I was really afraid of transvestites. How would I introduce myself? As a customer? As a tourist? As a confused student searching for her gender identity?

In spite of my previous experience with transvestites and transsexuals in Brazil, I did not know how to behave here, in an English-speaking country with different cultural codes. In Brazil, I used to play the role of a snob and extravagant woman, which fit perfectly with major cultural expectations. But here, I was afraid of being considered a competitive model or cruel evidence of the natural whims of biology. "I am a real woman . . . am I?" I remembered Judith Butler's criticism about nurture and culture, but at that moment I was thinking that Butler's writings were very useful during academic meetings but not OK at a dancing establishment.

I felt Andrej's words giving me the strength I needed to cross the gender barrier. I approached the woman, using the Spanish language as a bridge between us. I introduced myself in Spanish: "Hi, I am Bichat." But I stopped because I did not know what else to say. It was not necessary to say anything else. It was obvious that I was not a customer or a drag queen, so she relaxed. She did not care about my existential doubts, and as soon as I took a seat close to her, she smiled very kindly, as if sending me a signal of friendship and approval. She was glad just for my presence and started talking with me. Her name was Vivian. She was a fat, Latin American transvestite, probably in her forties. She wore a short black skirt and tights of the same color. The contrast between her big body and her tiny clothes was almost hilarious. However, Vivian was a very deep and sad person.

I started asking about her, and she referred directly to her role in her family. Vivian was the oldest son in a Puerto Rican family of six. Her father left them in complete poverty when she was eleven years old, and Vivian took care of her brothers and sisters while her mother worked outside just to maintain them. This role division with her mother provided her with a deep maternal feeling expressed in caring toward others. Vivian told me four or five times: "I was the real mother for them. I cooked, I helped them with the school homework; everything that a mother does I did." She also told me that she was still playing that role. At the moment, she was living with her mother, a married sister, and two nephews. She added: "I take care of them. I buy toys for them,

I take them to the doctor when they are ill, and they love me, they love me and for me they are as my own sons."

After talking for about twenty minutes, a guy who was sitting at the same table tried to get Vivian's attention. I was listening to him, but I could not figure out what he was doing, as I had my back toward him. In addition, I did not know what to do, and I worried I could be an obstacle for Vivian's business. I asked her if I should leave. She answered: "No, stay here. It is not our business if he does not behave as a gentleman." But the guy was more and more insistent, trying to talk to her, interrupting our conversation. I felt very strange, as if a competition between the man and me were taking place there.

However, I pretended that nothing was happening, and I followed Vivian's instructions, but suddenly she stopped paying attention to me and started talking to him. I left and returned to my friends. However, ten minutes later, I saw Vivian alone, and again I approached her. Once again she was kind and talkative, and she started complaining about the guy's behavior.

I was astonished. It was very clear she wanted to present herself as a lady in front of me. My interest in her provided her with the opportunity of raising her self-esteem by showing me that she deserved the best. I was her ally. She said something like: "If he wants to talk to me, he has to behave. I am a lady. I don't accept men who think we are whores. If he doesn't behave properly, it is better for him to stay away from me." But in spite of her strong conviction, the guy came back, and once again she paid attention to him. I left. It was too much for me.

I entered the bathroom. In one of the cabinets, a long-haired transvestite was urinating with the door open. In the main bathroom, other transvestites were talking and gossiping. They represented an explicit token of feminine identity. They use the bathroom as women do: as an intimate space to recognize themselves as similar to and different from one another. Bathrooms are the most ritualistic areas for representing female identity. We women need bathrooms. Bathrooms provide us with a cruel confrontation with ourselves and also with a weapon to confront the environment.

Comparison, seduction, competition are preinstituted in restrooms and facilities. However, women also use bathrooms for better reasons: for confidence, solidarity, and free expression of their inner feelings. During the field trip I was not clear about these motivations, but after my first visit, I realized that it would be the "key" space to develop my research abilities. I came back there [the bathroom] at least four times that night—not only because of my sociological motivations but also because of the effects of the beer. Nothing special happened during the first three visits, but the last time I met four transvestites talking, doing makeup, and fixing their hair.

One of them—a tall blond transvestite—was trying to comb her hair, an effort that was giving her a really hard time. Suddenly, and spontaneously, I tried to help her, and I did, but as I was standing behind her, she did not realize who was helping her until I had finished my work. She turned her head, discovering me. "Thank you," she said. "What is your name?" "Bichat," I answered. "Okay, Bichat, my name is Gina. Please, take this for a while." She gave me a coat to hold and entered the stall.

Gina was impressive. I guess she was trying to look like Rita Hayworth. As the film star, Gina had glamorous blond hair, a tight dress, and a challenging attitude. The other transvestites were hanging out there, talking, smoking marijuana, laughing. I was quiet and contemplative. Nobody paid attention to me, and I felt the sweet compensation of the feeling as if I were a sculpture. Everybody noticed my presence, but nobody paid any attention to it.

Gina came out of the bathroom and noticed that I had behaved exactly as she had expected: I was waiting for her. Showing me her leadership, she entered a conversation with her friends, talking about men, hairdressers, and so on. It was not very clear to me, but I got the impression that they were negotiating areas of influence. In other words, they were dividing the outside space, and space meant men and potential customers. They were also expressing their different aptitudes as they were flirting among themselves. Again, I was relegated to the status of a silenced spectator.

However, Gina tried to comfort me, sometimes looking at me or smiling. Suddenly, somebody noticed my presence and asked very bitterly: "Who is this?" I did not know what to answer, but Gina replied, "She's my friend," and hugged me with her strong arms as she was saying that. I felt dizzy and tired when I left the bathroom, and I could not find my colleagues. So I decided to stay close to Gina—just in case. But she did not take notice of me anymore. She was trying to enter into a conversation with two guys. She realized that I was behind her, so she told me, "Oh, you still here. Listen: I can't take care of you anymore, I have to work." She was rude, but immediately she added, "You're not here alone are you?" "No," I told her, "but I think everybody I came here with left." "OK dear, listen, try to find your friends, and if you don't see anybody, I will be around." I felt sad, as if the roles had been exchanged, as if the situation were not in my control anymore. Fortunately, I saw that my teammates Sam, Anette, and others were still in the place. I was happy. We left together.

Bichat continued her fieldwork at Edelweiss:

We met at around 9 p.m. for dinner, then went next to Edelweiss, which could be defined as a transvestite/transsexual bar where both customers and workers establish different kinds of relationships, based on the idea of a pick-up joint.

The transsexuals and transvestites were interesting because the kind of reality they reflected of women was remarkably prefeminist. More than anything else they seemed to be recreating women in their own image, so that the final effect was one in which they appeared to be somewhat like women but much bigger than life and too overdone to be considered "real" (meaning biological) women.

Clearly, the sexuality of the end of the twentieth century in the West, and particularly in New York City, has increasingly emerged as being both a contested and fluid terrain—in which simple definitions of sexuality are clearly obsolete and even anachronistic in certain contexts. Incidentally, if I were to choose a name, as Williams suggested in our discussion that we do, for such an elastic type of city, I would name it "The Protean City."

Deck [one of Bichat's contacts] talked about an incident involving a transvestite, since he "knew what they really were," that took place at a club in the Village. However, he confessed that it could be incredibly difficult to always know a person's sexuality. He said he was dancing at Webster Hall, and after his performance he went out and danced with a "gorgeous and very feminine woman" in the crowd who asked him to accompany her to the fourth floor.

When they started touching each other he realized, to his horror, that the "she" was a "he." He then informed her he was dancing in the next set and "ran away as fast as I could" from her. Some prevalent and recurring images included the mirror on the dance floor and the constant importance this mirror had on the "girls'" view of themselves.

The heightened self-awareness and self consciousness of the "girls" manifested itself through their distinctive walking style while they watched themselves in the mirror. The mirror enabled them to appear simultaneously narcissistic and flirtatious and was certainly a significant focal point in the club. I also noticed several posters of Marilyn Monroe throughout the club. She seemed to be the epitome of womanness for the transsexuals and the transvestites. More specifically, many of them seemed to want to imitate the kind of oozing yet very "girlie" sexuality that characterizes her so well. The movies that were playing on the screen were *Sunset Boulevard* and a drag show.

This seemed to be a fairly significant focal point for most of the people at some point in the evening. I noticed one rather buxom transsexual (or transvestite—I can't tell) bartender who occasionally would run her fingers on top of the screen in a motion that suggested that she would like to covet, be part of or be near the images of the drag queens. They appeared to be the ultimate to emulate for aspiring transsexuals and transvestites.

And I could see why: they were amazingly striking. The importance of the audience watching. Can you really be a drag queen without "admirers"? I suppose you could, but it would probably be a real drag, no pun intended. Their identity, I believe, can only be fleshed out by being seen, especially by men who are interested in engaging in some sexual act with them. Kind of a yin/yang and complementary thing. The German philosopher G. W. F. Hegel in "Lordship and Bondage" [a section of *Phenomenology of Spirit*] champions the conception that "I am who I am only insofar as I am understood to be so by some other. The self that I am is nothing which exists in isolation of other self-conscious selves. The self is essentially social in its very construction."

Judith Butler makes similarly salient points in *Gender Trouble* when she analyzes Divine, the actor/actress of John Waters's film *Hairspray*:

Her/his performance destabilizes the very distinctions between the natural and the artificial, depth and surface, inner and outer through which discourse about genders almost always operates. Is drag the imitation of gender, or does it dramatize the signifying gestures through which gender itself is established? Does being female constitute a "natural fact" or a cultural performance, or is "naturalness" constituted through discursively constrained performative acts that produce the body through and within the categories of sex?[5]

Bichat is an extremely acute observer with a warm, engaging sense of humor. She is very curious about what the trans(vestite) phenomenon is all about; since she has observed cross-dressing in her native country, her observations are all the more interesting when applied to the scenes in New York City. She writes: "The notion that one's identity is created only via others' affirmation of it seems particularly applicable to the transvestite/transsexual population."

Here she continues her notes from Club Edelweiss:

"Deck" was what he told me to call him. I couldn't seem to pronounce his entire name, so he shortened it to "Deck." He couldn't pronounce my name either, so I shortened it to "Gee." Clearly, a reciprocal beginning. He claimed to be Irish but sported a thick accent that didn't sound at all Irish to me. It sounded more as though he had developed a speech impediment from the recent ingestion of drugs. But in any case, he told me he had been in the United States for six years but remained "very proud" of being Irish.

He also added, at this point, that I was probably proud of being indigenous Indian. Ten minutes into this mundane conversation, which was progressing painfully slowly given that I wasn't able to decipher what he was saying, he abruptly said:

"We're not going to have sex tonight, are we?"

(This was the most clearly enunciated line he uttered all night. I unfortunately had no trouble understanding it.)

I replied, "No, we're not."

He asked, "Why not?" I replied, "Well, first of all, I'm a lesbian."

Deck responded with, "You are?"

I muttered, "Yeah."

He commented, "Well, that's OK. It should make it more interesting."

I replied, "I'm sure it would."

Then he made some statements to the effect that he had no trouble with my being a lesbian and wandered away. I ran into him once again that evening, and he told me that I was "cool." At least that's what it sounded like.

I seemed to have a perpetual problem with people's names this evening. The second man I encountered said his name, and it sounded like "Boo-Nation," which, I know, sounds absurd, but he repeated it three times and I swear it sounded like this. (I was too embarrassed to ask him a fourth time.) He was a twenty-six-year-old African American who in the course of the conversation routinely raised his hands (four times) and touched his chest, affirming, "I know what I am. I'm a man. I am a heterosexual man." People definitely seemed to be forthright at this club (as I should have figured out from my buddy Deck), and about ten minutes into this conversation, Boo-Nation lighted up his joint and gave me a multiple-choice question: "Are you a transsexual, a transvestite, or a straight woman?"

Feeling bewildered, somewhat embarrassed, and slightly complimented by this, I decided to be game and challenged him. "Why don't you go ahead and guess?"

"I can't tell at all," he said, "because of the lighting. I have to believe what you tell me."

Anyway, Boo-Nation proceeded to tell me that it wasn't until two years ago, when he was looking through a porn magazine, that he realized his attraction to transsexuals and transvestites in general. According to him, he "couldn't tell the difference" when he had sex with a transsexual. He professed an attraction to transvestites or transsexuals who had "bubble-butts"—if they didn't possess this feature then he emphasized that he/she had better have a very attractive face.

I asked him who he thought was the most attractive "girl" in the club, and he pointed to a white "woman" who did, in fact, have a pretty face but, regrettably, a "flat" ass. It seemed he was generously overlooking this flaw because, as he put it, "there's just something about her." Then looking at a very tall African American "girl" he said, "See her? She's sweating me." Not knowing this expression (and suddenly only able to think of flies), I asked him what this meant.

He said it meant that she desired him sexually. Later on in the evening he looked bitter because a different African American "girl" (who I happened to notice had both a lovely face and a "bubble-butt") responded to his come-on line with "That'll cost you" and then bounced away to flirt with another man. I guess she wasn't sweating Boo-Nation. One last point that he made (when I asked him why he liked coming to Club Edelweiss) was that in the club he didn't feel discriminated against as a black male, whereas in the "real world" women just wouldn't approach him because they were racist.

I noted Bichat felt this was an important point because American society is full of racists.

Soon after this, a man in drag who referred to himself as "Cindy" approached me and asked if I had come to the club with some friends. "Cindy," who is a computer programmer, was easily one of the most loquacious individuals that I have ever met in my life. His need to talk about himself, especially about his sexuality, and to be understood was initially interesting but soon became utterly exhausting for me. His wife, Debbie, was upstairs, and he told me that he first remembered wearing women's clothing in junior high. His parents knew and, predictably, didn't approve of his predilections, but ever since he and Debbie got married, his parents seemed more comfortable and "just didn't want to know or ask" about his "other life."

Finally, we come to a young, attractive man called Vinnie, an Italian and a dancer at Webster Hall. He was waiting for two of his friends and said that he felt no attraction to transsexuals or transvestites. I should say I noticed at least one "straight" couple in the crowd who seemed to be "getting off' on the bizarreness of the situation. I could only conclude that they came to gain vicarious pleasure for their own monotonous sex life.

We all know how tempting something can be when it's "off-limits" or "taboo," and I think part of the interest and prurience for the "Johns" at Club Edelweiss was because of the culturally and socially transgressive nature of engaging in any sexual act with a person whose sexuality is so undefined and amorphous.

I have to agree with Terry's remark in one of the conversations we had that there does appear to be a sexual revolution of sorts occurring throughout the city. What I saw at Club Edelweiss strongly suggests that not only may we see New York as a plastic and malleable city but that the sexualities that inhere in it are similarly elastic, fluid, and negotiable. Binary oppositions, when it comes to sex, are tricky to negotiate in an arena that profits from ambiguities of gender and through overlapping and transgressive boundaries. Gender is meant to be an illusion and a fantasy all evening at Club Edelweiss; this is essentially the raison d'etre for the existence of this club.

Bichat's writings at Club Edelweiss provide brilliant empirical support for the idea of the "look," since the "look" is of crucial importance here.[6] In this case, Bichat manages to combine her observations with some theoretical notions that build up a brilliant final account. She challenges preexisting notions about the latent homosexuality of the clients, stating that the performers at Edelweiss work to achieve looking like women and that clients, too, are seeking that resemblance.

Moreover, she constructs a picturesque description of how the lives of the trans-vestites who work there go on during the daytime, helping the reader understand how these practices are attached to life itself.

Her writings open the door to some interesting ways of conceiving of sex, nature, and gender. When speaking about transvestites and transsexuals, I often theorize about how transvestites seek to recreate women, work to look like women, but aspire to something "overdone" in their efforts to resemble, to be paired to real, biological women.[7] Taking some ideas from Butler, I question established ideas about sex and gender, asking if being female constitutes a "natural fact" or just a cultural performance. This suggestion is strongly backed up by Bichat's field experience at Edelweiss, where transvestites manage to look like women and are approached by men who are looking for something, for someone who more or less looks like a woman.

CONTACT: BILLY JOE, CLUB GLAMOUR (2003)

As Bichat's episode closes, another opens, as a new contact/informant reports on the transgender scene at another club. We meet Billy Joe, twenty-seven, who is white and living in the Chelsea area with a friend, although he recently ended their relationship. He's tall and the studious type, with slight, androgynous fea-tures. He says he's not afraid of interacting with new people.

It is a Wednesday night at Club Glamour, and there is a tranny party going on tonight. I thought that arriving later in the evening would be best because I assumed there would be more people and I could just mingle among the crowd and remain anonymous. However, this was not the case at all. I arrived at Glamour around 11:30 p.m., and while paying to get in, I was already getting looked at by this blonde tranny that was working the door. The look that he/she gave me made me feel like an outsider, and I knew I was. I was just hoping that there would be more people inside so that I could sort of disappear into the crowd, but there were about fifteen people in the whole place, maybe.

The layout in Glamour consisted of a dance floor with a small stage as you walk in; off to your immediate left, the club wraps around into an L-shaped curve where the bar is located along with a fireplace and some sofas. I stood for a while, but I felt that all of the eyes in the place were on me, so I decided to take a seat at the bar as soon as one opened up. As soon as I sat at the bar

I felt more comfortable and began to try and take in my surroundings. The bartender was the only real woman (biologically speaking) that I saw that whole night, from what I could tell. But then again, looks are deceiving. While sitting at the bar I immediately noticed that this was the main cruising zone for people trying to hook up.

When I first walked in, I thought that the look I got was due to my being maybe one of the only men in the entire place. However, that theory was proven incorrect rapidly because the place was filled with men. I think now that I got this look and other looks during the course of the evening because of how I was dressed. The other men and the trannies that were in the club were all dressed very well for the most part. Long gowns and dressed in sexy outfits, while the men wore suits and semicasual clothing. I was definitely dressed down in my T-shirt and jeans, which I normally wear when I go out dancing. But no dancing tonight; this night was all about finding some action. While at the bar I noticed the interactions between the men and trannies that were taking place.

The men in the club seemed to be in the late thirties-to-early fifties range as far as age was concerned, and it looked as though this was a place that they came just to find some fun on the side. From what I observed, the men that would come in would go to the bar and get themselves a drink. They would then be approached by a tranny; the "ladies" usually did the approaching, and if the gentleman liked what he saw, he would offer her a drink, and they would begin a conversation. Some of the men in the place, the ones who were obviously spending more money, got more attention.

Some of them had two to three girls surrounding them as they would just buy drinks and continue to talk. This went on all night long. The DJ and the dance floor were ignored, despite some high-spirited diva-ish vocal house [music] being played. I was tempted to dance, but I knew that this would make me stick out completely. I fought the urge, remained at the bar, and kept listening in.

After being at the bar for about fifteen minutes, some of the "ladies" began to approach me as well. Some were more subtle than others. One tranny walking behind me passed his hand over my ass while I bent over to speak to the bartender. Another ran her hand through the back of my hair while walking by. These were some of the more subtle gestures. However, a young tranny, who was Puerto Rican as I found out later and into Latin men, was slightly more outgoing.

She came up from behind me and licked my ear, then sucked on my earlobe for a few seconds before whispering, "I wanna suck your dick baby; I wanna lick your balls and take you into my mouth. I'm gonna deep throat you, baby. I bet you have a nice big hairy dick, don't you? Let me suck it . . ." She simultaneously reached down and grabbed my crotch and kept squeezing her hands around my crotch to emphasize certain words she was whispering into my ear.

We have talked before briefly about escape strategies, but I think I was slightly ill-prepared for this because I cannot recall the "what do you do when a tranny has got you by the balls" conversation. So I played it as cool as I could, let her finish speaking, then I turned to her after holding her hands and said I was very flattered but not interested in her offer. She then looked me in the eyes, somewhat standoffish, and said, "What . . . you don't like girls?" To which I replied, yeah, I am sorry, but I have a love interest right now. She then said to me, "You don't cheat?" to which I replied, "No, sorry." She then said, "Fine, what is it, you like boys or something?" and I stated, "Yeah, I have a boyfriend." She said, "Alright, fine." And walked away, somewhat angry, it seemed.

I continued to get attention from the "ladies" as I watched the interactions between the older men and the trannies. Then a few moments later, a tranny who is partially responsible for throwing these parties, "Valerie," I shall call her, came over and also started talking to me. However, just as our conversation started, the same Puerto Rican tranny came over and said to Valerie, "Oh, he ain't into girls, don't bother with him," to which I felt the need to defend myself and clear up this partial misunderstanding. I then said, "I never said I didn't like you girls, I just said that you were not my preference. I have no problem with anyone here."

Then Valerie chimed in and said, "Well we love everybody in here so just like what you like and have a good time. That is all that I want, for everyone to have a good time." With that said, the other tranny decided that she wouldn't hold a grudge anymore; at least that is what it looked like to me. So then after speaking to Valerie a little more I found out that the following Friday she was going to help throw a Carnival party (Brazilian) at Club Glamour and told me I should come. I told her that I would try to make it.

I only stayed at Glamour for another half-hour or so and then decided to leave, since most of the people in the place were already paired off or had found their sex/love interest for the evening. As I was leaving, I looked toward the back of the club beyond the dance floor where the bathrooms are located, and I saw another tranny leaving the ladies room. I thought it very interesting that they all used the ladies room and not the men's room at all. As I got my coat I was handed a flyer about the Carnival party by the "lady" that was going to be the main performer for that party. She was going to be in full Carnival regalia and surrounded by exotic male dancers. She was also on the flyer itself. She told me I should make an appearance the following week for that party, and again I said I would see what I could do. I then left and walked down the stairs, but not before getting another semi-shady glance from the tall, blonde tranny that had given me that same stare when I first walked in.

There are few places more appropriate than this bar, whose "front region" is where performances are given, as Erving Goffman suggests in his book *The Presentation of Self in Everyday Life*. "A region is any place that is bounded to some degree by barriers to perception. Given a particular performance as a point of reference, it will sometimes be convenient to use the term 'front region' to refer to the place where the performance is given."[8]

Now we turn to another club, one in many ways quite the opposite of the Glamour Club. We meet Trigatri and Vanessa.

CONTACT: TRIGATRI, GRAY GARDENS (SPRING 1995)

Trigatri is one of the smartest of the new crop of hipsters I have come across. She speaks with knowledge beyond her years, and I found her intriguing as she talked about gender-related matters. She has a stern demeanor and a sense of concern on her face. Gray Gardens is a gay/ transvestite bar located at the art installations of in Irving Plaza, a theater located at Irving Place and Fifteenth Street. Shows take place every Saturday, beginning at 10 p.m.

I went there [Gray Gardens] with some friends also interested in the study of gender identities. The gender dynamic is something I would like to explore. The place is primarily a huge room with a stage at the back. The tables are located at both sides in the dancing area. From the ceiling moving screens were playing erotic films. The environment reminded me of the sophisticated atmosphere I found in other bars, the opposite of the kitsch assembly of Edelweiss. The place was also left in semidarkness, with some small tables decorated with white tablecloths and tiny white candles. The customers also constituted particular clients, closer to the "yuppie" New Yorker stereotype. Beautiful gay men, sophisticated women, extravagant transvestites. There was a show performance in which transvestites and women danced together. They used colorful ornaments, leather, brilliant knits, and the spectacle was based on the comedy as a way of dealing with gender identities.

That was one of the most distinctive characteristics of the place. People were mixed up. The transvestites were both actors and customers and not sexual workers. Transvestites were playing seductive strategies not very different from gay techniques or those practiced by heterosexual partners. I spent a lot of time dancing with my friends and other people (including gays and a couple of transvestites), especially because the music was very loud and also because I could see almost nothing. In the dancing area, gays, women, and transvestites danced alone or formed a confused human mass, as a kind of paradise of sexual mixture.

After dancing for almost an hour, I was tired. I entered the bathroom. This was a very "heterosexual" restroom, in the sense that most of the people were "women" in the biological sense of the term. The facilities made up a huge space divided into three areas. I remember that I had drunk at least three beers and was very tired and suffocated by the smoke at the dancing place. I'm clear on the effect of beer on my body, so I did not search for other psychological explanations.

The environment was very hot, and I started washing my hands. I also decided to wash my neck and my shoulders with cold water. I took off my shirt in order to protect it from the water, but I kept my bra. After washing up, I took some paper towels and dried my body. When I started putting my shirt on again I heard a kind voice besides me: "Please baby, keep doing so." I was astounded. I turned my head and I saw a woman looking at me. It took me two seconds to realize that this girl was a transvestite and that he/she was masturbating himself/herself. I did not know what to do, and the first thing that came to my mind was a confused feeling of being a participant-observer and a damaged woman being used as a sexual object.

However, my sociological role was stronger than my feminine subjectivity, and keeping calm, I asked, "What do you want from me?" "Nothing in particular from you . . . I just want to see you. Please, don't leave." It was too much for me. I did not know whether I should feel pity, anger, or nothing. I felt treated by someone who was pretending to be a woman, someone like me (female), but in fact was using her/his appearance to take advantage of a female place. I also asked myself if my ignorance of what was happening was the key to the real answer. A third factor was the surprise of discovering that I could be the erotic object of a transvestite. In spite of all these alternatives, I was there in front of the mirror listening to a voice next to me: "Thank you, thank you."

I did not want to turn my head to see what was going on, but it was impossible not to recognize her figure in the mirror, as he/she had an absolute erection. After a couple of minutes I decided to change my role. I asked, "Why do you need me here?" He did not answer. He was very concentrated on his dick, and I thought that he probably had changed his object of desire. "So," I added, "I'm leaving." He reacted, "No, don't leave, what are you asking me?" I answered, "What do you need me for?" Suddenly, he/she stopped, putting his/her two hands in front, showing me his/her anger. "Oh, silly baby, are you asking me, why do I need you here? For nothing, I just got the illusion that I could fuck you. Is it OK for you?" He/she was very ironic, very sarcastic, and I felt that he/she was right, that my questions were really very stupid. Suddenly, I felt she was not a woman anymore; she was a man. I left.

The question becomes: Are people just "surfaces to each other"? As the Loflands write: "That surface therefore becomes an object to be evaluated and styled according to aesthetic criteria."[9] Does sexuality simply make people surfaces to one another? Are they just portraits, as Lucian Freud argues?[10]

CONTACT: VANESSA, FIELDWORK OBSERVATION: VISUAL GAZING (1995)

Vanessa is twenty-six, Italian, and lives in Brooklyn. She is eager to learn about the Soft City and explore all its themes, from heteronormative behaviors to S/M, dungeons, and lesbian sex. There is some link between Trigatri's experiences and Vanessa's.

"How can I observe when I'm trying to avoid any kind of eye contact that might establish a connection?" She poses this question as we talked about "men" in a place near the university. "Those dozens of men milling past . . . I can feel the strength of their sheer will trying to exert a pull, a magnetic influence on my gaze—pulling it toward them—as if it were a real, material thing itself. I feel it necessary to fight against that. A strange kind of role reversal. Often enough, on the streets of New York, I feel myself the object of unwanted, violent (what I consider nonsexual in its violence) attention. All New York is male."

It is important to note that describing events chronologically forces the researcher to obtain a more representative sampling of events, acts, actions, and reactions than would result from a selective rendering of just those items of information that are most memorable. By avoiding recording only the most "spectacular" items of information, the researcher tries to provide a well-rounded view of the events/acts/actions and not focus only on some popular, sensational, or overly personal interpretation. I also would like to note how it would be better to return, in some capacity, to the observations from the opening of the chapter about the shifting climate for discussing transsexuality and the changes in New York City over the past few decades. For instance, the previous chapters contained a rather mournful look at the disappearance or alteration of spaces that were formerly sex clubs. However, unfortunately I do not have knowledge about what Club Glamour, Gray Gardens, and Edelweiss look like now, since they have all closed. The Soft City is fleeting.

chapter 4

Peep Shows

Behind a closed curtain was lotion, a condom wrapper, paper towels, a bottle of rubbing alcohol, a heart-shaped pillow, and a clock. I was curious what a peeping room looked like.

—Peep Show View

The peep show derives from the old nickelodeon format, "nickel" referring to the five-cent admission price and "odeon" the stem from the Greek word for "theater." Nickelodeons were makeshift facilities housed in storefronts; the first opened in Pittsburgh, Pennsylvania, in 1905. They showed films for one hour. Originally identified with working-class audiences, nickelodeons appealed increasingly to the middle classes, and as the decade wore on, they became associated with the rising popularity of the story film. Their spread also forced the standardization of the films to the length of one reel, one thousand feet, to facilitate high-efficiency production and the trading of products within the industry.

New York's Soft City was and is home to many such establishments. One of the most popular was a place called Show World Center, now permanently closed, and like most such establishments, it had conspicuous signage, small window displays, and at one time had its street window painted a dark color to prevent peeping from outside.

Focusing on questions of masking and concealing and how these phenomena play out in the sex business, this chapter begins with a discussion of how peep shows and access to other types of videos facilitate the contemplation of disguising or covering up sexual practices.

4.1 Peep Show booths. Times Square.

This chapter begins with field notes from Alex, twenty-seven, male, white, followed by my observations from 1980 of the Times Square scene of a much earlier era.

CONTACT: ALEX, TIMES SQUARE (1995)

I wanted a research subject that was relatively accessible and one in which there were several examples to compare and contrast. The peep shows provided this, as they are among the most plentiful sex-related venues in the city. Finding the right kind of peep-show house is sort of a hit-or-miss venture, save for Eighth Avenue between Thirty-Fourth and Fiftieth Streets and the West Village. The venues are not advertised via traditional channels but rely on passersby and word of mouth.

Partially because of time constraints, I concentrated my research on the area of Eighth Avenue between Thirty-Fourth and Fiftieth Streets, on which there were no fewer than twenty peep-show houses, all contained in stores that sell pornography. I felt that concentrating my research in this neighborhood was appropriate because there are so many different peep-show houses here. I did visit one show in Lower Manhattan and found that it was not much different from those on Eighth Avenue. I conducted the majority of visits between 10 p.m. and midnight, hours during which I thought there would be a decent traffic flow in and out of the booths.[1]

At each show I visited, I attempted to document as many objective features as possible, for the sake of comparison. I documented the approximate number of selections each venue had or purported to have, how much viewing time one was given for one dollar, and the types of pornography available in the booths. I also noted the presence or absence of buddy booths, which did not seem to have an effect on whether the particular venue appeared to be a hotspot for gay cruising.

The peep show is oddly well suited for covert note taking. It is private, and the glow from the television monitors provides adequate light for writing. I kept my notes in a small notebook and spent much of my time in the booths writing down different features of each establishment, timing how long my money lasted, and surveying the types of porn available in the booths.

As for choosing which establishments I would go into, I had no specific criteria. If a place looked interesting to me, if they claimed to have a large number of selections in their booths, if they claimed to have twenty-five-cent shows (of the establishments I surveyed, only Show World Center had them), if I liked the sound of the name of a place, or if the window displays looked good, then I would go inside.

The pornography available in the booths ranges from the simplest male/female sex to every perversion imaginable. I saw heavy S&M, golden showers, and bestiality in one booth, and every establishment I visited had a wide variety of different fetish porn. The act of entering a peep-show booth and inserting money is akin to the act of confession, except that in the case of the peep show, one confesses his desires to himself instead of to a priest. The fact that the peep-show booth is very similar in size and appearance to a confessional in a Catholic Church is the proverbial icing on the cake.

Entering Kinematics, it seemed to be a porn-video store like any other. All the walls and racks (which were standing in the center of the store) were full of porn-video covers. But taking a closer look while walking around I realized that the videos were of mainly one variety, what one might call S/M videos. (There might have been some "straight" stuff, but I didn't see it.) Most of the covers displayed, speaking in S/M insider terms, scenes of dominant/submissive relationships (male/male, female/female, male/female, or female/male) and other S/M motifs I cannot recall in detail. Most of the videos also showed various kinds of S/M equipment in action. In addition to the videos on the shelves were folders at the counter available for inspection and containing copied video covers.

There was no S/M equipment besides the (various) ropes in action. All in all, this experience left me quite confused. The movie began to bore me, and I left the booth to explore the rest of Kinematics. I counted twenty-two booths and while doing this realized the extent of the store. In the back of the booth room was an aisle on the left leading to another room. Here all kinds of S/M equipment were displayed. I saw, for example, leather and chain wear, whips, hot-water bottles with pipes, spanking paddles, magazines, artificial vaginas, dildos, and vibrators in all forms and colors. Before I left Kinematics I talked briefly with one of the staff, but he wasn't very accommodating. I just wanted a few questions answered about his customers but realized that these questions might be construed as business related and may be uncomfortable for him to answer. He was reluctant to respond to my questions and finally pretended not to understand me. He handed me a flier for another venue and said I should go there; he said I could get more information from the people there.

Whenever I am in these sex establishments, be they bars, stores, or whatever, my pressing wish is to get out as soon as possible. The man behind the counter might have been willing to answer some other interesting questions about his business if they had nothing to do with his clients. But I felt I was getting a bit too nosy and decided to move on. I did see one guy who came from the booths and washed his hands. I assumed that some of the customers who came in had been masturbating in the booths and then washed their hands in the sink.

I did wonder why there were so many booths, and perhaps this would be one of the reasons. I had a few other questions. Why does the store specialize in S/M, and why locate the shop in this particular part of the city? I then asked one of the three male staff persons how the video system worked. I wanted to know how one watches a video. He told me that half an hour would cost eight dollars, and if I wanted to, I could watch even longer for additional payment. My next question was which of all these videos were available for watching (because I assumed that many of them were for sale only), and he told me I could watch any one I liked. So I looked around to choose a video for watching in the video booths. While I was walking around, not only to choose a film but also to experience the atmosphere of the store, I became aware of the groaning and moaning coming from the back room of the store where the video booths were located.

Listening to these sounds, one easily could tell that it was the characters in the films groaning, not the occupants of the booths. Then I saw another man, a customer probably, coming from the booths in the back; he too washed his hands in the sink (which I suppose was either for customers' use or at least not restricted to staff use only) and then left the store. A man in his fifties wearing a well-fitting, respectable suit was the next object of my attention. He was glancing through the folders, maybe choosing a video for watching, buying, or renting. I suppose video renting is possible in Kinematics.

By the 1990s, the Times Square peep-show scene was geared primarily toward isolated, individual patrons; it was something customers did alone and covertly. In the 1980s, the earliest peep shows often were not isolated from the rest of the

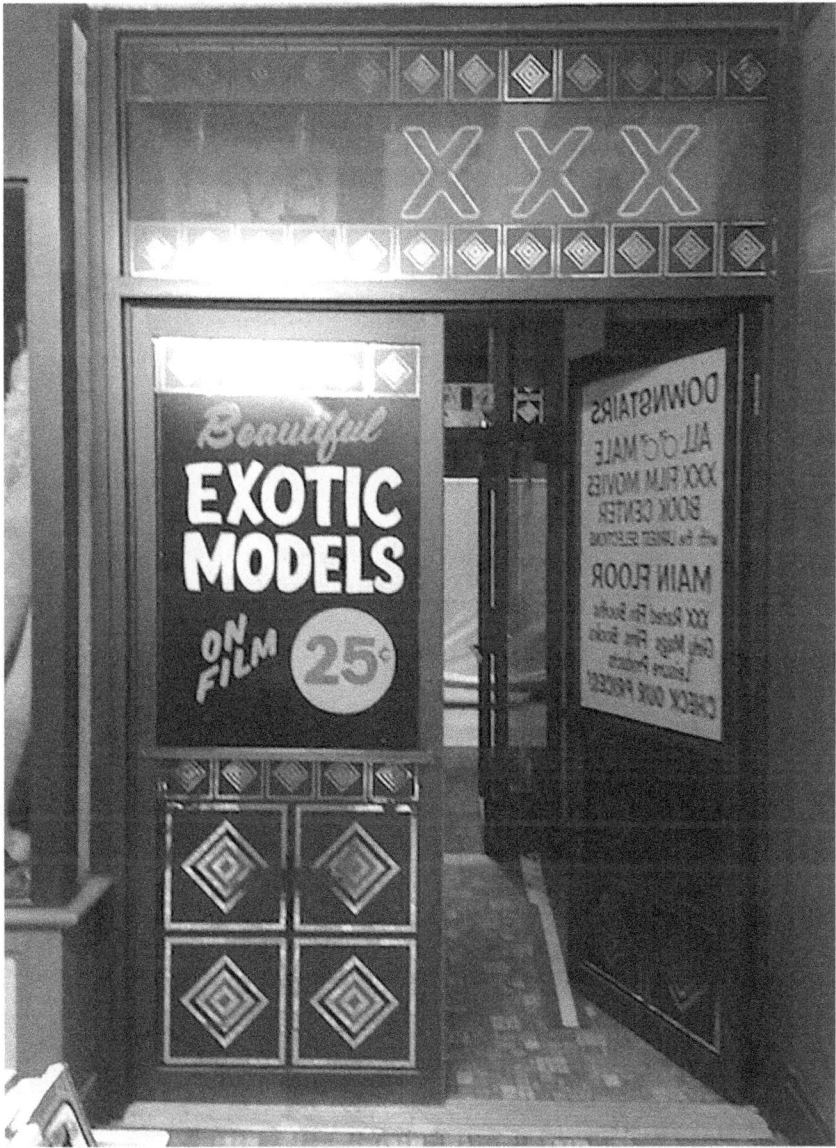

4.2 Show World Center. Times Square.

store and offered little to no privacy. The introduction of curtains and then doors has increased the privacy of the peep-show experience and contributed to its recent success and expansion. For a mere eight quarters, some places offer a private, direct, minute and a half of live visual and verbal contact with a woman or man, who works in a small space just in front of the client's booth. The customer may express a fantasy, deliver insults, or watch in silence.

One thing is clear: the growth of such live peep shows undoubtedly contributed to the decrease in burlesque in Midtown and in some late-night movie-theater going as well. I felt the reason pornography and peep shows are considered "dirty" today is not because they symbolize sex but because they symbolize desire. It is not socially acceptable to have sexual desires. One can have sex, but according to the Catholic doctrine, the only socially acceptable purpose is procreation. The media portrays sexual desire constantly, and this is the subject of much controversy and scrutiny.

The old pornographic movie theaters on Eighth Avenue showed actual sex acts taking place, so they were seen as dirty and dangerous. However, Samuel Delany, a frequent visitor to the theaters for years, says in *Times Square Red, Times Square Blue* that acts of violence in the theaters were rare. Everyone just wanted to get off. These theaters, because they devolved from places to view pornography (a discourse) into places where actual sex took place, were shuttered and replaced with sex shops featuring individual pornography-viewing booths.

WILLIAMS FIELD NOTES: ROXY THEATER, TIMES SQUARE (1980s)

I arrived at the Roxy, a raunchy peep show theater at the edge of Eighth Avenue. The place reeked of cheap perfume, ejaculate, and harlotry. The theater has pay booths. A man sits, taking money and giving back red tickets like the ones you get at a country fair, carnival, circus, or Coney Island. The show at the Roxy was a ride of a different sort, hardly what I'd expected.

I walked into the thumping sounds of Jimmy Cliff's "The Harder They Come" and saw a big black guy ferociously fucking a small white female on a tiny stage for a mostly white male audience. Neither she nor her muscle-bound partner, a man around twenty-five, appeared to be faking. They were enjoying their act. The man stayed erect throughout the entire twenty-minute performance, standing her up on his dick, then laying her down again, spreading her legs, and fucking some more. After a few more minutes, which seemed exhaustively long for those who are "no-studs," they stopped. The audience was silent.

Around the left side were curtains and small chairs or little divans, but they were quickly hidden by a curtain. After the black stud had removed the mattress from the stage, the crowd began to clear: in the back of the theater and to the left of the entranceway, six scantily clad women, four white and two black, stood up to make their presence known. They then sat in chairs with their legs crossed or opened; there was little doubt why they were there. One of the women wore a G-string, which made her appear nude; others wore negligees or scanty panties covered by see-through blouses.

After the lights came on, I could see that the chairs we sat in were pockmarked with cigarette burns. The air was smoky and the floor a bit sticky in parts. A palpable funk oozed from the armpits of the room. Dingy, garish, red velvet curtains lined both sides of the theater.

A tall blond woman in her mid-twenties approached me. "Hello, honey, don't you want some company? Wanna join me in my private booth?"

"Where is your private booth?" I responded.

"Right behind there. Come on, I'll show you."

"What can we do in your private booth?"

"We can do whatever you want. We can have sex, talk, drink, whatever you like."

"Well, what'll it cost me?"

"It'll cost you ten dollars now if you willing to go with me, then it'll cost as much as you're willing to spend after that."

"Thanks, but this whole experience is stimulating enough for me, maybe some other time."

"Okay, but you don't know what you're missing."

Peep stores have doors on their booths for viewer privacy, and in many instances they have a red light over each door, which goes on when the machine is in use. The basic charge is twenty-five cents for ninety seconds of a film. To see more of the film, the customer must continue depositing quarters into the machine. Most customers know what the film is about from the title, a representative still, or a short written description posted outside the booth.

I offer my notes on the peep-show industry from the 1980s to reveal how these particular venues have changed since then.[2] Something that has emerged is how the main action in these spaces engages some kind of physical, sensual stimulation, one derived from some aspect of the scene itself: the smell of leather, semen, perfumes, cigarette smoke, powders, body odor. Other sources of stimulation include body motion and touch, taste, and sound. The music is often raunchy, ribald, and risqué. A song heard at many of the S/M venues I encountered was Nancy Sinatra's "These Boots Are Made for Walkin'":

> These boots were made for walkin'
> and that's just what they'll do
> And one of these days these boots are gonna walk all over you

It could often be heard blaring through the wall speakers, a teasing melody, no less a knowing one.[3]

WILLIAMS FIELD NOTES: FRISCO CLUB/PEEP SHOW, TIMES SQUARE (1980s)

I walked upstairs at the Frisco and was greeted by three characters in this jerk-off joint: the first was a young black woman in her twenties wearing a black ballerina's tutu. She was neither amusing nor particularly sexy or attractive. The second character I encountered was a muscle-bound money changer with a mean disposition. He was quite talkative and wearing a too-tight T-shirt, babbling on about club rules, listing what people can or cannot do. I asked myself: why do people with bad breath always seem to have so much to say? The third greeter was a Puerto Rican man who must have weighed three hundred pounds. He was mopping up around the booths; apparently, he was the janitor. He too was surly, but I could understand why. I was later told the guy was Sri Lankan, not Puerto Rican, and that most of the Frisco's employees are Sri Lankan, Black, or Hispanic.

One notices with striking regularity the large number of Black employees in the Times Square porn industry, although I must be careful and not assume their ethnicities. Notably, these employees play many different roles: bouncers, guards, sex mates, money changers, floor sweepers, dancers. Here at the Frisco they are employed as dancers, performers, coin changers, and cashiers.

The burly man I met at the entrance was speaking harshly to a customer who happened to have stepped into the wrong area without a token. You must purchase a token ($1) in order to go into the booths with the women; apparently, this poor slob had not done that. I don't think he spoke English either, which didn't help his case any. I went into one of the booths, and as soon as I had dropped my token in, a young white girl with a busted lip who was about twenty or so stepped in and pulled down her underwear.

"Do you wanna sexy show?"

"Yes, go ahead," I said. I had heard this line from several of the women.

"Well, it'll cost you two dollars."

I hesitated.

"It will cost you two dollars," she repeated. "If you want me to give you a sexy show."

I paused and considered her offer. "All right. Do you take quarters?"

"Yeah. I take anything if it adds up to two dollars."

I pushed the eight quarters through a plastic door with ten different slots, and a small screen opened. She bent over, picked up the coins, pulled a chair up, spread her legs and fingered herself, all done with a demure, matter-of-fact half-smile.

"Why don't you come over and play with yourself," she said to me. "Oh come on, let me see your dick."

I didn't want to show her my dick, because she was not paying me; I was paying her. So I told her, "If I do it, it will cost *you* eight quarters." She looked at me like I'd stolen something, and the window slid slowly down until her face disappeared. I went to another peep show before heading up the street.

In these two cases involving the Roxy and the Frisco, I, paradoxically, am the one objectified. That objectification is necessary for the sex worker to exercise some kind of power over the patron. The sex worker charged two dollars for a peep show. When she asked me to take out my penis and I then suggested that if I did we would be *performing for each other*, I was violating the terms of the implicit agreement we had entered into, namely, that I would be the objectified one. She indignantly acted offended, and the show came to a stop. This constitutes a perfect example of the power that the desired object exercises over the one who desires it and how that dynamic serves to problematize the idea of objectification, of who is objectifying whom. The sex worker expects the client to do, for free, the same thing—that is, masturbate—that she does in exchange for money. If this does not happen, the relationship is broken. These two cases (at least for me) provide a new way to think about power in relation to sex work. Perhaps because penetration—or any physical contact whatsoever—is not involved, the power dynamics instead play out in communication, contentment, and engagement.

WILLIAMS FIELD NOTES (1970 AND 1975)

I came to Thirty-Seventh Street looking for Kinematics, expecting a store no different than any of the other porn shops one sees in Manhattan. I was surprised to find a doorway discreetly marked with an awning; there was no show window or neon sign shouting for attention. I walked up the steps and entered the store. At that moment, I realized why the store keeps such a low profile: it is an S/M fetish store.

I noticed a tall counter on the left where the cash register was situated. In the first room of the store were video booths, along with several large racks filled with more booths. In the glass case at the counter, I noticed what seemed to be the only "straight" porn videos in the store. Along the walls and on the racks were probably several hundred videos; the titles indicated the fetish depicted, such as bondage, slaves, spanking, rubber/latex, and caning ("British" discipline). I noticed that most of the videos seemed to be centered on a violent act with a definite "top" and "bottom." Curiously, most of the booths also had pictures, many of which seemed to include religious (generally Christian) imagery. One of the photos depicted a man bound to a cross; another depicted a woman bound between two columns. Some of videos had titles in foreign languages: French, German, Japanese, Dutch.

The store was laid out such that a person browsing the racks could have a relatively large amount of privacy. Few customers were in the store with me. Based on the few people I did see (all men in business suits) and given the prices and gender orientation of most of the videos and magazines (the videos were forty to sixty dollars each), the general clientele is probably upper middle class. I did not speak to any of them.

While there were dildos and vibrators for sale as well as women's outfits, these items seemed secondary to the S/M merchandise, both in stock and on display. An overview of the titles and covers of the booths and magazines did not really display a dominant or submissive gender as a group, but in most of the nonviolent fetish products (leather, vinyl), there was a definite majority of products with women as the subjects.

For the most part, the porn sold here differed in that it seems (judging from the titles) to be less about what most would refer to as "sex" than straight porn. Most would probably call it violence. It was also often centered on an object or type of object (canes/whips, leather/vinyl) as opposed to straight porn, which centers on an action, usually intercourse. At the end of the room opposite the entrance was a doorway from which the sounds of slaps and screams emanated. I walked through it and found a room lined with small booths containing video screens. Three of the booths were closed. Small red lights above the doors glowed, indicating occupancy.

I left through a doorway in the back of the room, which led down a narrow hallway with glass cases containing enema kits and various outfits (maid outfits, vinyl lingerie). I entered a room with a large counter on the right, holding several magazine and bookracks. On the far wall were several dildos and vibrators for sale. On the magazine racks in the center of the room were titles such as *Bound and Gagged* and *Bondage Babes*. Most of the other titles had to do with bondage or leather and latex fetishes.

One observation I might note is that the physical environment of the store is arranged so that eye contact with other customers and with employees is easily avoided (as with the magazine and video rack arrangement and the elevated counters). Also, the darkness of the room with the video booths added to the possibility of avoiding interaction with other people and contributed to the anonymity of the environment. The lack (or even fear) of interaction illustrates how marginalized and deviant the porn in this store has been conditioned to be seen in its larger social context. Although it has less to do with intercourse or nudity, this porn is even more taboo.

In general, the place has been designed to be as low-key an environment as possible. The store draws little attention to itself from the street and significantly less than most other porn shops in the city. The discreetly marked awning gives the impression of exclusivity to the clientele, and it certainly is not a very effective advertisement for the uninformed passersby, because it gives little information as to what lies inside.

The changes in our society about the role of sex have had an unmistakable impact. The freer sense of self and the concomitant liberated views about sexuality have sparked a revolution in the attitudes of men and women about the meaning of sex. Most of the men who make the porno parlor their daily ritual have a basic need for compulsive, noncommittal, nonemotional sex, yet they all see everyday life as itself erotic.

The peep shows you have just read about are merely the public tip of the iceberg. Sex was always well developed in New York City. As peep shows and live sex shows became more important industries, they began to spill out of the Soft City and into other communities in expected and unanticipated forms. This sea change took place under Mayor Giuliani's designation of a specific area of the Village as an ipso facto red-light zone. Police pressure before the naming of the Village area as a red-light zone was specific to the Times Square area, parts of the Bronx (Hunts Point, for example), and to small sex-related "strolls" in and around the city. Still, the largest marketplace for sexual goods and services in every borough was underground and remains so today.

These less visible locations comprise the most significant way sex is managed and controlled in the Soft City and reveal how difficult, if not impossible, it is to eradicate. Because of police pressure before this designation, there is a visible manifestation of a far larger market for sexual goods and services. This has only continued to flourish in the underground of lower Times Square and other areas of which the Soft City is the southern frontier. One has simply to purchase a copy of Screw magazine, the unofficial organ of the sex industry in New York, to learn that the idea of a single place to go to for sexual services, say, a stroll and a series of retail stores, has become obsolete. This is an era of cell phones, credit cards, escort agencies, apps, and virtual reality. The hooker's stroll still exists, as do pimp bars, and as these shift their locations (depending on where police pressure is most strongly felt), the peep show remains a mainstay of a changing industry.

chapter 5

Escorts and Clients

And he felt that he was hers utterly: he would have abjured everything, to possess her for a single hour that very night.

—Emile Zola, *Nana*

In this chapter I reflect on the overlap between visible sex work and more "discreet" practices. The new approach to prostitution in the city is referred to as "in-calls," which involve young women using their apartments, hotels, and other locales to meet clients for sex. The more traditional practice, which still exists as well, is an escort agency through which transactions are mediated by a madam or a pimp.

Sex workers operate under the rubric of providing fast sex in the city. Although sex work is not as visible on the street these days, it is still quite common. New technologies such as pagers, cellular phones, and the internet have made less visible forms of sex work thrive beyond the reach of traditional street-level police crackdowns. However, police surveillance and crackdowns do still occur. This poses many problems, as my contact Ruby Love, who is now known as Madam X, and other contacts we will meet will discuss. In escort agencies, many women act as their own pimps: the woman hustles herself and keeps most of the money. She gives a portion to the man behind the door who protects her from the "crazies," aggressive clients who refuse to pay or who want more than they pay for. Businesses such as the one Madam X operates, although they are independent, are often aided by lawyers, crooked cops, and boyfriends. If they begin to make big money, what they call "cheddar," they might be "taxed" by local organized crime syndicates.

WILLIAMS FIELD NOTES (2012)

In the 1980s, the administration under Mayor Edward Irving Koch began a cleanup campaign to regulate prostitution. Koch wanted to avoid being labeled as "soft" on gays and on sex, largely because his bachelorhood and sexuality had been campaign issues in 1977. Koch also wanted the city to be "tourist friendly," since he saw the tourist trade as offering one of the remedies to the ailing city budget. "In 1995, the city council adopted a zoning ordinance establishing regulations barring adult entertainment from residential zones and most commercial and manufacturing zones, and mandating that where permitted adult businesses had to be at least 500 feet from houses of worship, schools, daycare centers and other adult businesses."[1]

Even though New York City welcomed millions of tourists every year, Koch felt the city had a reputation for being dirty—meaning literally full of trash and poor sanitation. Koch also felt that the sex shops along Forty-Second Street and elsewhere in the city were too prominent as tourist attractions and, though he wanted tourists to visit Times Square, that these venues took away from other, more "proper" tourist destinations in the city. Another bone of contention or area of concern at the time was the growing AIDS epidemic. Along with San Francisco, New York City was considered a center of the epidemic. Koch began closing sex venues—BDSM locations and gay clubs, more specifically.

In the mid-1980s, I began conducting more formalized, multisited ethnographic forays into the Soft City. One of these included an escort agency, for which I became a driver. This job allowed me to see firsthand how the street prostitution business was moving indoors, fronting as tattoo parlors, Swedish massage, tanning salons, facial parlors, and the like. As this fake nomenclature was emerging in the culture, communications technologies were changing as well: beepers and pagers, the arrival of the internet, and videotapes and laserdiscs. Further, crack-cocaine markets changed the character of street prostitution—or, more broadly, sex worker commerce—as well: the most substantial change would leave minority sex workers on the street and move higher-end sex workers (mostly white women) indoors. The internet also had an impact on the race game: while the black/Latinx (Blantino) street prostitute continued to be viewed as just a "ho," the white prostitute moved indoors and began to take on a viable "career identity" as "sex worker."

The term "career" normally refers to those within a respectable profession, but in this case, the term broadened to refer to any economic pursuit undertaken by an individual that expressly involves behavior considered deviant. Prostitution's move indoors made it possible for many of the women to become "collaborators," and they could network and identify as "workers" with distinct careers. One contact the reader will hear from shortly, Ruby Love, talks about this pursuit: "We are hos with a purpose." Katherine, another contact who was commenting on a small-sample ethnography I conducted at the time, stated,

> Many of the women Williams interviewed considered their work at the escort agency a career, some long term, some short. The rules accompanying employment at the escort agency also created an atmosphere of professionalism, from basic strict procedures regarding your arrival and departure when dealing with a client to the financial and proper workplace attire in order to represent the business in a professional manner.

What contacts like Katherine noted was an internal hierarchy within these agencies, one based on attractiveness: This value was seen as both a form of sexual labor and as erotic capital. This idea is intimately related to the concept of "sexical labor," elaborated to mean the way sex is used as a medium of exchange and how women use their sexuality to their advantage to acquire illegal items (for example, drugs), which ultimately suggests an economic arrangement. In this case, women use their "erotic capital" in a predominantly male world to gain leverage and power.[2]

Comparisons can also be made to a career in modeling: with natural good looks, kept up through proper grooming, there was ample room for moving up, which most of the women felt meant eventually owning their own agency or starting their own business. I note here that Ruby Love (aka Madam X) in her operation mostly employs Latinas. I think this is a reflection of Madam X's place of operation and/or of the communities she wishes to support through her business. Her clients also prefer Latinas because, as she says, "They are pretty, exciting, and eager to please, plus they are fiery, hot-blooded, and extremely sexy. These values connect with the fact that the money is also what one would refer to as 'cheap dates,' since only a few hundred dollars will get the client what he would otherwise have to pay perhaps a thousand dollars for if it was a high-end white model."

Culture matters to this house: these Latinas represent a cultural component in the selection of these particular women. I think this is a reflection of Madam X's place of operation and/or of the communities she wishes to support through her business.

Ruby Love (aka Madam X) was the first in her circle to start her own agency as an independent:

> I started my own agency, and I kept a lot of stuff Melissa [the former owner] used to set up her business up with. I wasn't gonna sit around and play that game of putting out forever, because you don't look good forever. You age quickly in this business, because every guy wants a "teeny bopper" if they can get one. What's gonna happen when I'm twenty-five, thirty, and can't please them anymore? I'll tell you what. I'm fucked, that's what, and not in the way you usually get it.

The sociologist Arlie Hochschild makes note of the importance of emotional labor in jobs such as airline steward or waiter, industries that require routine relations with the public. In this regard, escorts have a job that is not just about making the client happy but doing so by having sex with them. Several women told me that most of their male clients didn't want sex at all but someone to talk to about things they could never talk about with their wives or girlfriends. Most of the women were not interested in being therapists, though they did do a lot of "pretending work," and not just the orgasmic kind. Ruby Love says:

> I'd sometime pretend to come [have an orgasm], but other times I didn't. It all depended on a number of things. How I felt that night. Whether I had got off that week with my boyfriend. You know, that kinda thing. Sometimes it's real, and sometimes it's not. But I do a lot of smiling and listening to them talk about how their wives and girlfriends don't perform this or that thing they like.
>
> Not working doesn't bother me as much as having to work a regular nine to five. I hate straight hours, time clocks, and superior bosses. Making illegal money is a whole different scene. It's part of what I categorize as freelancing.... If you can keep this life up and survive from it alone, you're doing better.

She perceives succeeding at the "street life" as "doing better" than her straight-world counterparts. Ruby Love also expresses that not having the everyday structure of a legal job and a boss to obey allows much more freedom over her day-to-day life and future. Katherine Zapert explains this antiestablishment philosophy, which she observes "appears in all of the data": "The majority of women in the sex industry begin to see their work as part of their identity. This of course contributes to their inability to imagine themselves ever being part of the legitimate work force." She argues that the women choose

> to frame their work as an attempt to break down the hegemonic structure, or the concept of patriarchy [that] is responsible for the "whore" stigma, effectively dividing us into "good girls" and "bad girls" in order to conquer. Because the work I do takes place within the structural confines of an escort agency or service, this sentiment is seen less when discussing societal norms, but appears when discussing the restrictions and rules of that operation, as all girls wanted to fuck the agency.[3]

It is no secret these young women, with very few exceptions, did not want their families to know of their choice of occupation. Many had started out with high hopes of being beauty queens and had been so for much of their early lives; they now faced the reality that beauty doesn't last forever and that their previous titles did not translate into steady employment. Regardless, most of them expressed a desire to keep their work a secret from family members and old friends. Unbeknownst to them, this reticence is one of the traps of this line of work and one of the reasons many end up in the sex business: pimps and other sex workers don't want them to connect with their families either. Family contact makes it more difficult for procurers to control sex workers.

Lisa, a tiny pixie brunette with a ponytail and snakeskin boots, sits on the hood of my car, waiting for her agency coworker. This is her day off. She is one of the women I found most interesting because her look is completely contrary to the way she talks: although white, she talks like a black person, using black idioms, gestures, and hand movements. She said she was raised around black people. We were discussing sex and her mother's perspective on her career.

> The motherfuckers [clients] be playing on sex. And everybody wants to get into your business any kinda way. Mom be playing on sex too in her own way because she sees the money I be getting. That's why I don't discuss my

business with nobody. Its gotta be an extreme emergency for me to do it with a client for the first time we meet, for example, so why would I discuss my life with my mom? As far as sex is concerned I'll do it [have sex], get my shit off and tell the nig— [she stops herself from saying the entire word] to get out. I say, "Put it in [her vagina] but no sucking on my titties and shit cause I be falling in love too much." Too easy with that kinda affection.

There is clearly ethical concern and cultural judgment regarding loved ones at play in Lisa's remarks. I recognize this as what the sociologist Erving Goffman referred to as a "spoiled identity." This is where sex work heavily stigmatizes women in such a way that others don't want to be associated with it because they will be branded whores, or worse.

Lisa's sense of becoming socially undesirable is in spite of what one older prostitute sarcastically told me one day while chatting about the business: "*When I started in this business, we were just hos; now we're sex workers.*" This is a sentiment I've heard expressed by others as well. Yet the altering of this status from "ho" to "sex worker" has changed neither the laws nor the attitudes of most people, who see the business as sinful, corrupt, vile, and unsavory and the people in it as parasites. Most everyday folk anticipate sex work as not only remaining illegal but also as always being considered immoral and stigmatized, whether indoors or on the street, whether they are called "sex workers" or "sex angels."

Katherine Zapert argues that women working in the indoor sex industry need to protect themselves because they are at greater risk for physical violence. This danger, Zapert tells me, is in part because of our society's acceptance of misogynistic and violent behavior, which "our legislation and legal precedents continue to perpetuate." She quotes a *New York Times* article: in 2007, a Philadelphia judge declared that when a prostitute was forced at gunpoint to have nonconsensual sex with three men, it was not rape but "theft of services."[4] Women do have problems with clients, but across my observations, the agency makes every effort to protect the women.

Gloria, a twenty-three-year-old Dominican woman, talks about what she was told to do on every "date" with a client:

Number one. Don't trust nobody. Check the room, under the bed and closets, and if you walk in and see more than one person, leave immediately. If the person is wearing sneakers, kindly leave. If they smell bad or been heavily drinking, leave. Just tell them you have to call the agency. But there are ways the agency tries to protect you because of the information taken before you arrive, name, phone number, address, credit card info, driver's license, et cetera. When you get there, make sure the person is who they say they are based on that information. I think if some girls get hurt it's because they get too eager to make that money and don't pay close attention to those kind of details.

One of the "girls" who had that girly-girly look all the clients desired once got into my car, looking shaken. In some of my interactions with other workers, I saw the usefulness of Gloria's advice. She told me about what happened:

Went to the hotel as I was told, and this guy, this man, wanted to tie me up, but I know he did not look right, a bit uncanny looking, so I decided to say I had to phone the agency. He looked visibly upset at that. I just felt he would hurt me if I stayed in that room. I just felt that for sure. We were told if we feel uncomfortable we should leave. I wanted the money, but I didn't want to die trying to get it.

Zapert writes: "Anyone familiar with American culture, and the sex industry (particularly the 'online' sex industry), knows that the sexualization of younger and younger women is nothing novel. I point out that escorts are known as 'girls' and many clients wanted girls who looked like their daughters or their daughters' friends. Babysitters were often mentioned as a desired fantasy object."[5]

I refer to escort agency work as *quasi prostitution* because the woman does not need to have sex with the clients if she doesn't want to. But there is a proviso, since there are different kinds of clients and different levels of danger. These layers of sex work and the agency these women possess in being able to negotiate these transactions transform the reality of their labor into a form of quasi prostitution.[6] The following notes describe work I recorded during the 1990s. At that time, I was both driver and sociologist, using the job as a way to carry out research and make extra money while working as an adjunct professor at the CUNY Graduate Center.

WILLIAMS FIELD NOTES (1990s)

A slow night because it's the middle of the week and a holiday as well, and nothing is going on. I'm reading my book and waiting for a young girl no more than eighteen. She's been to the car twice, saying her date is not in his room. I tell her to call the office, but she's afraid they'll tell her to come in, and she knows this client (he tips heavy), so she wants to stay and try one more time.

A friend worked as a booker at a Midtown Manhattan escort agency, and the manager needed a driver. She told her boss about me; I liked to drive and liked night work, plus I was training in martial arts. I went down, met the owner, and was hired on the spot. The salary was low, but my friend said the tips were fantastic. I needed money, but more than money, I saw it as an opportunity to do research on a relatively new social scene. I soon discovered the "girls" made up for any lack of a decent salary because the tips (as advertised) were very good. I made money, and by waiting for them or for listening to their troubles or adventures, letting them use my car phone, not looking in my rear-view mirror, honking my horn, or not telling the boss what they were doing off the books, all these little things turned into "tips" for me, that is, great material for my field notes. I also read a lot: Thomas Mann, Richard Wright, James Joyce, Edgar Allan Poe, Claude Brown, everything I could. I wrote copious notes.

After a while, all the girls wanted to "fuck the agency." Some got caught and were fired; others got away with breaking the rules because of the money they generated. Though escort agencies claimed they were not associated with prostitution, à la "call-girl" operations, it was assumed by many, including law enforcement agencies, that the escort business was basically a front for prostitution. From 1984 to 1986, major shifts began in the commercialized vice industry—increased competition, increased specialization, conflict between groups—as prostitution swiftly moved from the street to indoor locations. These shifts had as much to do with the official attempts to control prostitution as they did with the larger social mission in New York City to eradicate or at least contain prostitution by keeping it off the streets.

New forms of prostitution took shape in the city in locations like massage parlors, tattoo parlors, tanning salons, and, of course, escort agencies. Prostitution took on a new character and direction, camouflaged in locations variously hidden, and all kept indoors. Most of my research as a budding ethnographer had been conducted at night. My dissertation was on after-hours clubs where people hung out all night sniffing cocaine and partying. So this driving at night was just right for me.

One of the first young women I drove on a regular basis was a tall, dark-complexioned former model named Ruby Love. She had a client, a foreign attaché or diplomat, something like that, who lived or stayed at the St. Regis Hotel, one of the most expensive joints in the city. When he was in town, he always asked for her. She would go see this guy, who would pay her two, maybe three thousand dollars. She would be all high, zooted off coke, and say she had just fucked him again. All he wanted was for her to fuck him with a dildo and he'd pay her a few thousand bucks. Well, she was supposed to call the agency and report when she came on call and when she got off, but she'd say she was out in an hour when in reality she would stay for three. She paid Melissa and the agency for only one hour. Melissa would ask me where Ruby Love was, and I would say, "At the bar having a drink or dinner or something." Melissa knew she was lying, but Ruby Love brought so much money to the agency that a lot of her behavior was overlooked. I got a hundred bucks for ignoring Melissa's pleas.

My job was to drive the women to their "dates," wait for them, or if it was an all-nighter, see that the girls got to their locations and remain on call to pick up other girls who had completed their dates. I use "girls" here because all the escorts are referred to as "girls." Young women of every description, color, and shape, though rarely fat—chubby, yeah, but not really fat. Although some clients specifically called for "full-bodied women" or "big-boned women," they were not "fat fat," as it were. But even women we might call "fat" were sometimes requested, but the agency didn't really have "fat fat" girls in their rolodex.

Many of the clients wanted girls who looked like "teeny boppers," but it was all about *girls*: girls who were mothers with kids at home with babysitters, girls who had just gotten married but needed money to pay for charges made on overburdened credit cards, girls with boyfriends at home waiting for them to arrive with cash and drugs, girls who were graduates from private schools, and girls who had just missed the big time by one vote and ended up runner-up in the latest beauty contest. These young women were all well dressed, stylish, and smart because that's who the boss hired and what the boss wanted them to be.

"I always tell the girls to wear clothes with a good line to enhance their figure." This is Melissa, the boss lady, speaking to a group of new recruits. I'm sitting here waiting for her to tell me that I should be more responsible to her and the agency, not to the girls, and to let her know what's going on. She has just hired another driver (a woman), who I'm told is quite loyal to the agency. I suspect she got word I'm more loyal to the "girls" and probably heard rumors to that effect from some "bitch snitch." The fact that I have never ratted out or informed on any of the escorts since I've been driving gives these rumors some credibility.

Melissa was born in Brooklyn and was a former beauty queen herself, and she knew all the tricks of the trade. But I wanted to know how she dealt with the police and the public—and the mob, for that matter. I wasn't about to broach these subjects with her. I had to wait for the right opportunity. (It never really came.)[7] "One good dress or suit can be worn on several occasions," she tells the group.

> You will not be seeing the same person often. And don't wear anything you're not comfortable in, otherwise you'll be preoccupied with thoughts of making a good impression and therefore unable to focus your interest on the client. Dress with elegance and style. No jeans. Dresses preferred. Hair and make-up styled every season. Make the effort to coordinate the look with shoes, bags, accessories. The effort is worth it. Aim for the polished look.

In spite of Melissa's advice, many of the girls changed clothes in the car and, of course, asked that I not tell. Ruby had a client who she says paid her "extra" if she followed his orders. He had a script for her to follow, and that included wearing a very short skirt with no underwear, red lipstick, smeared.

A few months before I met her, Mary, at nineteen, became an escort. She says Melissa was obsessive to the point of telling her what she should have in her closet:

> She told all of us one day at a meeting that our closet should contain a blazer and skirt, feminine blouses, matching shoes and purse, accessories, casual outfits, evening dresses, but not flashy, and a weekend travel bag. She gave us tips about having perfect fingernails . . . if you have short nails, wear a clear or light polish or false nails, and to stay away from silk because it wrinkles too easily and our dry cleaning bills will be very high. Because of the beauty-contest years I knew all about this stuff. But she wanted us to get membership in a spa to control our weight, get a makeup consultation, and buy fashion magazines and "How to Dress" books.

I asked how she remembered all of that and she replied, "Melissa gave us the list to memorize."

The office is on the second floor of a twenty-story, nondescript building located near Ninth Avenue in Manhattan. The room is crowded: a bank of telephones and a switchboard arrangement are on the left side of the room, six small chairs are spaced around the back, and several folded chairs rest against the wall. Four of the chairs are occupied by pretty young women; two are standing. One, with a red beret and tank top, blows bubble gum and is obviously a regular; the others nervously wait to be interviewed.

The manager's (Melissa's) office is more comfortable: thick white rug, two big white chairs, a large round white sofa with several cushions. Her clean mahogany desk has neatly stacked papers held in place with a red rock. The front window is covered with a venetian blind; a potted plant wilts in the corner behind the phone bank. Melissa comes out, her words littered with a slight West Indian accent, and she begins her orientation with a rhetorical question: "How do I become a *professional* escort? We have prepared literature for those of you here for the first time and which I will give to all of you before you leave and will include agency procedures, rules, and hints. We will have a few meetings for the opportunity to get together and discuss questions, problems, situations and make suggestions."

Three other women arrive; one looks a bit older than the others but is dressed elegantly. Melissa glances at her watch but says nothing about tardiness. She asks the girls their names and tells them they will not be using their real names. Then she asks if any of them are "on call" and introduces me as their driver. One of the young women, who really did look like a girl in her teens, asked something about the secrets to being a good escort and for an estimate about how much money she could make. Melissa glanced at her and gestured with her hand for her to follow her into her office. She then asked if there were any other questions. "All our dispatchers are capable of answering your questions if I'm not around." The older woman asked about agency rules regarding clients and black books. It turned out this woman was Melissa's "plant." Ruby Love believed this because of the way she asked questions and the type of questions she asked. Ruby also mentioned that one of the dispatchers saw this woman walking with Melissa on Fifty-Seventh Street a while back.

There is clearly a moral and social ambivalence here for the girls. I started to wonder how the escort agency grew out of the conditions in the city. Were there certain urban conditions only this particular city could provide? If so, why? What is it about the city that creates these conditions, or is this possible anywhere and everywhere? Escorts hide what they do from friends and family, and as a result there is a rise and fall of escort agencies, sex clubs, and visible prostitution in the city. One of the girls told me:

> I never told my parents what I do because they'll ask too many questions. I just say I'm doing PR work or secretarial work, modeling on the side. It's not that I'm not proud of what I do; it's more like it's not really anybody's business on the one hand and a way to avoid having to get into details about this business on the other. Everybody knows what people think we do as escorts, so rather than having to explain it and get those looks from people, I'd rather not mention what I do.

Driving the women around gave me the chance to know them intimately; they talked about their clients, they talked about their families, and they ruminated on their likes and dislikes, the money they made, and the things they did to earn money. They spoke about Melissa and the whole "racket," as they called it. They said Melissa was emphatic about not using the word "prostitution," but they knew as well as she did this was a call-girl operation by any other name.

Melissa spoke briefly one day about how "this whole prostitution thing" was not something she liked to talk about. It was a taboo subject. But after reading an article in the newspaper saying all escort agencies were fronts for prostitution, she said she was "tired of reading this garbage. It's the same old thing, every agency in town gets lumped into the same dirty bag."

Ruby Love says that "Melissa always tells us":

> If any client ask for sexual favors, to leave immediately and call the office and all of that, but when a guy puts five hundred-dollar bills on the table and has a fistful more and says you can have as much you want, just stay another hour or two . . . who's gonna turn that down and call the office? Please! Melissa knows that, and we know that. Her lamenting about "no prostitution, no prostitution" is just to cover her ass just in case anybody gets busted, she can say "this is an escort agency, no, no," and "this is not a call-girl operation, blah, blah, blah," but who do she think she kidding?

The day the article broke in the paper, I talked with Melissa, and her words were very clear on this matter. Whether she meant them or whether the girls believed them was another matter. But in fact, Melissa was right, because the courts stated in the 1970s that as long as the owner is paying for some service other than sex—for example, babysitting, or housekeeping, or a maid service— the arrangement is not the same as or equivalent to prostitution. The girls are paid for "escorting" men to various events in the city; therefore, within the law, it is not prostitution.

Some girls develop "little black books" with clients' names and phone numbers; however, this is strictly forbidden, and any girl caught with this little item is immediately fired. There are many such rules and procedures. The escorts often talked about them because their lives revolved around them. Jessica, blond with green eyes and hailing from Minnesota, said that rules were made to be broken and that she was looking to land a rich husband.

> The booker tells us what to do, the manager tells us what to do, the dispatcher and Melissa tell us what to do. Everybody tells us what to do, but nobody tells us how long we should be doing this before we get a life of our own. I want to get married one day and have a family, and why would I not take advantage of this situation and find a husband? These guys are rich, many are handsome, almost all are successful, I would be foolish not to try and find somebody, and I don't care what anybody tells me, that's what I intend to do. You can have all the rules in the world, but you can't stop people from acting in their own best interests. And that instinct is to get ahead, that interest is to take advantage of situations and move on.

Sexual attraction or physical attractiveness becomes a value that can be traded or bartered for the advantage of social and/or economic gain. At the same time, as Ruby noted, unattractiveness can become a handicap. "All the older women and those who are not exactly raving beauties anymore, all they get is to suck dick and ass fucked. Believe me, I know: Suzanne and Barbara for example, you met them, they do the talk tricks too. But they don't get the kinda dates Jessica or Veronica or even Marianna gets."

These pretty women can capitalize on their "rank" by marrying, which provides some security against loss of beauty. We are aware that others enter the labor force in jobs where physical beauty is very helpful, and of course, some become prostitutes in settings less glamorous than escort or call-girl operations. So the question is not why so many of the girls don't become prostitutes but rather why so few of them do.

Others felt the rules were old fashioned and basically out of touch with the times. I spoke with the booker for the agency about the situation:

> This is the 1980s, right? The agency tells us that the client belongs to them. And it's not the agency's intention to make money or profit from fines and penalties they impose on us. But at the same time, they have all these rules that make it impossible to obey. For instance, if you stay with a client after the assignment is over without collecting fees for the agency, they fine you for each hour you stay with that client. Well, sometimes you just wanna relax and you like the guy and you're having fun and you forget about the time. Why should we be fined for that? Another thing is about drugs. Well, cocaine is at every call I go on. Really, I'm serious. All my clients have tons of coke on them, and if you get caught, you're fired. If you get caught stealing, okay I can under-stand that, but [being fined by the agency for] giving clients your phone number or taking a little coke? I don't think that's right at all.

I discovered that Melissa would use fake clients to see if the girls were break-ing her rules, but she employed this tactic only with girls who were not her best, and she often used the bust as an excuse to fire them outright. Ruby, for instance, brought so much money to the agency that Melissa would not dare try that with her. There were other rule violations that were grounds for dismissal as well, pros-titution being at the top of the list. Other types of violations were fined, with fines as high as a full agency fee (about $300), for example, for a "no show" with a client, down to a one-dollar fine if, for example, you called on a wrong line to the agency. If a girl was with a date and used a poor excuse to leave the date early, she was docked a full agency fee. Girls were to turn in credit card slips and checks on time. If a girl made a mistake on a check or credit card slip that caused the bank not to pay, a full agency fee would be collected in advance, and the girl's cut would be held up till the money cleared.

The names in table 5.1 have been changed to protect the identities of the pro-fessionals. Nevertheless, it distinguishes in a truthful way the original "profes-sional" names of escorts.

As the "girls" take on the role of "escort," they may stay for only a few "dates" and decide not to continue, as the following story attests: "On my fifth date I meet this creep," Vivian, a demure redhead with green eyes tells me. "I mean a real fuck-ing creep. He was mean, and I'm sure he woulda killed me if he had the chance. Lucky for me I had my phone in my hand and told him I had the agency on the

TABLE 5.1 Ledger of professional escort service workers

Name of Escort	Age (now)	Height	Weight	Hair	Eyes	Body measurements	Origin	Languages	Occupation	Hobbies
Marylin (Christina) (will call when on)	35	5'8"	120	Blond	Blue	35-25-36	German	German, French	Interior decorator	Ballet, literature
Rosemary (Rosemary)	34	5'8"	124	Blond	Blue	36-24-35	American	Spanish	Actress	Dance
Eleanor	28	5'6"	115	Blond	Blue	34-24-34	Swedish	Swedish, French, Danish	Dancer	Music, dance
Annette (Denise)	27	5'9"	127	Blond	Blue	36-24-37	French	French	Model	Skiing, travel
Elizabeth (will call when on)	23	5'10"	127	Dark blond	Blue	35-24-35	American	Portuguese, Spanish, French	Medical student	Dance
Mary (Kristan) (will call when on)	21	5'3"	106	Blond	Blue	32-24-33	American	French	Student	Sports, photography
Catharine (looks young) (calls when on)	33	5'5"	115	Brown	Green	34-23-34	American	Spanish, French	Actress, model	Sports

TABLE 5.2 Ledger of professional escort service clients

Name and address of client	Escort	Type of transaction	Amount	Comment
Henry H	Lorraine	cash		when escort there refused to pay
Archer	Eleanor	cash		Eleanor stayed two hours; client stole money from purse
John T	Mellina	cash		pulled knife, took money, client met her in lobby
Rocky	Leanna		500	drugged the escort
Michael	Holly	debit card	255	got very rough with escort
Steven	Rhonda	credit card—declined	750	credit not good
Morty	Clarissa	cash		rough—do not use
WH	Gena (new girl)	credit card	500	extremely rough with new girl
William	Denise	cash		weird and dangerous
Mr. Luzzi	Eleanor	cash	250	has many aliases, uses stolen credit cards

line, and that's the only way I got outta there alive. He was a raving maniac. I decided after that incident, this business is not for me." Others throw themselves headfirst into the job as escort and move quickly into the life. For some, life becomes "fabulous," filled with fancy restaurants, Fifth Avenue shopping sprees, exclusive nightclubs, and exotic trips, all with handsome, rich men.

The "girls" also carried around something called a "porta-print," which is a mobile credit card machine. All escorts had to carry the porta-print with them on every assignment and had to have a minimum of five credit card slips with them. The credit card should belong to the client and have been authorized before the assignment was given. If any additional money is given to the escort by the client, it had to be noted on a separate slip and authorized.

The "clients," as they are referred to, come in every possible type, though I've only seen a few of them and talked with even fewer. They are elusive but don't mind being seen in public with a beautiful young woman. But when a call comes in for a "girl," the clients are very much alike. They all want "youth." They want "beauty." They usually want white girls. There are some exceptions, but of all the young women I've driven around fit a certain pattern, and that pattern is what the usual client prefers.

I had a phone in my car and a beeper on my belt. I was privy to all the gossip and stories about the clients, learned about the fees, and heard about the fears and phobias of the clients and the girls. The main question I often asked was how they got into the business in the first place; only later did I get around to questions about prostitution. I usually got the girls to talk about this before long, and they were more than willing to discuss the matter.

I would ask them about sex in part because the high-end girls, I was quickly told, do not have to perform sex acts for money (not that they don't); only the lowest-paid girls put out. The minute I said that, they would immediately defend their position. Ruby once said the high-end girls "will suck dick and get fucked too, but they just cost more."

Many of the girls confirmed that most of the male clients didn't want sex at all but someone to talk to about things they could never talk to their girlfriend or wives about; others wanted someone who would do things sexually their wives wouldn't do. These things, many girls said, could be downright freaky and strange. "Some wanted me to shit on them or piss in their mouths." As far as how the girls got involved in the escort business, Ruby tells me, "I was in a beauty contest and came in second. End of story. What do I do now? The girl who won was sucking the judge's dick, and she's probably married to him now. What do you do when you're just another pretty face?" Ruby had a slight gap in her teeth, a Laura Hutton look; she says that was the reason she lost.

As I got to know Ruby, she revealed more about her clients, what they wanted, and what they were willing to pay. Tonight I drove her to the Waldorf; she says it's the foot-fetishist client. She carries a bag full of leather outfits and her old shoes.

He's actually a shoe importer. He gives me all the best, most expensive shoes, thousands of dollars worth of shoes; alligator, snake, lizard boots, suede, you name it, he's given it to me. He wants me to bring my old shoes because he likes me to put them on, and he jerks off when he smells them. He calls in advance and instructs me not to wash my feet for two days before I see him.

She uses a bag for other things too, but I never got to see what was in it. I'm sure it was the image Bunuel envisioned as his *sac de excrement* in his movie *That Obscure Object of Desire*. I ask Ruby about the other girls and she discussed the "regular girls," the girls who played the "tru-ho" role, and the girls who were just professional prostitutes.

> Well, I can tell you the tru-ho loves herself some dick. You got tru-hos who love big dick and will be completely turned off by dicks that don't fit her criteria, if you know what I mean; then you got tru-hos like Mary, who will completely lose herself to some good dick regardless of size, she's just a freak for fucking. She loves to fuck, no matter what. Audrey is the other type, a professional prostitute, that is, she will always go for the money, as it should be, but she's kinda cold. She is all business. Fucking for her is a job, and she's on the job and off the job. She wants to be paid and that's it. I think bitches like her are more into pattin' pussy [lesbian], but that's just my opinion.

Uruzaia (a pseudonym), one of my recent contacts, asked me if she could go to Melissa's agency to interview for a job. "She [the booker] assumed I was calling for an escort and asked what I liked. Once we were oriented, the statistics came in a recognizable order, for this was the third agency I contacted."

> **BOOKER:** How old are you?'
> **URUZAIA:** I'm twenty-three.
> **BOOKER:** Do you know what an escort service is? I mean, have you worked in this business before?
> **URUZAIA:** No. And yes, I know what escorts do.
> **BOOKER:** We provide adult entertainment. Height?
> **URUZAIA:** About five feet, two inches.
> **BOOKER:** What do you weigh?
> **URUZAIA:** I'm not sure. I'm small. I work out.
> **BOOKER:** Your name.

BOOKER: Uruzaia.

BOOKER: Hi Uruzaia. I'm Sandy.

URUZAIA: Hi Sandy. Once again, I'm not sure. I'm petite. I wear a size two or zero.

BOOKER: Oh, you *are* tiny.

URUZAIA: Yes.

BOOKER: Well, here's how it works, Uruzaia. We have a driver who picks you up and stays with you at all times. He waits outside the "out call" while you're with a client. We are very concerned about safety, hon.

URUZAIA: Yes, I am as well.

BOOKER: And where do you live, Uruzaia?

URUZAIA: In Manhattan.

BOOKER: Good, hon. And when can you work?

URUZAIA: Don't you want to see me at the office first?

BOOKER: Good god, no, hon; nobody comes to the office.

URUZAIA: But don't you want to see what I look like? How do your clients pick which girl they want?

BOOKER: We're a big agency, hon. We place all our girls. No, the driver will take a picture of you, and on the first call the manager will be in the car to meet you. What's best for you, days or nights?

URUZAIA: I'm going to school, so nights are better.

BOOKER: Do you want to start today?

URUZAIA: No, I can't. I never thought it would be this quick, so my weekend is already booked. May I call the driver on Tuesday, in the daytime, when I don't have classes, and then start the next weekend?

BOOKER: Sounds good, Uruzaia. Just call this number. You may not get me but anyone here can take good care of you.

While driving these young women around for six months, I started to distinguish among three types of escorts. The first type was the "high-end" supermodel-type escort who would charge upward of six hundred bucks for a "date." She may or may not have sex with the client. The "second-tier" girl charged about three hundred to five hundred bucks and usually did have sex with the client. "Third-tier" or "lower-level" girls were "party girls" who would do drugs, have sex, and do whatever else the client wanted; they were also called "regulars." There were also "voice sex girls" who would not be called as often as other girls and would do "talk tricking" in the office.

I heard about "talk tricking" quite fortuitously. One of the girls, Lorraine (pseudonym), explained it to me:

> The girls would talk about guys who would call and say nasty things to them or have the girls say nasty things back to them, and these guys called all the time. One day Melissa heard me talking to this one guy and she listened in and said it was the same guy who'd called the night before. She said if he called back again tell him you're gonna charge him, and that became a regular thing after that. I asked how they charged the guy, and she told me how it worked.

I learned in the pimping world this was called "talk tricking." The pimp, whenever he saw one of his ladies talking to a man for any length of time, would tell her: "The next time I see you talking to a man, you better charge him, because your time is my time, and I don't give my time for free. He's a 'talk trick,' don't you know? He's talking to you and getting off, so you gotta charge him or no conversation." Usually the guy would ask the girl to explain—in detail—what she would do for a certain fee. "Will you suck my dick till I cum? Will you lick my asshole? How much would it cost to eat the shit outta your asshole?" Meanwhile, the guy is getting off on the girl telling him these things.

Commercial sex is many things, not just oral, anal, and genital contact. It can also be verbal. Male customers frequently seek the verbal services of sex workers, who in some ways become paraprofessional counselors. Verbal interaction is apparently a key component of the encounters between men and women in not only the escort agency world but in the wider commercial sex industry more generally.

WILLIAMS FIELD NOTES: THE HOUSE OF MADAM X (2015)

Madam X, the owner, manager, and impresario of her own place, asks me, rhetorically: "What do I call this place, this house? Well, as a matter-of-fact, I call it my 'service house' because that's what I do. I service clients. The name of the place is the house where I escort women, girls, dates, johns to get service. I service clients. I do full service here." She laughs. "I say, if anybody asks what I do, I say I do body rubs or sensual massage."

Madam X told me that part of what she sells in her house is the look: bodily capital, erotic capital, human capital. What she is selling is partly ephemeral, part physicality, part personality. What, then, is the relationship between the model industry, the beauty industry, and the sex industry?

> Well, I can tell you this. The call-girl agencies, call-girl operations, sex houses, they used to be part of the glamour business. But there is an obvious connection to all of this because of the link between the body and emotion. There is also the fact that you must pay attention to your body, how you walk, how you talk, what you wear, how heavy or skinny you are. I feel safe in this house, and I mean 100 percent safe. As far as what the girls do, well it's all about acting, surface acting. They all do it. My girls are all educated. I would say they are educated with college creds. I can tell you this, many of my girls have decent work background outside of this sex work, and many are single mothers, about 50 percent of them are in that range. You asked about the time it takes for a client to be in here for service, well it's about forty-five minutes.
>
> The average time is forty-five minutes, but only about 40 percent of the women do it right. Most of them just want the money. I tell them to slow down, do it right. Extend the time, the extra time. The average? In terms of money? The average amount is $700 to $1,200. But anyway, I have a certain environment, and the girls have to conduct themselves accordingly. I must say this used to be a glamorous profession. This used to be a glamorous business.

In what follows, some of the self-descriptions of the girls, if not openly brazen, are sketches of damaged young people, though many are quite humorous; some do not fool themselves into believing things will get better. The girls do take certain risks, however much they are minimized by the careful monitoring of client interactions with cameras and the safe words used by the women if a client gets too rough or dangerous. "Only girls who are into S/M let the man pull her hair or slap or beat her."

Madam X is quick to point out to me that this kind of body cruelty is basically rough trade and that this is not allowed unless the girls who like that are paid extra money for this service. Madam X writes about the social production of value in the world of modeling and studies the markets. The former model Ashley Mears sees this modeling business as a form of body cruelty and says the value comes simply from being in the sex industry, since all these industries are connected to body cruelty.[8]

Ruby Love went from casual sex to becoming madam of her own service through a series of lucky—or unlucky—events. I met her during the disco days on the east side of Manhattan. At the time, I recall her talking about what her life was going to look like: she would be an actress, a model, a housewife, rich and famous, and the like. But the best-made plans of mice and men often go astray. Just like the woman who said, "I used to be Snow White, but I drifted."

I guess you could say she drifted. But in the discos men—and women—loved her and would approach her for sex. She would have the sex, along with the drugs (mostly cocaine), and move on to the next party. After a year of this, she decided to charge a fee, "gifts, really," for these adventures, and this led to her meeting another girl who worked for a Midtown escort agency called Melissa's Girls. From there, she slowly began to do sex work as a freelancer for money.

I didn't think of it as prostitution at first because, well, anyway I was giving it away before I started with Melissa. It was either give it away or charge for it. So I decided to charge for it. I then went into the agency business thinking I would make even more money.

At sixteen I started meeting hustlers, men, because I was after fame and fortune, started hanging out with an international crowd of boys and girls. I had a very interesting lifestyle. I guess you could say I was a spoiled little kid from early on. My parents put me into a very progressive Manhattan Day School in kindergarten really. I was four or five and was at Walden shortly thereafter. I had a mean teacher who mistreated me. She would pull my hair when I disobeyed or pinch me when I would step out of the line, things like that. So every day all of us kids would go on the roof to play games and this [one] day she stood at the edge showing us something and as she turned her back near the edge I ran over and tried to push her off.

I was taken out of the school. So you might say my delinquency started very early. I became one of the lost girls in the city at that time. That incident is in that school's lore, I'm sure. I remember distinctly her treating me badly. They told my parents, and I had to go somewhere else. I then went to Sacred Heart Academy after that and made good grades but cursed out my teachers there and was expelled. I was always bored. My father made a very good salary because we had everything we needed, the cars, the house in the suburbs.

I was always gravitated toward those things that are not socially acceptable. I grew up early with a big chip on my shoulder and basically resentment with the hypocrisy in the society and this attitude or philosophy of mine made me feel like I wasn't doing anything wrong. My mother was a housewife taking care of my brothers and me. It was said back in the day if you were one of the lost girls, as I was, you were part of the "girl problem."

Madam X's is referring to the "girl problem," a term that named a phenomenon in 1930s New York: Young girls would assert themselves and hang out, prostitute themselves, or spend their time in bars and night dives, beer joints, all in search of recreation. She continues: "We were called 'fast girls,' and, by the 1980s, we had many allies with the women's movement, and girls could do whatever they wanted. Discos, like the earlier period in New York cabaret life, came about with the beginning of speed culture, coke, fast drugs, acid trips, fast dancing, disco, hip-hop, fast cars."

The arrival of the "fast girls" ran parallel to the increasingly "fast" nature of American life and the growth of "fast sex" (oral sex as a mainstay). Escort agencies flourished, as did other elements of modern-day life, such as drugs, open sex, and freer attitudes. I began to see prostitution as part of the sexual services industry along with a host of other sex categories: sexual faddism, such as the black big booty fetish; boy pussy pimps; male whores; escort girls; street hookers; sex junkies; madams; and crack cocaine.

So by the 1990s my nuclear family was missing, and I had a nervous breakdown. At the end of the breakdown I was derelict and homeless. I woke up one day at Creedmoor Hospital. I was Ruby Love, and they had only one name like mine in the telephone book at the hospital, so I told them to call that number, and they refused at first thinking that it could not be the same family name, but they did call and it was my father. . . . It was the same family as that name. I had lost my childhood around that time, and then my father came to get me. This was around the time that I lost time, which was in the 1980s to 1990s.

My experience on the street in the 1990s was the beginning of problems for me because I did not have my family support, my brothers and friends and others, so I returned to drugs and got into the crack culture. But even at that time the dealers and the cops did not want me to be out there doing crack, because I was this little innocent chick that they felt sorry for and liked my spunk. So in those situations they treated me as if I was a star. I was always in a privileged position. This was the kind of thing that I was used to, being deviant, engaging in deviant behavior. The crack thing brought me to my knees, though.

Ruby Love did not get involved with a pimp, madam, or anyone else—in fact, she has never worked for a pimp. She was a little too smart for that, or maybe too independent, too brave or foolhardy to need that sort of protection. But she did do call-girl work, and that is perhaps where she got her start at training in the rules of the game, the proper etiquette required of the girls Henry James called *femmes du monde*. This was her "turning out," her introduction to a school of misbehavior where she learned techniques of sex work, sitting at Melissa's knee as one of her "girls."

But since Ruby is smart and quick on her feet and has had early upper-class instruction, she figured out a lot about life on her own. "I called it using your head [taps her finger to her head, sticks out her tongue, and laughs] when I was a mere teen," she recalled when I asked about her sexual escapades in the city clubs and bars before she was twenty years old.

The house she ran in 2014 is small, with only ten to fifteen girls, mostly Latina, older than most house girls, all very pretty and physically endowed. These women are not your typical "turnouts," since inexperienced in the sex realm they are not. Their average age is twenty-eight to thirty, they are of average height, and some speak only broken English.

I made contact and went to see her at her new location and office space. It took me several days to track her down.

WILLIAMS FIELD NOTES (2014)

The snow had been falling all day but stopped before my arrival. I drove to the parking lot and was instructed by phone about which house I should to go to. I walked two flights up, and at a small sliding door a woman in a black negligee peeped through, beckoning me in with a finger. I still had my phone to my ear as

I entered, removing my snow-covered shoes. I sat down and rested my feet on a soft beige carpet.

A small cat purred from underneath a multicolored blanket on the floor. "She doesn't like men," the woman said. She giggled while telling the purring cat to "hush up." She asked if I wanted anything, juice, water, wine, and I heard Madam X call from another room upstairs, "Get comfortable, I'll be down in a few."

I sat back and took a better look at my hostess. Latina, perhaps thirty, with ample breasts and a warm smile. Shoeless, wearing a black negligee to reveal a nipple, hair pulled back with manicured fingers, no jewelry. She understood I was to interview her and the others and inquired what kind of questions I might ask. I explained to her the basics: I was writing a book about the sex lives of New Yorkers and the life of Madam X, a woman I knew back in the escort days, and I wanted to get her story and the stories of some of the women who worked in the house. Easy questions. She thought that was interesting but before she could say anything else, the phone rang. After the call, Madam X came down to greet me and said she had to do a few quick things. I could talk to one of her consorts to kill the time.

I asked Madam X what the women she works for are called. Without hesitation, she replied, "I call them hos because that's what they are." I looked at her, surprised, and she reiterated, "Yeah, I'm sorry to say that, but it's true, they're hos. What is the definition of a ho?" She answered her own question.

It's a person who have sex for money right? Well, that's what they do. They have sex for money. You can't pretty that up. That's the cold hard fact. I should say they can't wait to make money. It's as if the money is everything. I tell them not to jump at money and be too quick to leave the clients. Be patient, the money will be waiting for you. But they don't listen, they just want to make the cash. Get that one out the door and bring in the next one.

By the way, the first girl I want you to talk to is my best girl. This girl sucks dick like no other. She can suck a golf ball through a garden hose.

Madam X smiles and shakes her head.

A coupla times I've had guys come around and I notice what kind of shoes they're wearing, and I can tell if they are cops by what they wear. And if they are cops, they can't take their clothes off. So I ask them to flash, which is, I take a photo of their body parts, and that assures me and my girls that they are not cops because a cop can't compromise himself that way and get a conviction. And if they choose not to do that, I ask them to leave and go out. Another thing is if a person wants to talk about money, mentioning cash or dollar amounts, that sends a trigger that something is up, and so I avoid talking about money, only contributions and donations. I never accept money in my hand. I always ask the person to put the money down on the table or on a desk. I watch them count it out and go from there. This is done only after they are fully undressed.

Many or most of my clients are regulars. Now, that is for many reasons. First, my girls are clean, and they are nice and polite. I teach them to treat the customers well because they are our bread and butter, you understand. Second, if clients keep coming back, we must be doing something right, and that's important for longevity in this business. But this business is not what it used to be. It used to be a much more glamorous business. The clients and the girls. Clients were diplomats and famous actors and big-time businessmen and -women; the girls were models or model wannabes and you got six hundred bucks an hour and you might not even get your dick sucked for that if the girl didn't want to. But now it's a whole other story.

The first of Ruby Love's consorts I interviewed was a Latina from South America.[9] Nana is twenty-nine, with shoulder-length black hair, about five foot three, with a strong accent and keen sense of humor. Her dress is casual: this is too early for clients, and she "has not made up yet." She walks with a twist in her step and what is known in the sex trade as a "hos walk," which is a swishing move from side to side many women use to advertise the trade. It appears much like a normal walk, with a bit of emphasis using the hips to swivel. She smiles and asks me what the interview would be about. I say I would like to know about her clients and what they desire from her.

"Most of the men want easy sex, but that can be my hand or my mouth. I use my hands to work them. Or they want my mouth, which I do very well for them, and some want my asshole but I always say no to that." She puts up one index finger and waggles it back and forth.

No, no, not for me. Some girls do that for sure here, but not me. I like to be in control of the situation and so I prefer the man on top of me, not dog style either. The many girls who do the back-door sex have to get more paid. They get extra for that move. I do have the client who just want company, you know. They like to hug or kiss or something like this. Company, yes. They tell me they are bored at their house. Or they have a problem or no problem. They say they want to talk and hold me. Do you understand my English, no?

I say yes, and she laughs. I thought this a good moment to ask her about the dick-sucking comment Madam X made, but for some reason I chickened out; I just got cold feet and regretted later not asking. But on the other hand, I felt it might change the mood. I thought about asking her several times but never did.

"Sometimes I like to drink with them. I like a little cocaine, too. But more and more and more it's a massage. But I am with my clients very close, no? You know, what I say." "Affectionate," I say, and she agrees.

NANA: Yes, affectionate. I am very sweet and very nice and sweet and close with them. Lovely, you know? But some women like back work, to be spanked . . . but not me, no. I can't work like that. Sometimes I have difficult client who want to have sex with no condom or if they want the *culo*, no? But not for me. Some women they like it, but not for me. I don't like it. The other thing that is difficult for me is the sadomasochism. Some clients like this, pull the hair, and I don't like this. They pay extra money for that. Yes. Some clients they give you big tip for doing that. But not big tip, really I mean after you give them massage they give you twenty dollars, thirty dollars, sometimes a hundred dollars. It all depends. It depends what the client like, you know. But when they say about the sadomasochism, I say no.

TW: Is it that the client wants to spank you, or does he want you to spank him?

NANA: No, he want me to spank him.

TW: How long is a session?

NANA: They change because sometime one hour. Sometime, half-hour. But sometime they want two hours and they will pay for that. It depends on what they need. I tell you this one thing. I used to work at another place and I had this old man eighty years who liked me very much and all he want was to hug me, drink wine with me, laugh with me. All he want to do is talk, talk, talk, for three hours. He just talk and play, drink for three hours. I need to touch him [massage the penis] because he like that too. I think this is a nor-mal situation. It is not very different [unusual]. When I'm in a session, I'm in control. I like control. Me [laughs], I like it because they want to control me and I don't like doggy, because they in control because they behind me and they in control.

TW: Suppose they ask for a session like doggy style, what do you do?

NANA: Well, I try to escape. You know. I say I have headache or I don't feel well like that.

TW: How much is what you do with a client pretending, like a performance, and how much would you say is real? How sincere are you in these sessions, and how much are you pretending to be sincere?

NANA: I pretend. I don't feel. When I do that [sex] I don't feel, you know? But with some clients I do. When I know my clients I feel more comfortable, then I feel, but if I don't. No feel anything.

TW: Tell me about your work routine. How often do you work?

NANA: When I come here I work four days a month. I have another job where I work in an old people [home]. I work for a company there. I go to the nursery and wash them and bath them and that's what I do three days a week, maybe four.

After an hour, the phone began to ring and clients began to arrive, so I had to leave. Before I left, I was promised another meeting with Madam X and her consorts, a class visit. Two other women said they were willing to be interviewed, but that had to wait until my next visit.

CONTACT: SILVA (2017–2018)

The next contact we meet is Silva. I consider him a "bridge person" in the work I do because he connects me to a world I am trying to understand. Like my other contacts, including Ruby Love, he is a translator of the heart. He makes it possible for me to help readers get to know the Soft City intimately. As I noted in *On Ethnography*, "It is this relationship, more than anything else and certainly more than my presence in the field, that makes possible the depth, the 'ring true' quality of the visual page."[10]

Silva tells me he is making notes with the intention of eventually writing a book about his experiences as a customer in the sex trade. He offers rare insight into a dark and hidden corner of the Soft City.[11] How do I know if Silva is telling me the whole truth? I've wondered about the honesty of many of the personalities I've encountered. I knew Silva as a businessman, and I know about his family, though not intimately; his father is a politician and his mother a dressmaker. Beyond that bit of information, I can't say more without putting him at risk with the authorities. I cannot vouch for every incident he says happened, but I can say I have found him to be truthful, as I have been able to verify independently some of what he has told me.

Silva is twenty-two, short, and stocky, with a bald shaved head. His head is shaved because, he says, "I like it that way. It gives me luck." He considers himself lucky because he has never been in any trouble with the law and has enough money to keep the women he "desires" happy. He says he sees the women because he often feels lonely. He has no visible scars on his face but furrows his forehead as if feeling the aftereffects of a bad emotion. The corrugated brow gives him a nervous look, even though he is quick to laugh. He has long fingers, with one little fingernail uncut; the others are bitten down to the nub.

Silva's Journal 1 (2017)

Here are notes written by Silva regarding in-calls, transactions in which the client goes to the escort's place of business. Since I am interested in both the "sex worker" and the "sex client" in the sex industry, several points must be made. First, Silva is someone who solicits sex from women. The women he pays to have sex are basically trading sex and consider their trade as "sex work" or "working." Second, Madam X refers to her consorts as doing "hustling," "pro work," "prostitution," and "tricking," and many of these women call it "escorting" and a way of surviving.

This was by far one of the best hassle-free in-calls I have ever been on. I called her. She answered the phone. We agreed to a price. She texted me her address once I got off the phone with her, and after I got to the location, I called her, she gave me the room number, and I didn't have to deal with any crazy hotel staff asking me questions. This place was located in [omitted] in a drive-up motel opener on [omitted]. I honestly didn't even think things like this even still existed. I walked into the "lobby" because it was literally just one room, kind of similar to the tollbooths on the freeway, but she asked me,

"What room honey?" I answer and kept walking. "202" she responded, "up the stairs to your right."

Now this going into strange hotels has always been scary to me, because I can't afford to get busted. I have a very busy and demanding life, and I can't afford to get caught with these girls and be in jail for even one day. I haven't been able to even take a vacation in a few years (another discussion). I say all of this to say that when hotel staff asks me what room, I get a little scared, because I'm sure that these girls have many guys come see them during the day. The hotel staff would have to be complete idiots not to wonder what is going on in the rooms. Unless they are in on it? Or maybe they just don't give a damn? That is one of my biggest fears along with getting an STD. Back to the story.

I knocked on her door, and she opened it, and the funny thing is that this girl hid behind it. I don't know why girls do that. I walked into the room with an elevated bed in the center of the room. And the TV was on and she watching the Tyler Perry TV show (can't remember the name off the top of my head). I paid her and commenced to take my clothes off; she went in the back of the room, which I think is where the restroom was, and I guess put the money in there, then she came out and began to take her clothes off.

She was so hot, she was about five eleven, light brown with long hair; she was very skinny but had a nice little bubble. She also had these really big eyebrows, but anyway it didn't matter at this point. I hopped my ass on the bed and put my head on a pillow. My penis was not erect, I honestly was kind of taken care of last night, I took care of myself, but I saw her on the page [Backpage.com, an escort website now seized by the FBI] and thought it would be cool to come and see her. She commenced to put the condom on and start the sucking of dicks.

When she first tried to do it, she didn't put it on right and it hurt. Her pupils dilated and she looked at me and "Oh my God, I'm so sorry." I said to her, "I'm okay, are you comfortable with doing this?" She responded "yes" and commenced to put the chrome on the dome. After about five minutes she said to me, "A short stay is fifteen minutes." I responded, "Okay, I'm about to come." She started sucking again, I could tell that either she wasn't that experienced or she wasn't into it, or maybe that this is another sex con.

I noticed that after about two minutes of the caroming [slang term for fellatio] of the dome it didn't feel as good, and my dick began to lose its erection. So I said to her, "Could I just touch you," which was the reason why I wanted to touch her. Because I wanted to see if my penis would get hard again, but unfortunately it didn't. I just wanted to touch her—her abs, her ass, her chest, her light brown skin was so beautiful. I liked to create some sort of small talk with her, but she was not even interested and she didn't even want to touch me.

She then said to me, "your time is almost up." I then asked her how much of my thirty-minute session was left of the $100. Luckily I had an extra $40 dollars to pay her, so she took the money and went in the restroom and then came back. When she came back I told her that I would like to put my rod inside her pod and swim around for a little while.

She was like, okay, then she got on the bed on her back, and as I was about to try to put my penis inside of her, she accidentally poked one eye out and had this look on her face as if she was very uncomfortable. I then asked her, "You look uncomfortable. Would you like to get on top?" She responded very fast, "Yes, sure," but all of this moving around and just her disinterest in me made my penis go down again. I landed across the bed and tried to rub my penis against her vagina, but there was nothing. I then asked her if I could hold her and touch her again.

I sat up. She got down on her knees and rested her hands on my shoulders and I caressed her beautiful titties for about five minutes. I tried to create small talk: "What's your favorite food?" She responded in a not-so-nice way, "Chicken." Everything I asked her about she was being very short and distasteful with me.

After about five minutes of this exchange, she was like, "I think your time is up, let me check my phone." She said, "Yeah, your time is up." Then I said, "Oh, well, can I have my $40 back?" She responded, "You really want your $40 back?" I said to her, "I've only been her for ten minutes since I paid you the extra $40, but I understand if it is going to be a problem." Then she walked toward the bathroom and said, "Can you come out here?" I realized very quickly that she wasn't talking to me when I heard a deep, medium-tone but authoritative voice say, "Let it go, my dude." Now I had already started putting my clothes on before he [the pimp] spoke, but once he spoke I put on my clothes Jessie Owens fast.

After he said that I said very softly, "It's fine, I understand." Then the girl shouted at me in anger as she put on her pink sweatpants that looked so good on her, "'It's fine,' yeah, you went over your time. If you wanted to have sex, you would've had sex." There was a short pause as she put back on her shirt, then she yelled at me, "It niggas like you that make this job hard," and then commenced to open the door while I was still putting on my pants. I left the hotel with the condom still on my dick, and she waited behind the door until I left.

I did the same like I do to most or all of the girls I see: I thanked her and said, "Have a nice day," and then BOOM! She slammed the door. This kind of had me feeling down once I left the space. For some reason my dick was like "No, we're not fucking today," because I was very much attracted to her and wanted to fuck her, but my penis wouldn't stay erect and then come to find out that there was someone else in the room the whole time. It might have been her lack of compassion, of interest in me at the time, or could've been that I had my dick sucked the night before, but I still had an urge to get some pussy. This has been happening with more than this girl, someone who I'm generally attracted to, my penis doesn't get hard, or it gets hard for a little while and then it shuts down. More on this later.

In the next set of notes, Silva describes his continued encounters in what I see as a quest for love, a sentiment not often expressed in the sex trade. I think Silva was in fact seeking a way to love and be loved, but unfortunately this quest could also be called a series of hundred-dollar misunderstandings.

Silva's Journal 2 (2018)

Honestly, I love going to see her! I always leave and want to stay longer, because I always feel as if we are in many ways working to get each other off. I like when she is satisfied, and I hope that she likes when I am satisfied. I'm not sure how genuine it is, and if it is not, then she should certainly pursue a career in acting.

Last time I saw her left me very curious! Because that was the first time I had ever fingered a girl before fucking her, and it was good to feel that way from a "non penile" way. I was curious how a vagina felt on the inside with a finger in her. But I also wanted to see what it tasted like, and I thought that she would be the perfect person to try this with considering that she is always clean, smells great, and she sucked my dick last time and I came in her mouth. (Lord!!) Last time I left I was saying and speaking all kinds of things.

Anyway on with the show, so I arrive, get to her place, pay her, take off my clothes and hop on the bed, and ask her, "Is it cool if I eat your orange?" She responded with a giggle, "You want to?" I said, "Yeah, I would like to try it!" She then replied with a smile, "Okay, we can try it, but if I don't like it I will ask you to stop." I was like, "Okay, cool." I lay on the pillow, and she got on top of me with her legs on the sides of my arms and my legs in between her torso.

BOOM there it is! Right there that beautiful orange. I wasn't hesitant at all and I went right in and started eating! I started by just licking the outside of her vagina, and the very top where the clit is located, then I started to lick the inside of her vagina, and I was quite surprised to find out how good it tasted. I kind of tasted to me like fresh spring water with just a hint of lemon or just the right amount of tart. I honestly enjoyed the process, and hearing her moan just made the experience even more fulfilling. Normally when I go over there she often reacts calmly to everything that I do, which is good I guess, but this time it was a little bit different.

After a while she sat on my face and started to grind on my face, and began to moan even louder. While I was enjoying the pleasure, she was recovering; I was out of breath, and had to ask her to get up for just a minute. "Are you okay?" I said, "Yes, I just need some air."

Then we went back to trying to get each other off. She began sucking my dick again, and then I was eating her out like a fat kid in a candy store. She kept moaning and moving around on my face for about five minutes. This prevented her from sucking my dick, which I was fine with, because I was thoroughly enjoying eating her orange. After a while she got on top of me, where I could see her face. She began to ride the shit out of my dick. I should say the first time I came over and we did this position she came all on my leg and pants.

I was laying casket style on the bed while this was happening, and then I got up and we both locked torsos and began to move together. She put her arms around my back and began to sweat. We kept going faster and faster to the point where we were both tired. I didn't come, but I so enjoyed myself. I asked her, "Are you tired?" She said, "Yes," then she laid her torso on the bed with her skinny brown legs on my shoulders.

I put my finger inside her vagina, and she moaned for a little bit but abruptly ended my attempts to still pleasure her and said, "I don't like being fingered." Then she took a break.

Now I have been wanting to talk to her for a while, because I have been seeing her at least four times and always enjoy myself every time. She is also from down south [omitted] way, and this I found out upon my first visit when she noticed my accent and my phone number being a [omitted] number. Me and her were both naked, and her legs were on my shoulder as we began to engage in conversation.

I started by asking her what is her favorite position or what is it that gets her off. She said to me how she is very immune to sex and how it's just sex. She also mentioned to me how she used to have a boyfriend a year ago, but she had to get out of the relationship because it was "toxic." She also talked about how her past boyfriend's brother came to see her one time without her knowing who he was, and he threatened to tell his brother about what she does on the side.

She does have a job, by the way: she works at a [omitted] firm in [omitted], where she is basically a runner girl for this firm. The firm represents a lot of landlords in the neighboring states, and she is the assistant to someone there, and she mainly just posts signs on buildings on apartments where people are being evicted. According to her, the job provides her with a reduced-rent apartment, and her apartment is a large studio, almost loft-like with big windows and also a decent pay.

She got the job because of her sugar daddy, who started out selling property in Africa. She mentioned how she and her ex-sugar daddy were close for a while but not now. I wanted to ask this question from the beginning, but I'm sure that she gets it a lot: "How did you get into do this? Because it seems like you have a job and make good money?" She replied with, "One of my friends started doing this and told me about it and said how it was a way for her to make some extra money on the side. But even though my regular job pay good, but I like to have some extra."

"Plus, I don't just want to live and just make enough to get by."

She asked me how I got into Backpage.com, and I told her I work a lot and I try to do things the right way and wait on the right girl to date. I told her I like to get to know someone and be with someone I really like rather than be with somebody I just met and meet with lots of rejection.

So anyways, one day as I was venting to a friend about how I almost got close to having sex with someone, he told me about Backpage, and that's how it has been ever since. I then went on to talk about how from my experience and dealings with my many friends how we don't really have an understanding of love and relationships. I can assess that my generation is blinded by the false relationships, what we see on TV and movies, and that we have no real idea that relationships take work and time.

A relationship with anyone (whether friends, sex partners, dating) is a commitment that needs to grow with someone. Everybody wants to be with someone, but not everyone wants to work out the problems of a relationship, because, believe me, I know it takes work. It's hard work to stay and grow in love and I personally believe that at this age (twenty-one) I really know that until I'm about twenty-seven, twenty-eight I should not try and pursue anything serious. I should just have fun and let the chips fall where they may.

This began to spark a conversation about emotions and feelings. She said to me in a nutshell how I was correct on some parts, but I have to be careful about my emotions and other people's emotions. Which I totally agreed with her, after that I told her as I caressed her beautiful chocolate legs and torso, told her how much I love coming to see her and always wish I could see more of her. She mentioned that she likes me as a customer and is very comfortable with me sexually. My stay with her ended up being a lot longer than a short stay. I was at her house for approximately, oh, forty-five minutes, and we did about fifteen minutes of fucking and about twenty to thirty minutes of talking, which was awesome. I asked her when she might be available again so that I could come see her, and she said "usually toward the last two weeks of the month into the first week. Sometime I need a break." I said okay and commenced to put on my clothes and leave. We hugged for a little while, this time a little longer than usual. She was still naked and I had my clothes on. She walked me to the door and said, "See you next time."

Silva's Journal 3 (2018)

For some reason I really had a yearning to running up in something, and I have been in these rehearsals for this play at the theater for the past six months and have not had any real time to do the things I need to do for me.

Today was the last day of the show, and I knew I was cutting it close by doing theater, but I really wanted to have some good pussy before the show. I'm sort of skeptical about giving my dick to someone I don't know or paying for more than a short stay for someone who I am seeing for the first time, but I wanted to try and take this opportunity, and there is a "ho"-tel right by my house in the city.

I've been there a few times, mainly for BJs because the girls there don't always look as hot as they do in the ads, plus they are professional dick suckers, I mean professionals. I remember over the summer I saw this one girl, and it normally takes me at least five minutes to come, at the least with her it just felt so good that I couldn't hold it in, she made me come in a minute, two minutes. I mean the come was all on my arm, all over her face and the bed. Every time I have been here, I have never left unhappy, I think that the hotel knows about what goes on there. There are two main ho-tels that are where the hos hang out and that's Simpson (Super 8) and 165 and Brook (Days Inn) [both fictitious places].

I was very mixed up about this girl, because I figured she would be fine for me to get an erection and handle that business. Damn if I was wrong. I walked into the hotel and went straight for the elevator. The lady at the desk didn't say anything to me, and I pushed the second floor. I came out of the elevator and walked down the nice carpeted hallway, and there she was sticking her head out of the door with a shower cap on her head.

I get to the door and I was blown away, as the song says: "This girl is fiiiine." She was short, but not too short, probably about five foot five, about my shoulder height with the perfect body, had a gumdrop, onion booty. I assume had to be a D-cup breast. When I came in she was wearing a black Brooklyn Nets swimsuit with the shower cap on. I walked into the room, put my stuff on the dresser, and paid her. I noticed there were two suitcases in the room, one on both sides, and there were two beds. She later mentioned to me that there was another girl in the room and how she didn't want me to be surprised or uncomfortable.

I continued to take my clothes off and sat next to her on the bed. I touched her. She pulled away and said in a very soft and sexy voice, "Your hands are too cold." She then got up from the bed and walked toward the TV, threw me a condom, and said, "Put it on." I honestly hate putting on condoms, partly because they have this terrible smell, almost like burnt rubber! However, I understand that without them I would have no protection.

While I was struggling to put the condom on she got out of the bed and with her back facing toward me, she slowly took off her Brooklyn Nets jersey swimsuit and began to move in a very seductive way, I guess what we would consider "whining," which I was very turned on by! Then she turned around, locked eyes with me, and slowly walked over to where I was on the bed, put one leg on the bed over mine, and then put the other one to get on top of me. By this time my penis was fully erect and went right in. She felt soo good inside! I can't honestly describe what it feels like. I just know good pussy when I have it. It's like having a massage on my penis and with just the right amount of tightness, moistness, and body temperature.

I could feel the heat of her insides before I was in. Once I was in, I wasn't ready for what I was about to experience. Normally most girls when I see them and they get on top, they have a few moves that they will do such as grinding, moving around my dick in a circular motion, but she on the other hand had some other moves that honestly my penis could barely handle, it was almost as if she was doing Jamaican whine on my dick, she would move up and down, but she would also smack her ass while this was happening, and then she would pivot and OMG it was soooo good.

All through this process I was feeling all over her well-toned, sexy body, and feeling her D-cup breasts. Now she didn't necessarily make too many sounds or moves to make me come while my dick was inside of her except toward the end, when she was riding me so hard that I couldn't hold it anymore.

Once I came I immediately started laughing, which is not my usual reaction, and then I asked her, "Did you just whine on my dick?" And we both started laughing! I then asked her if she had a towel or tissue to go take the condom off with. I took the condom off and started to put my clothes on. I asked her when she might be available again. She responded, "I am always available, I'm either here or at Simpson." I said, "Cool, I look forward to the next time." She said, "Cool." She walked me to the door and I touch the lower half of her torso and ass and said, "Thanks."

As I began walking down the hall toward the elevator, I heard someone say, "He had a big head!??!?" Another female voice responded, "That nigga had a real big bald head?" followed by a loud sucking of the teeth. I'm not sure why she did that; with the door still open it was blatant that they were indeed talking about me! I wasn't offended; I got on the elevator and went downstairs.

Keep in mind that this is a person writing his own story in his journal, in an attempt to understand his own psyche. In the novel *Nana*, Zola points to the character of Muffat: "Whilst he was passing along the boulevards, the rolls of the last carriages deafened him with the name of Nana: the gas-lights set nude limbs dancing before his eyes—the nude limbs, the lithe arms, the white shoulders of Nana. And he felt that he was hers utterly: he would have abjured everything, sold everything, to possess her for a single hour that very night."[12] Silva, like Zola's Muffat, is in search of love. He speaks openly not only about the recognized necessity of overcoming his scruples and his fear of contracting sexually transmitted disease but also about the importance of his goal of obtaining sexual pleasure. His notes reflect his complex psychology: on the one hand, the man whose pleasures and desires have to be managed with "call girls," but on the other hand, the man in search of love, of physical intimacy that went beyond the mere commodity traded between "clients" and "sex workers" in the Soft City.

chapter 6
Smell, Touch, and Participation

As a sociologist, I have thought for years about how the observer is *observed* perhaps even more so than he or she is *observing*. "There is nothing surprising there for after all, the ethnographer is a stranger—someone new whose position is always peculiar."[1] In this chapter, I begin with the connection to the mind and with the kinds of observation that are based on smell and touch.

As I make my way to a club, odors greet my arrival: piss-stained stairs, the smell of leather and sweat. The odor orients me to the environment, entices me to become part of the action. I imagine eyes as cameras aimed at exteriors, watching the teeming movement of passersby, the busy streets, and ears as microphones, listening for the narratives that expose interiors. Then the smells emanate, and they help define the setting, since smell owes no allegiance to the space and moves freely throughout. Smells bring out emotions in people. The odors, perfumes, and funk of these places do not repel the nighttime devotees—as a matter of fact, the funkier the place, the more popular. I see each individual, each person, framing the attitudes and passion of those stories as they provide the tone and tenor of what is seen and sensed.

We don't only want to see things; we want to smell and touch. Smell is one of the classical five senses (though there are perhaps six or more). The receptors in our noses get stimulated by odor-bearing substances, and these nerve impulses pass up to our brain. Our brain can distinguish between thousands of odors, and some odors are more pleasing than others.[2] Throughout this text, I introduce various characters as voice, mediator, interlocutor, and ethnographer; they tell the stories of their lives as I tell my story of this moment in their lives.

This is both biography and autobiography of the city. The following voices and vignettes are passionate, raw, tender, and perverse, and in the process of listening to their stories, I fashion my own story as I continue to ask the question: What is desire? In the Soft City, desire is more than voice, more than a narrative that accounts for the biographical or the autobiographical. Desire is also about action. The key point about the action that people engage in or seek out in the scene is that it is purely physical or sensual stimulation, which in the sex scene

6.1 The Fabric Factory, foot fetish worship, c. 198?.

stems from a myriad of places, most notably sight, but also smells, odors, and aromas, emanating from leather, pleather, rubber, shoes, socks, boots, bodies, sweat, tobacco, marijuana, crack, semen, farts, spit, beer breath, shit, alcohol, bad breath, wine, feet, funk, perfumes, vaginal deodorants, and blood. Other stimulation derives from sounds, tastes, body movements, and fantasy, yet touch and smell might exceed these senses in potency.

As Largey and Watson remark, "Odors function partly to maintain the boundaries of social setting or the appropriateness of the relationships engendered within the setting. If the perceived odors in a setting clash with its routine definition, an individual would probably feel 'dissonance anxiety' and difficulty in sustaining any bona fide identification with his setting."[3] In the Soft City, instead of sensorial avoidance, be it olfactory, visual, or haptic, some people are more likely to greet these locations with pleasurable acceptance—but certainly not all.

CONTACT: DINA, BODY SHOP (2001)

Dina is a shy twenty-year-old from Lebanon who spoke almost inaudibly about issues important to her. She wrote:

> I took a taxi to the club called the Body Shop on Twenty-Sixth Street. The club has several floors and is laid out neatly with little back rooms, and some red chairs and a lot of equipment, a bench and a chaise-like hanging apparatus thing. Each item of equipment is placed by a wall as if it is an important piece of art, with some spotlights shining on it. There is ample space around the equipment so that people can stand and watch. The place is spacious, with booths for people to have drinks and ice cream. The lighting is nice and dark but not too dark. There are mirrors around and a huge mural of bodies that look like action comic heroes but with their genitals exposed and their body parts protruding and enlarged.
>
> It smelled heavily like disinfectant, which really bothered me. The whole club smelled like some type of bathroom. However, one could see that it was extremely clean. Tables and chairs look very clean, and the floors are spotless. It is comfortable to walk around. Then people begin to arrive. Everyone was happy to be there and dressed neatly. However, one thing I noticed was that they tended generally to sit too close to me. When we sat down, they would pull their chairs close to mine and at times would brush their arms or knees

against me. There were times when they would just leave no space around me, and I felt claustrophobic. They would pull their chairs around and sit very close. One thing is that I would smell them and it was not good.

Most of them had a strange smell that just bothered me very much. This was the second time in my life when I felt like I needed to get out of that space and go to another. It reminded me of the first time I felt claustrophobic. I was in a plane. The seats were extremely small, and I was boxed in to the side of the place with bodies all around me. And soon I discovered the smell of the man beside me and felt like I was going to suffocate. I felt the same way, as soon as this man sat in front of me, his knee almost touching mine, and he began to speak, and I smelled him. I thought that it may be his feet or his whole body. Then I spoke to others. I wanted to give them some mints, but I had none, and I wanted to tell one guy that if he took good showers and brushed his teeth that he would get many more girls than he is now.

The people were very nice and very sweet and welcoming and kind but when they got close to me there was extreme discomfort. Somehow I think that it was the smell that is given off when hormones are activating. I get the feeling that the men who did give off these smells were sweating and charging their bodies to soon ejaculate. The ambiance was of readiness for sex. With their sweat came the smell of smoke, whiskey, salt, and oil. Sitting among them, I saw them focusing on me and watching me carefully to see my reactions, and they all soon discovered how they could speak to please me, and they would ask me if I wanted to be spanked. They were very adamant but not forceful. They wanted me to feel comfortable with them so they sat close to me.

CONTACT: ONELLA, HELLFIRE CLUB (2001)

Onella is a rather quirky young woman. She's twenty-one. Her hair is purple; she tells me she spent last year in Spain hitchhiking. She speaks several languages and chats confidently.

I have no fears about going into the Soft City.

I was so comfortable at the club. I walked around with confidence and met many people. I wanted to see and hear the pains and screaming and moaning and ahhhs and ooohhs. I wanted to see the beautiful people who just feel "touch" with their bodies, and I felt that I was going to meet some honest people. One guy looked like a student. He told me he was "just curious." He was not an interesting subject. Yet he was, because he was "geeky" and so "normal" looking. I wanted to see his sweet smile and sunshine face turn into pain and lust and utter joy. This time I had less makeup, and my hair was simple so people were not mesmerized. This is not to say that people are usually mesmerized by me, actually never.

But when it's a slow night at the S/M club and no women are around and suddenly a young-looking little girl walks in, there is bound to be a lot of attention on her. Also because of the fact that this time there was a lot going on, I did not get the same amount of attention as last time. However, many eyes were on me. And the feeling of people being so aware of me being around them made me try to act very casual, and thus they did not grab me or harass me.

A man suddenly showed up in front of me in his jeans, no top, and a leather mask that covered his whole head. He appeared in front of me and with energy, with a quickening of step with his head turned completely toward me, he just stared. I ignored him; he went away.

There were women chained and men playing with themselves and putting on a show since many people watched. There were also some men who were getting whipped by women, but not that many, and they were not the main spectacles that night. The main one was a tall woman with light-colored hair, a curvy body, fatty stomach, whose arms and legs were chained. Two men took turns whipping her and finger fucking her. They also stuck clothespins on her nipples.

There was one man who was tied, and there was a woman who was whipping him, but not too hard. There was a woman who got her clitoris pierced. She seemed to enjoy it. Her pussy was not so big, and she did not have much hair. In fact, her pussy looked childish because the lips did not look developed enough, and she looked very young. She had a lot of makeup on. I was at the time just watching her, talking. I wish I could sit and observe. When I did, men would come and watch me and jerk off. I was just afraid that they would cum on me because they would stand so close.

People were so relaxed, and the feeling of sex, open shirts, loose pants, slow-moving people, sensual looks, gazes, soft eyes, slow walking, it was nice. Even the ones who were whipping each other, their faces were relaxed and their breathing deep. They were in a dream of ecstasy, but a slow one with bursts of pleasure with each other.

I met this older man who liked group sex, but he said not much was going on. For another guy, meeting women and playing with each other was a thrill. Another guy wanted to take me out for dinner. I said no. Maybe I should have gone. Ah man, I missed an opportunity to interview him fully. But somehow I may have made the right choice because he really wanted to have sex and maybe it would not have worked well. However, maybe just talking to him about himself would have done the job.

All night he followed me. I stared at him and he stared back, and I made him feel self-conscious of what was going on because I was able to stare him down. Haahhah . . . I was never able to do that before, and now I can do it and I see what kind of effect it has on people. It was all surreal, as the people's faces were so sweet toward me. This one guy would whisper when he spoke. He was so well dressed. He was cute, long dreads, and a nice smiling face that looked calm, happy, and just nice.

He said that he liked everything. We sat on a bench in the back while another guy stood by and stared at me and gave himself a hand job and stroked his very long dick with Johnson and Johnson baby oil. He also looked kind. His face was red, his neck veins were protruding, his mouth was a bit open. He kept his face and head still and stared at me, breathing deeply and making small sighs and making prolonged deep sounds of "ahh." He was really enjoying his time, and I was happy about that. But I thought it was funny because his act, which was because of me, was somewhat whimsical in that he had somehow deceived me while I was not watching; he had perched himself comfortably and was taking on a ritual, a simple ritual of joy. I thought this was funny. I could not help but laugh.

That was really weird of me to do but I could not help it, it just came out. It was not because of discomfort. I was fine; the Johnson and Johnson set me off. How unprofessional and immature of me. Back to the guy with the dreads. We spoke, and he spoke very nicely in that his voice was soft and patient, and when I laughed he said that people are pretty humorous. He was very relaxed, and he liked me a lot, but he was a little troubled because he liked me. You see, all of them were troubled because they liked me. They were so alone, so longing for physical affection and touch that they would be willing to be with me.

There is nothing wrong with me but they have no idea who I am. And I find that troubling. But then again, it's all a fantasy. And fantasies are not real. So the dreads guy walked with me to the back and we stood by the doorway, our backs toward the men who had followed me, excited that I may perform in the little room. He took out his dick with my permission. It was slanted and dark. As Richard Watts writes about pretension, he was not a "fraud who assumes a love of culture that is alien to him."

He knew what he was doing, which was being patient so that he could see if "we could play." So I stroked his dick softly with a finger to make him happy and also, it was like I was in a store, stroking to show the salesperson that I was not just window shopping and completely disinterested, so that she would continue giving me info. The Power, I felt, was not anywhere. The rooms were full of calm sexual energy and blowjobs, and now I am tired and must sleep. Goodnight.

Some girls perceive lounges as "meat markets" where people mainly go to hook up with someone, and they report that it is usual that men touch hips, legs, waists, and butts. While these touches considered in the context of daylight are perceived as sexual harassment, they are "perfectly normal when you're a little drunk and in a club—these sorts of things are expected to happen."[4]

CONTACT: ONELLA, TRUTH CLUB AND THE WAREHOUSE (2001)

Onella's focus on touch expands to a focus on touch and smell through her interactions with what she called the "rubber guy":

I went to the Truth tonight. It's a club on Twenty-Third Street, off Madison. At the bar I met a man named Jeff but whom I will call the "rubber guy." I was getting ready to leave the club when he asked me casually if I wanted to go in the back of the club where I could put ice in his latex clothing. I said okay, and we proceeded to the back of the club, but the back is not separate; it's just a little space beside the bar by the wall that is darker than the rest of the club. It is the little hallway where the entrance to the back of the bar is; therefore it is quite accessible but not completely visible. So he stood with his arms on the wall and his back toward me, and I held him in my arms and ran my nails over his body, played with his hair, held his chest, squeezed his shoulders, kissed his neck, and pulled on his rubber top and rubber gloves and made sounds with the rubber.

I pulled his shirt zipper down slowly while playing with his exposed skin and hair and dropped ice into his clothing. I danced with him and made his body sway from side to side. I did not feel anything. I was just doing it for the mere experiment. However, I would not be able to do it if he smelled bad. In the beginning when I met him, when he spoke, I did feel like there was a special repulsive smell on his breath, but then he had a beer, and I guess, I don't know how, but the smell was not there, or somehow I was able to avoid it.

Anyhow, whatever it was, this smell was not there, and that allowed me to show affection toward him. Otherwise, I would have been repulsed. He became somewhat passionate in his movement and could not keep his arms on the wall any longer and began to stroke my legs and butt with one hand while the other held onto the wall. So then his hand that was on the wall slipped and hit the light switch several times without our awareness until some bouncer guy came and chastised the poor guy for turning the lights on. So then we sat on some couch, and I played with his hair as he sat.

He just sat with his head bent forward, his arms dangling between his legs, sometimes gently stroking my knee, his head swaying with the movement and pressure of my hand, his face in pure calmness, his eyes closed. He looked like he was sleeping and was in a dream or just meditating and forgetting about any type of pain or pressure. He was so relaxed. Then I left him and went to the dance floor and danced to some jingle and other type of good music, and he joined me. He was completely free. He was in his latex gray pants, his latex top with a zipper, all very very tight, wearing eyeliner and lipliner. We danced and danced with crazy movements, not touching each other but in some type of role play where I was more in control and a bit less crazier and he was out of control. It was fun.

CONTACT: VICKIE, HELLFIRE CLUB (1999)

In this part of the narrative I elaborate on the sociological value of focusing on senses beyond sight. I see scent, odor, musk, as a kind of collage of the senses because they cut across observation. And the next set of notes does register and find the presence of those senses, since they are included in the same way as is sight. These notes are also about the coupling of smell and touch, since these two senses are related in some way as presence.

Vickie, twenty-four, has tiny freckles and dimples and is quick to laugh. She wanted to see Hellfire because others had told her about it. The first time, she was not impressed. The notes that follow describe the next time she ventured out.

The first time I went to Hellfire was part of a group of friends from my neighborhood. The second time I went with just my friend Judy for fun. We'd each left our houses with the desire to do something different. She'd had the misfortune of seeing her ex-boyfriend at the Clit Club, where we started our night, with a date, so she was in a state deep in her own mind. This was the first time Judy and I had socialized outside of [class], and I was glad for the experience. After the first time I'd gone to Hellfire I did not think much about it, and I certainly never thought I'd go again. . . . But this time it was inching toward three in the morning and just as a joke I said to her, "Let's go to Hellfire," which was right down the street from where we were walking.

The fact that there was no cover charge for us made the decision all that much easier. I mean, what did we have to lose? We were both itching for something interesting to happen, something out of the ordinary, and for us that apparently takes a lot. We had relatively little fear of bumping into note-taking, nonparticipating mates, and we were left to our own devices. So in we walked with the distinct feeling that we were not novices this time around. I was wearing dark denim jeans and chunky bad-girl boots. Judy was all in black with a diva coat with a collar turned up. My knee-length coat had fur on the collar and the cuffs.

I mention this because we kept our coats on the whole time we were there, as if taking them off would show off that we really were women, and I was not interested in baring my tank-top-wearing body. The coats also added to the allure of how we looked, two bad asses looking for trouble. The crowd was sparse and predominately male. I would have guessed there were under fifty people at the club this Friday night. I walked in, not afraid. I had emotional and physical armor on and was with someone who I was certain would not judge me. We walked into the second play room at the back of the club, and porn was playing on the television above the bar. Women were voraciously sucking dick. I remember not only feeling exposed being the only women but empowered by all this. It was not long before we were approached to play.

A white man in his mid-thirties attired in a fatigue-like ensemble approached us. He was amiable and did not reek of desperation. He asked us if we would like to trample him. Not knowing what that was, we asked for some clarification. He wanted us to walk on top of him. I thought I probably could do this but needed some prodding. I asked him if it hurt and if I would be able to keep my shoes on. He asked us the proverbial: "Is this your first time here?" I was able to answer in the negative, which I assume gave us a bit more leeway in his interaction with us. It was his casual attitude that enabled us to continue talking for a few minutes and eventually engage in the activity with him. He wanted us to trample him. Now, at first I envisioned someone jumping on top of him, and I definitely was not signing up for that. This, how-ever, was not the case. He wanted us to walk on his chest. Judy and I looked at each other and silently agreed that we would indeed do this.

We followed the man over to a corner in the club where there was a cross-shaped stock. It was wobbly, presumably from enthusiastic usage. He laid himself on the ground with his knees bent and his potbelly protruding. I was not sure of the shoe etiquette: Should they remain on or off? Luckily, we were to leave them on. I went first. I gingerly stepped upon him, as if afraid of hurting him. I took baby steps on his chest, toward his arms, which were under his head and back down toward his knees. This required some control and balance on my part. I asked him if he was okay, and he responded that he was.

There was a faint sheen of sweat on his face. When I got off of him, I noticed that a small crowd had formed. I took my place among the crowd and watched as Judy trampled and interviewed this man. He wanted both of us on top of him. I was concerned about the weight. I thought he was about to handle about 230 pounds on top of him. I figured he knew what he could handle, so we held each other for balance and took turns stepping on him. We did not trample him but rather took small deliberate steps over him. We asked him where this particular fetish came from, and he told us that an ex-girlfriend had done this for/to him. Only she'd done it wearing stilettos. I wondered if in some sense we were conjuring her and his desire for her. Were we surrogate feet? I myself did not ask any of these questions, but I am sure Judy had, as great minds think alike.

Even though a small crowd of men had formed, I was not bothered. I had no compunction about doing this because I felt I was losing nothing. There were no fluids exchanged, nor did I feel like it was sexual to me; it may have been to him, but that was incidental as far as I was concerned. Once again I was in the environment in which I was doing something I'd never known or thought about before. I'm not certain of all the elements that were in place for us to engage so seamlessly this evening. Perhaps it was a combination of things. While we were more familiar with each other, we also did not have a spattering of mates to hold us back. Could it be that after only one visit we were desensitized to all that is Hellfire?

Was there a full moon out? At any rate I imagine that it was a combination of factors that helped us to engage this evening. While I'd been busy trampling, another patron asked Judy if I would be interested in spitting on him. Whether he thought I'd be interested in that because of the very fact that I was in Hellfire and already trampling one man, I don't know. She suggested that he ask me himself, and after I "disembarked" Judy relayed this message to me. While discussing the gross nature of this, the potential victim wobbled over to us and disrupted our tête-à-tête.

I'd actually seen him earlier in the night. As we were doing our first once over of the club, he was in one of the concrete stalls masturbating. I was thinking this man fits my stereotype of someone who might watch child pornography. He looked desperate in that room jerking off by himself. He was wearing a large white T-shirt that fit only the circumference of his belly and was tucked inside black sweatpants. He was slightly creepy, and I had to wonder about his hygiene because he looked a little greasy. He was tall and round mostly around the middle; needless to say he was not very attractive.

When he asked me, I thought, "absolutely not." I'm trying to discern exactly what I thought was so unseemly about this act. The act of spitting was usually associated with men spitting out, chewing, or men hurling spitballs out of their cars they're driving. Was spitting on someone in conflict with my idea of femininity? It probably was more than just that. Spitting, like masturbating, is normally a private act. Now people would be privy to it, and I assume an audience would form to watch me. Perhaps I was concerned with what the patrons would think of me for spitting on this man. Should I have cared what they thought? I mean, after all, they were there too. Would they see him as the victim, not me? So I told him I would think about it, and due to my nervousness my mouth went dry, as if to throw off the act. In his zeal or desperation to get me to comply he went and bought me some water; the seal was intact when he returned with it, so I drank some. I figured I might as well try it. I mean, what were the odds I would be asked to do this again?

He went over and sat on the bench in the room. He took off his shirt and then asked me if it was okay if he played with himself. I thought, "What is he going to ask me to do next, swallow or something"? For some reason I thought this was not an unreasonable request, albeit a fairly repugnant one, so I said yes, and he grabbed on to his nubbish penis. I asked him if I could close my eyes, and he looked petulant and said that he'd prefer them open. So I accumulated some saliva and shot; it landed on his arm. I repeated and then he asked me for the piece de resistance, to spit on his face. I braced myself and spat on his face, and he groaned with pleasure. I did it two more times before he spread his seminal fluid over the concrete floor of Hellfire. Words don't often fail me, but the best word I could come up with for this was "gross." With that I walked away. The man we'd trampled remained with us; I wasn't sure if he just enjoyed our company or if he was acting as a bodyguard of sorts. I thought it prudent to get away from this last scene as soon as possible, so we went to the bar room.

CONTACT: LORRIE, FETISH PARTY, PARASOUL CLUB (JUNE 2003)

Lorrie, twenty-three, lives in Manhattan and is visiting this club for the second time. She does not consider herself a fetishist, though she likes to adventure when she finds the right vibe.

I decided to revisit the fetish party from a few weeks prior, as it was an overabundance of stimuli and cheap to enter. A friend attempted to attend a week earlier, but to no avail. After some investigation, I learned the party had moved from club Opaline to Parasoul, both of which are on Avenue A in the East Village. The website offered no explanation for the move, but I assumed it was to keep it underground and to keep more "mainstream" participants like us at bay. But that didn't work.

Unmarked and illuminated with red lights (a pattern among many of these events), I approached the party with my girlfriend Nurcille and a small Asian/Black man, Circa, who admittedly "fits into the most peculiar of circumstances." There was one party upstairs of which we knew nothing, and the overweight white guy and fanged Asian woman duo from my previous visit greeted us at the top of the stairs. We came dressed in all black, as I'd learned that contributed to reduced admission. Unfortunately, we forgot the "flyer" I'd printed out on the internet that would've allowed Circa to enter for $5 instead of $10. Nurcille and I entered for free as it was before eleven o'clock anyway.

The stairs led down to a room of no more than 150 square feet. Extremely dark, the only light came from tiny track lights on either side of the room that illuminated a captivatingly professional series of bondage/S&M/erotica photographs. The front of the room housed the DJ, with the bar and its bouffant blond bartender in black vinyl at the rear. Around fifteen people were present when we arrived. The gender ratio was almost even, with just a few more males in attendance. Red velvet couches lined the two sides of the room, with no other chairs or tables.

The participants were forced to face each other in a direct manner, and the circular nature of the small venue created an intimacy not felt in the other club. More clearly partitioned and constructed of multiple levels, Opaline provided a more open, slightly better-lit arena for the night's events. Parasoul, however, was bereft of the stage, the huge movie screen, the cozy round tables, the ample space for dance and performance. Yet it was not deficient but, rather, different and even more inclusive. The main focus upon arrival centered on a white man with a fit, healthy build who was escorted to the center of the room.

The same leather-panted MC hosted the evening's events, giving the crowd a play by play of the fetish action occurring throughout the venue, recruiting, making fetish matches, and inserting one-word commentaries like "ssseeeeeexxxxx" or "sexual!" in a husky, provocative tone during a performance. He explained that the man whose face was completely covered by a black hood (I kept wondering if asphyxiation was part of his fetish and couldn't determine the exact opacity of the hood from the inside), wearing nipple rings with a chain connecting them, his hands handcuffed behind his back, his ankles chained together, and wearing nothing but a leather and silver-studded G-string had been a very, very bad boy.

A dominatrix in a collar and black vinyl corset guided him belly down onto some red cube cushions. Massaging his butt with her hand and paddle in a manner I've come to recognize as a sort of S&M foreplay, she prepped his rump for a series of patterned spankings, intermixed with more caressing. Unlike many of the spankings I've witnessed heretofore, this exchange seemed to involve a bit of role play. Although shackled and blinded, he dramatized an attempt to rise and escape after each series of blows to his backside.

She feigned a sort of aggressive dominance that failed to permit mobility on his part, warranting another spanking session, due to the insurgence of "bad behavior." He was gently grasped by the dominatrix and another participant and guided back to the couch, where his nipples were titillated via yanks on the attached chain, and several people touched, caressed, and prodded him in a fashion that yielded no squeamishness or apparent discomfort on his part. He was eventually left to rest, still hooded and chained, upon the couch, where he remained for a considerable amount of time.

After what seemed like hours, he removed his own handcuffs (a testament to the fantasy part of the party, as he was in no way technically disempowered but rather just giving off the illusion of disempowerment and acting accordingly) and de-hooded. We all took a second look, as the last remaining element of the man's body was disrobed, revealing (to our utter astonishment) a man with thinning gray hair in his late fifties or early sixties.

His body and energy were easily that of a twenty-something, and his assumed youthfulness was not even questioned until the unveiling of his head. He put on his wire-rim spectacles and brought out a small leather suitcase filled with neatly folded "conservative" street clothing, among which he selected an ensemble to his liking and disappeared to go change, never to return.

Meanwhile, another participant evidently enjoyed the style of the dominatrix and begged her for her services. Bending himself over the same red velvet cubes at the center of the room, he hurriedly pushed down his already sagging baggy jeans and boxers, which peeked heavily over the waistband. The style of spanking was not unlike the last exchange, but the submissive showed no signs of resistance and even embraced the dominatrix in a loving hug after rising.

Only one more spanking exchange occurred, again at the center of the tiny room, this time between a random submissive and a woman I thought was a professional dominatrix but later realized was simply a woman wanting to spank. Dressed in a red miniskirt, platforms, a red T-shirt that said "Princess" across the front, and a bandana with yin-yang symbols, the large-framed black woman mimicked the spanking style of the previous dominatrix, switching off with her at times. It was not until later, when I witnessed her in an argument with a guy that appeared to be her boyfriend, that I realized she was more of an eager participant than a professional.

The only other dominator present was an enormous black man who was present at the last Flesh Theatre party I attended. While he had previously spent the entire evening servicing one woman, tonight he circulated for the better part of this evening until finally situating himself on the couch with a large white woman in a black bra with fishnet stockings on her arms (a popular look for the evening). She was draped comfortably over his lap. A cup of ice at his side, he numbed her back with its chill before scratching her back in a calculating, methodical manner.

A young girl in a schoolgirl costume took center stage periodically throughout the night. Using a small, round table as her stage, she danced provocatively for the crowd and herself. Her blond hair was pulled into pigtails, which she later took out as the night progressed. Her white oxford shirt not buttoned but rather tied in a knot revealed her midriff and later her white training bra; this, too, was later discarded. A white G-string was revealed beneath her extremely short plaid skirt as she bent over to adjust her white-laced anklets and Mary Janes. A lacy garter on her right leg collected money by a myriad of participants as she danced, and she took the liberty of gagging herself with a piece of fabric for the duration of a few songs.

We remained in one section of the long couch, close to the DJ area, for most of the evening. It was apparent upon our arrival that the MC recognized our "outsider" quality. However, this fetish party welcomes and enjoys individuals of the sort, as long as they are open to experimentation and nonjudgmental. It is a venue for exhibition and an outlet for many people who enjoy being watched. Hence our valued contribution.

After short whispers and direct eye glances from the MC and the bustier-clad dominatrix, the dominatrix approached my friend Circa, while the MC made his way over to Nurcille and me. She introduced herself and asked Circa if he would like a spanking. As it was his first time in a club of this sort, he asked if it would be acceptable if he waited until later. She said no problem and left immediately. The MC asked Circa if he would like to spank or be spanked, to which he answered "spank," and a young girl I recognized from the previous party took a seat next to him. She tied up at the last event, but this night she was more than a little interested in receiving a spanking from my friend. She continued to follow him throughout the night, but never received the punishment for which she yearned.

A woman on the opposite couch enjoyed a foot massage from another participant. The MC motioned to the action across the way and asked us if we were interested in a similar massage and a free drink (the drink was contingent upon the massage, a sort of payment from the massager, a sign of his gratitude). I watched the other exchange in action and could identify nothing "out of the ordinary." It appeared to be your run-of-the-mill foot massage. As I am a sucker for massages, especially of the foot variety, and was in disbelief that I not only didn't pay but was given something in gratitude, I couldn't refuse the offer. Nurcille declined the offer, as she had promised her long-distance boyfriend that she would "not participate" in the events at which she gazed.

My mind reflected on the previous week's argument with my boyfriend. We had decided that lap dances were unacceptable . . . but what about foot massages? I considered the dynamics: in a lap dance, I was the one paying (in theory anyway), and the intention was that it was for my enjoyment; the girls were doing their jobs and probably drew little erotic pleasure from most of the exchanges in which they engaged. There was "heavy petting" and kissing (albeit not directly on the mouth) in such instances—obvious grounds for discomfort on his part—but the boundaries were somewhat clear. But a foot massage as a part of a foot fetish was much more complex and cloudy.

While I received "pleasure" of some sort from the exchange, it was not what I would categorize as sexual—or even sensual or erotic, necessarily. However, I assumed that for the massager, it was an experience comparable to sex in its orgasmic quality for them. Was the acceptability of the situation, with regard to my own romantic relationship, contingent upon my perception of the act or theirs? Nurcille concluded that their deep enjoyment on the erotic level made it unacceptable for her. Circa, however, likened it to a hypothetical situation where he was profoundly turned on whenever I wore black.

"You could continue to wear black every day, and I would continue to be turned on, but that doesn't mean you were doing anything wrong." I contemplated his argument. While it made sense, I wondered if the involvement of direct touch, flesh-to-flesh contact, altered the scenario in any way. After a short spell of deliberation, my academic and personal curiosity, in conjunction with my weakness for a massage, won, and I accepted the offer. (And decided to avoid a potential problem in my own relationship by simply omitting it from our conversation about the night. Dishonest, perhaps, but a detail I didn't recognize as pertinent to our relationship.)

The same individual I watched massage the girl on the couch directly across from us approached me and settled on the floor at my feet. Previously unable to identify him because of the overwhelming darkness of the room, I didn't recognize him until he expertly grabbed my left foot. It was the foot worshipper I described in my previous visit. He stuck out to me at the last party because of his unique physical profile among the group, which remained consistent at this party. He wore a baseball cap that hid the decidedly Asian features of his face, and he revealed his slightly bucked teeth only when he smiled bashfully on occasion. His enviably muscular arms displayed a black tattoo that encircled one bicep, revealed in its entirety by his white, loose-fitting Air Jordan tank top, and he finished off the ensemble with baggy blue cargo pants and sporty yellow and gray New Balance sneakers. He set a bottle of Poland Spring water and a bottle of Corona beside my legs and focused on my feet.

I asked if he preferred to start with one foot in particular, which he answered in the same way he answered all my questions: through gestures. I wore black ballet slipper shoes and little black Calvin Klein "peds" (small socks used to line one's shoes and give the illusion of no socks). He went straight to my left foot, removing first the shoe, then the sock, which he placed neatly in the shoe. He massaged in an aggressive, firm manner that I greatly enjoyed and attempted to express to him; I received no verbal response but rather a knowing nod. He made a kissing gesture toward my toes, and I asked if he wanted to kiss my feet.

I laughed, uncertain as to whether or not I wanted to allow it, and then decided I would permit it—but no sucking. He gently kissed my first few digits and returned to the massage. Harmless enough, I thought. It was yet another example of attempting to define boundaries. I was confronted with questions and actions I never previously considered. My own personal rules were in question; I had no precedent to which I could refer. I had only my instinct. I defined as I went along.

The MC announced the "virgin foot massage" that was occurring, focusing the group's attention on our exchange. An unassuming guy in his twenties, dressed in a tight black T-shirt that accentuated his defined arms, approached the MC. By their direct glances, I knew their discussion centered on me and, most likely, my now abandoned left foot, as my current massager had shifted to the right foot. The MC first propositioned Nurcille once again, hoping to sway her after my praise of the action I continued to enjoy.

She stood firm in her decision, prompting them to beg for my other foot. It seemed a bit excessive or indulgent or something I couldn't identify, two men simultaneously groping my furthermost appendages, but I once again agreed—partly out of curiosity, partly as a glutton—to the act. He seated himself on the floor next to the other guy, silently massaging my left foot. I stared down at them, and they appeared as children seated on the classroom floor. One, the guy on the right, working diligently, intently; the other, the guy on the left, almost playing with my toes and feet, inspecting them, discovering them as if for the first time. Their styles were strikingly different.

While the first one kneaded my feet like fleshy dough, the other caressed and applied pressure in more isolated movements. Both fixated largely on my toes, which created a bit of my problem when working on my left foot, as I had acquired several blisters on those toes the day before. While it created a significant discomfort when they were rubbed, I was timid in communicating this and shied away from detracting from what I assumed was their tried-and-tested technique. I opted to endure the pain.

The simultaneous foot worshipping continued for an extended period of time. I looked to Nurcille and Circa for advice. How long had they been at it? Twenty minutes? An hour? I had no concept of time. How long would they continue? Were they waiting for me to dismiss them? Every boyfriend I've ever had could give a massage for around ten minutes before tiring, but these guys were like machines. They showed no signs of slowing. "Do you want to stop?" I finally asked. "No," they replied in unison. "If he gets tired, I'll keep going," replied the man on my left. "I could do this for hours. I love it. You're beautiful and that beauty radiates through your foot. I feel a chemistry and a connection with it and with you; it puts me in a trance-like state."

Unsure of how to reply, I took the opportunity to chat with the left worshipper, as the other guy refused to utter a single word. I asked him, Jim, as he revealed his name to be, if he always felt that or just with me. "With you. Sometimes I see a beautiful person and I want to rub their feet, and then I realize 'Oh, it's bad,' and I just rub it for a while and leave. But with you I felt a chemistry." This led into a discussion of attraction and sexuality. "Does this turn you on? Is it a sexual experience for you?" I inquired. He thoughtfully considered the question. "It's erotic but not sexual. It's sensual. It depends on how you define 'sexual.'" Interesting. I could tell he had put some thought into this. "If sexual means 'wham, bam, thank you, ma'am' for you, then, no, it's not sexual. I try not to masturbate or anything because I feel morally stronger. I like the self-control."

He continued his discourse, with little prodding on my end. "This is personal and intimate, like looking into someone's eyes. I come to know you through your foot." Intrigued by his statement, I furthered his analysis, applying the literary term "synecdoche" to it. "What?" he questioned. "It's when a part, like a foot, represents the larger whole, like the body or the individual itself." Obviously impressed, he asked for an exact spelling and vowed to use the word himself in the future. I asked him if he enjoys receiving as well as giving. "It's not something I ever wanted, but I know reflexology and I figured I could benefit from experiencing it myself. It was alright."

A believer in reflexology, I questioned him further about his use of it in his massages. "I can feel certain parts of your body when I touch various areas of your foot." (At one point he hit a particularly sensitive area on my foot, about which I inquired, and he answered, "That's your shoulder. It's on your left foot, corresponding to your left shoulder. You've been holding up your leg and it's making your shoulder tired. Cross your leg like this." He repositioned my leg. "Is that better?" It was. Much.) I reflected on the strikingly different styles of the two guys. Before speaking with him, I assumed that the other massager had a background in reflexology because of the intensity of his touch. But then I realized the methodical nature of Jim's touch, almost exploring the specific points of my foot. He was subtle yet accurate.

I asked what he did for a living, and he admitted to a career as a massage therapist. How appropriate, I thought, and yet, what a venue for a potential conflict of interest. "Are you aroused by your clients? Do they turn you on when you're working on them?" He said he sort of separates himself from his clients. "I don't give them all my energy some of the time. When I do, I come home and I'm really tired. Just like this, I either feel a connection or I don't." But is that "connection" sexual—or sensual, or erotic or however you want to define it? "I think of it as a very spiritual experience; it's very mystical." He didn't give a clear answer, and I'm not sure there was one to be had. He told me he was finishing an undergraduate degree in exercise physiology and hoped to go to school for naturopathy, a type of alternative medicine doctor, in the future. Again a fan of his discipline of choice, I applauded his goals.

During my conversation with Jim, I somehow excused the other massager. (I'm unclear as to what exactly convinced him to finish.) "Can I ask you something?" he finally uttered to me, leaning over and speaking quietly into my ear. "Sure," I replied. "Was I good? Did I give you pleasure?" he asked timidly. "Then," he continued in the same hesitant manner, "May I ask you permission to keep your stockings?" Again taken aback and unprepared with a "usual" answer to such a request, I did my now regular "startled laugh" and decided in the affirmative. What could it hurt? He had asked me earlier if he could have permission to sniff my feet; he promised not to slobber. These were the only words he spoke during the hour-long massage.

He then revealed his impetus. "The feet exude the most pheromones," he stated expertly. "What I really like is the smell of the feet—the socks and shoes. There's nothing sexier than beautifully pedicured feet [which mine were not] and a pair of high heels [a far cry from my ballet slippers]." I entertained visions of his home, surrounded with a collection of stockings and shoes, which my Calvin Klein "peds" were about to join. "Okay, enjoy!" I thanked him again and returned to my discussion with Jim.

He returned shortly with a drink. "Thanks," I said. He continued to massage my foot, while watching another man fall to the floor beneath a woman on the opposite couch. That man placed her foot on his face and remained there for a lengthy period of time. "Your friend's a foot-fetish guy, too?" I asked. "Uh, he likes to drink. I think he's more into that," Jim admitted, a statement he immediately followed with, "I don't think of myself as a freak...I think I hit a low when I started to attend these parties." I tried to get him to elaborate further, but the music pulsated, making it difficult to hear the already jumbled manner in which he attempted to explain his statement.

It was getting late, and I think Jim could tell I would depart soon. "So, um," he began in hesitation. "Maybe you'd like to do this again sometime...we could get together again or something." "Well, I have a boyfriend," I stated bluntly. "Oh," he said with knowing resignation. "But," I continued, "I'd love to get your number and talk further with you, if you'd feel comfortable. You could speak anonymously if you like, but I'm very interested in your ideas about fetishism and your thoughts on feet." "And I really like sociology, too," he continued in earnest. "I come from a family of philosophy and literature." By one o'clock we exited the front entrance. A group of smokers were assembled in front of the club, an interesting mix of trannies and fetish participants. We said our goodbyes and dispersed in different directions.

CONTACT: BETTY, FIELD NOTES (2008)

Betty, twenty-two, considers herself a "budding intellectual" and wanted to learn as much as she could about the Soft City. She expressed her ideas eloquently in her notes.

As I jumped into the cab one quiet Friday night in New York City, I unknowingly entered into yet another spirited conversation about sex in our city. I had just emerged from the outing to La Trapeze, and my cabbie was quite familiar with the club and what it had to offer on the inside. After I had given my cabbie my address in Brooklyn, he looked at me through the rear-view mirror and exclaimed how happy he was to see young people emerging from La Trapeze. "This is exactly what we need, young people to keep the scene going and to keep places like this around."

The driver looked to be in his late forties. He was a Black individual, but I couldn't quite locate his country of origin. He was so excited and energetic as he drove me back to Brooklyn, and he gave me accounts of how New York used to be in the "good old days" when you could go somewhere and see a woman so excited that her gushing fluids were visible from feet away. He and others missed the sex and the freedom. He also told me of his dream to find his perfect "slut" out there so that they can be "crazy sluts together." One of the most interesting cries for a soulmate that I have had the fortune to come across.

No one can argue against the notion that much has changed in the wonderful city of New York and that the Soft City, as some have come to know it, which has been so well looked into, has faced much change and adversity. It is an interesting combination of both an attack on the Soft City as well as the interest of capital and the capitalization of these practices. In addition to a rather conservative political era and the further controlling of the body there has also been the great influx of capital into this realm of sexuality, desire, pleasure, and taboo. The sex market has not only boomed but also come a little more out in the open.

What used to be traditionally an underground economy has become somewhat acceptable in particular forms in society. We still hide our sex stores, still don't want them near schools or churches, and still find a way to stigmatize the customers, but it has become slightly easier to get what one is looking for. While sex is fun and is something done and enjoyed by most, there has been a dramatic influx of business into this supposedly private and spontaneous realm. One could go into a store and spend a hundred dollars before they know it. In addition to being concerned about certain new aspects of these experiences, such as the astoundingly high entrance fees, I found myself very interested and concerned with the clothes that one wears to and at such events as an important part of the experience.

The entire process was intriguing to me intellectually and personally and was also felt in my wallet, which is something that brought about more questions in my head regarding the fetish subculture. I found there to be a blend of reasons why clothes and fetish gear were so important, the two most important being status and desire, which will be explored in this account.

At most outings for the class, both with the class and in escapades otherwise, a lot of thought and concern was put into what was going to be worn that evening, which was important at the level of acceptability as well as at the level of being erotically stimulating. To a certain extent, I'm sure this was something that I was solely concerned about, but I usually did end up in a dialogue with others about the clothing, both outer- and underwear.

The Soft City has its own set of norms and mores, and it is important as a member of that community to understand those guidelines. Even more so, I would argue, as a new person to that community it is important to address these norms in manner and dress as to foster acceptance in the beginning of one's adventures.

In regards to the desire aspect, the prelude to the tactile part of sexuality and sensuality is the visual. Dressing in such a way that sends a visual image to spark desire is an important initiation. Additionally, stimulation is also fueled after the initial look by touch, by the sensation of different fabrics, textures, etc. It would be an error not to acknowledge the importance of the other senses as well in this aspect of fetish and everyday play. The smell of certain materials, the sounds they make, and I'm sure for some people the taste of them all fuel desire, pleasure, and, at times, pain. A man once told me that he could sniff leather forever. Just fill a room with it and he would be in bliss.

While the spectacle of sex stores in the city has dramatically been reduced in the last several decades, there are still many places that cater to the sex market where one can find sex toys, novelty items, and, of course, clothes and costumes. Not all sex stores are created equal, and there is a very wide range of stores that still exist. Part novelty and part necessity if one knows where to look, they are easy enough to find. The variety of sex shops leads to different experiences and different market aims. I have lived now in the same apartment in Brooklyn for the past two years, and I am right by Third Avenue, which has the BQE [an elevated highway] right overhead. The marked difference between Fourth and Fifth Avenue and then between Third and Fourth Avenue still amazes me somewhat.

When we first moved into the area, we immediately noticed all of the sex shops that run along Third Avenue. They seemed to have the range of merchandise, with many of them having twenty-four-hour booths for customers to use. A couple of blocks down Third Avenue is a nudie bar, and apparently there is also a swingers club in the area.

After we had settled into the area, my roommate and I decided to head over to one of the shops to check it out. Now, I have been in various sex shops in many different cities, so I had an idea in my head of what to expect. But the stores that line Third Ave. definitely have a nonfemale customer in mind and conjure up all of the negative stereotypes out there about these stores. The second we walked in, we knew it was not the place for us. And the leering demeanor of the sales guy behind the counter was more than we could bear. Clearly this was not the place for the random bridal-shower supplies run or the somewhat shy and uncomfortable female customer.

This was an interesting moment, since these stores never make me uneasy. When compared to shops in Manhattan, namely in the Washington Square/ Village area, it is evident that the act of shopping, picking out merchandise, and purchasing items is a very preliminary, but important, part of one's sexual experience and is also important in the fetish process. If uncomfortable when in a store, it can start the entire process wrong.

When contrasted with one of my favorite stores in the city, it is amazing what a difference the experience of shopping and nice help can make in becoming more excited about your purchase and then more excited about the endeavor out. From both my own interactions as well as the observed interactions with others and discussion with the people who work in the stores, the presentation of the store and staff can help ease first-timers into new territory and can also be an enjoyable place for seasoned veterans to want to go to over and over again.

It must be noted that at all times the gaze is present in these stores, no matter which one you choose to go in. To a certain extent, the feeling of comfort that one has in a place compared to another place is a bit of an illusion. While the guy in the store on Third Avenue might make one feel instantaneously uncomfortable, there is just as demanding of a gaze in other stores, where managers oversee their staffs like hawks. To a certain extent this gaze is always sexual—how could it not be—but it is better managed and much less threatening in different contexts.

To start with a personal story, here is an account from one of my last outings. Before heading out to the stores, I had a very particular idea in my head of what I wanted to get. This is the usual way that I shop for anything. I had a vision in my head of what the end product would look like, and dammit, that is what I would emerge with. I always start shopping with this false confidence. About 80 percent of the time I leave a store with what I picture. The rest of the time it is some variation thereof, with which I am only sometimes thrilled. Especially in the realm of shopping for an outfit to go out in (to a club, etc.), I often times let the salesperson take over.

It's a combination of not totally understanding all of the merchandise that is available out there and still not being totally comfortable with my body and how I want to present it. I also feel, and this may be wrong, that while whatever I purchase should be enjoyed by myself, I am ultimately dressing myself up to evoke the desire of someone else, another, and this other is what ultimately needs to approve of the presentation that I am offering.

What does this say about my fetish? Well, to a certain extent we can all agree that my desires are not of the most dramatic level of fetish and that my fetish might lie just as much in the other as it does in the objects that I buy.

Perhaps this makes me more mainstream, more of a novice, but my infatuation with my image or the corset that I buy only takes me so far. It is the validation in the other that brings me to the next level, which makes the whole event exciting.

That said, I do think that there is much excitement in imagining an event, in purchasing the correct outfit or toy to make that event exciting, and, of course, in the process of donning the clothes and the look. Walking out into the world with that confidence does a world of good in setting up the night.

I have shopped both in stores and online for merchandise, and while there is an ease to online shopping, it is not the same as walking into a store and looking at the merchandise in person. Interestingly, one cannot fully try on clothes in a sex shop. Usually it is done over the person's clothes, if at all. But there is still a better ability to get a feel for the merchandise there than from online. Also, there is the personal interaction. It is fun to go in and talk to the people who work there or maybe get into a chat with another customer about a product or item. I understand why people would choose to go in and physically purchase their stuff. Especially those who are much more ingrained in the scene. They can have customized items, as some of the S&M shops offer, or there is also the ability to have a relationship with the salesperson, someone who knows how to fuel your interests.

After many trips to sex shops in New York City I eventually found one that I very much liked. Good merchandise and good salespeople. Two very important things in any shopping experience. By this point in time I knew where I wanted to go, so I headed straight to the corsets. I had an evening planned of paddles and I wanted something to wear. I wasn't ready to go in there in full gear, not just yet, so I wanted a variation thereof. Maybe something stellar to wear with jeans, as I was concerned both with my dress as well as how much money this venture to the store would be.

As I approached the part of the counter that I wanted to be at, there was a couple in my way. They were fun to observe, the two of them assessing corsets and talking with one of the salespeople there. I stood next to them and eyed the merchandise as they finally settled on some white lacy thing. Not my style, but hey, whatever floats your boat. I wondered if it would be more fun to have my significant other there shopping with me. I have yet to bring him along. I usually tend to surprise him with stuff. I wondered how much that would change my experience. Would it be more fun? Annoying? A turn-on? A bicker match? The couple under observation seemed like they were having a good time. Wonder if they were turned on.

As I was watching this exchange and also looking for my own outfit, a salesperson approached that I had never seen before. I told her what I was looking for, and she immediately showed me things I would like. The big question was what color. Black. What else? That's not so true: I already had a purple one. The patterned one I was eyeing apparently was not made by a good company. So black it was. She offered to fit it for me, so we went to the backroom, where the vibrators and cock rings were, and she kicked out the guys looking at stuff. She needed the space.

Corsets are messy business and require grunt work. As she was pulling the strings and cutting off more and more oxygen I once again went down the road of imagination to when women wore corsets every day. What a different life. Breathing was such a novelty. But as she pulled the strings tighter and tighter and I could breathe less, my silhouette looked better and better. It's amazing what we do for fashion, for a look. But it got compliments in the store and it was very well received later that night. The texture of it, some sort of satin feel, and the look of it, the lines it created, were appreciated by all and only fueled how I felt.

These types of stores have a "busy season," which to a certain extent highlights the way that the general public perceives such shops. A salesperson once told me when asked that they get "very busy at Valentine's Day. And also at Christmas. I would say that Halloween is one of out busiest times." The information about Halloween is very telling about how the general public views these shops, but, clearly, there needs to be some regular clientele, or these shops would cease to exist. It is these people that I am interested in, both academically as well as personally.

Who are the people who live this lifestyle—and also find this aspect, the dress, toys, etc., important enough to spend their hard-earned money on? What purpose does this gear serve in their sexual and sensual exploits? Does it stay in the bedroom, or do they bring their toys and garments outside? And what excitement, if any, does shopping for these items bring them? And lastly, why in this age of the internet do they still choose to go out of their way, to a physical store, to get what they want?

As a way to briefly test the waters about these questions, I posted a couple of my questions on the infamous craigslist.org, one of the easiest ways to make connections for most Americans. I decided to post a thread on their NYC kink/BDSM community thread. My questions were as follows: "Where do you shop for your clothes and gear in the city? Do you prefer to shop in stores or online now? What materials turn you on? What do you decide to purchase?"

It was pretty amazing how quickly responses started coming in, not to mention how quickly additional posts were being put up. The activity on this thread, which I put up around one o'clock in the afternoon, was much more than I anticipated right off the bat. It was interesting to find that the suggestions and replies that came in indicated that people preferred to go shopping and that there were two stores that were mentioned over and over again in the city: Purple Passion and the Leather Man. There were also some suggestions for stores in San Francisco as well as some pictures and stories about the merchandise that people have purchased from said stores.

I decided to investigate this Purple Passion place. I had heard about it from various people in the past; when I was looking into the NYC BDSM community, this store was mentioned over and over again. They touted an online store, but the site insisted that they had a much better selection at their actual store, which was somewhat contrary to the way one would think it would be. Clothing in this shop runs from about thirty dollars into the hundreds. The shop is in the Chelsea area and is rather nondescript on the outside. Some thoughts on this outing.

The door is covered in black and posts a rather bold "you must be over 21 to enter" sign. Upon entering, I had the feeling that I was going into a Hot Topic [a store for goth and alternative clothing, aimed at teenagers], but clearly this place was going to be a bit more intense than that. And also wouldn't have teenagers. Sweet. The place was a lot smaller than they made it look online. Oh, the power of photography. But the smell that instantly hit the nose when you walked in was great. A little bit like leather, a little gritty, a little stale.

The place was about 80 percent clothes, 15 percent whips and other bondage gear, and 5 percent toys and books. They had an amazing collection of clothes and shoes. Different styles, lengths, fabrics, heels for women and heels for men, and various costumes. I could understand why people gave this place such rave reviews. And for the time of day, the place was fairly crowded. Which was fun. A couple shopping for an outfit together (guess this is a frequent thing) and a bunch of girls scattered randomly. I was struck by the female demographic of the store. I'm sure that is not always consistent.

People were rifling through the racks, getting a feel for the textures that were available. One of the most amazing things that they had was this rubber foam-like substance that was made into dresses. A woman stepped out of the dressing room in this hot red pleather number, exclaiming that she loved it. It was exciting to watch the other reactions. Unfortunately I couldn't afford such an outfit myself. Perhaps when I get paid.

I asked a very nice sales lady if the place draws in a decent customer base, and she replied that they are always crowded with a mix of new people and returning fans. I wondered out loud if she thought the internet helped or hindered their business, and she replied that it seems to stay busy in the store, but the online sales are an added bonus. She assumed that most people who go to the internet first either already know exactly what they want from previous purchases or are people who cannot easily access the store or perhaps live in places that do not have such well-equipped stores.

Purple Passion definitely had a more "dark" and "gothic" feel than other stores that I have been to. In discussions with people either in stores or at clubs it is interesting to see how many items have a story to go along with them and how important that story is to them. The more rare the item, the more excited they seem to be about it, as almost any collector of anything would be. The paddle or whip that no one else has, which they got in this little specialty store; materials that are hard to find, such as bone or ivory as an embellishment to the accessory and therefore the play. One person who has been in the scene for decades talked to me for hours about his collection, which pieces were good for what and what each piece meant to him. He told me, "The most exciting thing to me is a woman in ropes."

Clearly, almost anything can be fetishized, and some are more popular than others, it seems. Here, high heels and corsets will be explored, and their importance to the fetish world and to the general world will be extrapolated upon. The term "fetish" has changed over the course of its use, and authors argue that the sense of what we understand as a fetish was distinctly shaped by nineteenth- and twentieth-century discourses on sex, purity, and acceptability. Essentially, when one speaks of a fetish, what they are referring to is an item or particular part of the body that is the source of sexual stimulus and desire.

This item can be the most important part of the sexual experience and has the ability to eclipse one's partner entirely. There are variations of the level of the importance of the fetish; at times the combination of that and one's partner is important, and at other times the item alone is the most important and stimulating part. It is important to address the Marxist use of the term "fetish" in that part of what is being looked at is the commodification of the sexual fetish and the influx of capital into this market.

For Marx, commodities were assigned a value or meaning that allowed for them to become fetishized by the bourgeoisie, which led to the assignment of false importance to these objects and provided a distraction from their alienation. "Historical analyses of nineteenth-century fashion often employ an economic trope, and it is suggested that capitalism exploits the obsession with bodies in order to market new commodities."[5] To a certain extent, while this addresses fashion in particular, it can also be extended to the fetish. Certain materials employed by, or invented for, new fashions are adopted by the fetish world. As materials become more sophisticated, newer and newer commodities are introduced into the fetish world. Additionally, the "classic" fetish items are continually going through changes and being updated and augmented.

In addition to the Marxist economic way of looking at fetishized objects, the field of psychoanalysis also took part in constructing the understanding of the fetish and in diagnosing it as a disorder that has deep roots in one's psyche. The root of the fetish was taken out of one's alienation from their labor and placed in a more personal and individual realm.

In her book *Fetish: Fashion, Sex, and Power*, Valerie Steele brings in the idea that "fetishism is not only 'about' sexuality; it is also very much about power and perception."[6] In the BDSM scene, the relations of power are interesting to watch in and of themselves. People switch personalities and take on an "everyday" persona, and then while in the scene they take on a different persona, of the slave or master, etc.

Power is very much a part of this world; the power to inflict pain upon someone else, the power to control the pain that is being inflicted on you, and the power to choose what happens to you and where. Of course, nothing is ever 100 percent safe, but there is a very high level of comfort, respect, and understanding in this scene. If someone says the safe word, then it is all over, and the scene comes to a close. Perception was briefly noted earlier as an important part of the whole process. Perception can aid in turning a person on and making them feel sexual. But it also is closely related to status and privilege, and if you look a certain way in a club or venue, then that will equate into power and heightened desire.

When discussing power, it is important to bring Michel Foucault into the equation, as he wrote extensively about both power and sex. To a certain extent, sex and sexual situations always involve some sort of power relationship between the parties. In addition to the power on the individual level, there is also power at work here at the structural level. To a certain extent, this is where fetishes are even deemed to be so. The labeling of such is to make a distinction from the norm and to stigmatize a behavior or practice. "Moreover, this was the form in which it [perverse behavior] was manifested, more clearly than anything else, in the model perversion, in that 'fetishism' which, from at least as early as 1877, served as the guiding thread for analyzing all the other deviations."[7] Psychoanalysis and the medical field used fetishes and the created stigma of them to turn people's sexual practices into a problem.

Ernest Becker, a cultural anthropologist, wrote about the fetish. "Fetishism," Becker argues, "'represents the anxiety of the sexual act,' and the fetish itself functions as a 'magical charm' that transforms the terrifying reality of 'species meat' into something 'transcendent.'"[8] The definition of the fetish is actually very close to the way that fetishes used to be seen hundreds of years ago by relating it to a magical charm.

Before the rise of the commodity fetish, analyzed by Marx, people and tribes did put belief into objects, and these objects were thought to have magical properties or powers. In Becker's claim there is still that notion of the anxiety of sex and the need to change something about the reality of sex into something that is safe and clean for the participant. It is still not certain where this anxiety arises from, and it would seem that in some cases fetishists would contest the notion of anxiety that is brought up here.

Jane always loved her shoes. She prided herself on her collection. When she started to become interested in the world of BDSM, it was on very unofficial territory and primarily took place in the home. A little whip here, a tie there, etc. I had met her during one of my outings to the club, and our discussion had started because of her shoes. I had been looking for the perfect boots, and hers seemed to be right up my alley. While still timid in these situations, there is nothing like accessories to start a conversation.

I approached Jane after she was done with a scene and was just hanging out. By this time I had already become comfortable with what I liked to wear, and I was starting to become intrigued with others' choices as well. This was Jane's first time out, but her partner had much experience in the scene already.

Funny, I felt as though that was how I got my start . . . but I digress. I told her that her shoes were phenomenal and asked where she got them. "Oh, this place in the Village. I wish I could remember the name, I know I would remember it by sight. But aren't they amazing?!" And amazing they were.

They laced up past her knee and appeared to be made of the softest leather. There was an excruciatingly pointed toe, and I swear the heels were about five inches. Quite a bold choice. I decided to ask her what drew her to them. "They're hot. Look at the line of them, both on the foot and off the foot. I feel as though I can crush anyone, and the stature adds to my feelings of empowerment. To know that desire can be created by the point of my toe is awesome. I also knew that they were a look that my master would like.

"He loves leather anything, and these are very much akin to the pictures he has strewn about his bedroom. When I brought them to him, he just sniffed them with his eyes closed. I knew I had pleased him. And that turned me on. Though I can't show it. All because of the power on my feet." I also asked her what she thought made shoe love a "fetish." She replied that there was not much of a difference . . . but while she loved her shoes, housed them in their boxes, and told them how pretty they were, she would never lick them and get off. "So that has to be the difference, yeah?"

All of this somewhat negative representation of the fetish should be counteracted. It is interesting to grow up in a relatively mainstream world and be trained to have certain preconceived notions of people and normalcy. A person new to the fetish world might not know how to feel about what they see and what they are participating in. Even someone who goes into it excited about what they will be doing there can experience some dissonance in the beginning. Perhaps this is a mark of someone who does not have a true fetish or who is too ingrained in societal standards.

But the fetish world, like many other communities, is full of people who are nice and respectful and thoroughly enjoy what they do and the community that they have built up. Clearly, as with everything, there are a few people that are not always decent, but the comfort that has been created in every new situation I have personally been involved with has always been inviting and has offered a safe atmosphere to play in.

To move on to a particular item that is heralded in the fetish world, I wish first to look at shoes. Much work has been put forth about the difference that exists between someone who loves shoes and someone who fetishizes shoes.

According to people who study the phenomena of the shoe fetish, what makes the love of the shoe different from the everyday consumer's love of the shoe is the reaction that it evokes in the person. There is a sexual reaction and at times a sexual gratification; this is not necessarily common in the everyday shoe fan.

One of the most popular styles in question is the high heel. "There is a little bit of Imelda Marcos in many women, and many men exhibit an almost Pavlovian response to the sight of a woman in high heels." Imelda Marcos was the first lady of the Philippines and is known for her massive shoe collection. "Long before fashion emphasized high heels, fetishists did, and they have consistently advocated heels significantly higher than the fashionable norm. According to shoe historian May Trasko, fetishists have always emphasized 'the extreme and ignored fashion trends.'"[9]

What is interesting about this idea is that there is the constant push and pull between fashion and the fetish. Fashion ignored the corset after the turn of the century, fetishists kept it alive, and we saw the return of the corset in the 1980s. Also, fetishism is pursued by fashion as well. The new trend that is being seen from all of the high-end shoe designers for the summer 2008 season is five- or six-inch heels. Gone are the days where the "everyday" woman wears three- or four-inch heels; it is now trendy to be pushed to a higher heel walking down Fifth Avenue. If the idea that fetishists always push fashion is true, it will be interesting to see what the counter to this would be. Or, more so, if they will be the first to accept this trend.

To turn to psychoanalysis, "Freud thought that the shoe was frequently fetishized because it was the last (acceptable) thing the boy saw when he looked up his mother's skirt before his eyes met the horrifying female genitals."[10] Upon first read, this can evoke laughter, for it is so very Freudian. The phrase "horrifying female genitals" is very psychoanalytic in nature. As is typical of psychoanalysis, there is much fear of the body and fear of the genitals in particular, namely, the vagina and the glaring absence of the penis.

To a certain extent, if one is a follower of psychoanalytic theory, this idea is as good as any other to explain why certain people, namely, certain men, have a shoe fetish. To bring in a variation of this idea, perhaps in a certain era the fact that women's legs were completely covered up except for their feet might evoke the worship of feet and what they lead to, but I do not think that that is an adequate reason these days.

To leave Freud and bring this back to Foucault, we once again can locate this fetish in the realm of power, which seems to be a much more practical place to start. Shoes have the power to add height and stature to the wearer; these are signs of power. Extremely high heels also inhibit the motion of the person wearing them, thus bringing in an element of powerlessness, which could very well be a turn on. Also, shoes have the power to inflict pain, to crush, to dominate another person, the ground, and even the person wearing them. Perhaps these attributes in relation to the sexual act and what turns a person on exist in the very symbolism of the shoe and thus evoke the sexual stimulus without even needing a proper owner.

Corsets alter the body and can permanently change the person who wears them, both momentarily and, in some cases, forever. "The corset, like the shoe, was one of the first items of clothing to be treated as a fetish, and it remains one of the most important fetish fashions. But it is crucial to distinguish between ordinary fashionable corsetry, as practiced by most nineteenth century women, and the very different minority practice of fetishistic tight-lacing."[11] Tight lacing is exactly how it sounds and has always been a controversial practice in regards to the damage it can do to the wearer.

This is not a necessary component of the fetish, although it most definitely is one aspect. Many people enjoy corsets for the lines it creates, the fabrics and materials that it comes in, and for the power dynamic that it brings. "The meaning of the corset is contextual and constructed: 'The dominatrix wears her corset as armor, its extreme and rigid curvature the ultimate sexual taunt at the slave who may look but not touch. . . . The slave on the other hand, is corseted as punishment.'"[12] The use of the corset is varied and can represent multiple things at one time.

In a different vein, some women who have started to wear corsets regularly have trained their bodies to only be comfortable in a corset, and some now say they need it for support. Clearly, this is an extreme representation of the way one can engage in corsetry. It can be as simple as just wearing one out on a Friday night. They have become acceptable again in some realms of fashion, and for certain groups, let's say goths, they are a regular part of the wardrobe.

Many women who are into corsets pride themselves on having collections that they have put a lot of time and effort into building. Some women choose to wear these every day; others just use them for sexual situations. Here would be the dividing line I would assume between the *love* of the fashion and the *fetish* of the fashion. It is interesting to note that in both situations they do have the ability to make the person wearing them feel sexy, something that does not necessarily make one situation equal to the other. One woman I spoke with in the club told me: "The force of the corset crushing my ribs and stealing my breath is enough to get me excited and at times, orgasm. It is the psychological trip, the feeling of a million hands around my chest and the knowledge that I look amazing in it." How can you afford to have such an extensive collection? "You do what you can for the things that are important to you. I don't waste money on cigarettes, I rarely drink, I don't have to buy the latest gadgets, but I do love my corsets. If I couldn't afford it I wouldn't do it. I would have one corset that I used over and over again. Essentially it comes down to just being able to enjoy something. I can enjoy a few more somethings." This woman definitely has a different response to her corsetry than, say, the woman who is wearing it for the season's haute couture look. Overall, fetishes are interesting to observe because they do not always manifest in ways that you expect them to, and they also come to reside inside of oneself in a particular way. Going out to clubs, going to stores to try on different looks, and talking to people in the scene who are avid members of this lifestyle were eye-opening experiences for me.

The way I might enjoy a pair of heels, the corsets that I buy, or the leather that I wear is very different from a person that has a classic fetish for the item. But I think that one of the things that I have been privy to over and over again in the outings of the past three months, both in the BDSM clubs and other places, is that people's sexual appetites and desires range the spectrum. I have met many people that I would say have a fetish but do not fit into the classic idea of what a fetish is. I've come across many couples that have greatly enjoyed each other and the accoutrements that they use. There is a sexuality in their partner as well as what their partners are wearing.

A friend of mine was once told by a guy in the scene that she had the perfect body for S&M. He could see her in a scene already, and keep in mind that she was fully clothed. A large part of this, as with anything, is the imagination that is put into it and what just a thought of something can evoke in a person. There was no physical contact, and the woman was fully clothed in "normal" wear, but the desire was there, and the sensuality was built up in an idea. Fetish, sex, sensuality, and desire are all what you make of it. Is it a horrible thing that the market has entered these realms as well?

I don't think so, as long as people still have imagination. For those who have the capital to advance with the trends and then go crazy in a store, then this extra level of commodification works for them. Some get around it by making their own stuff, as a few of the people that I have met in the past few months have done, and some get around it by using their imaginations. As far as the connection to everyday fashion, the more there is the crossover, then perhaps the more fetishists win. They get to push their desire at all times.

It is not difficult to see why in these cases, a full participation of the ethnographer, through her own body, enhances her understanding of the situation. As Bob Marley shouts in his reggae lyric, *who feels it knows it.* To push the body into participation is beneficial because of the sensorial and bodily knowledge that accompanies unmediated experience; it opens up the possibility of seeing and understanding things in a new light.

In fact, it could be argued that participation is valuable to the researcher not because it allows him or her to gain a better understanding of others' experience but rather because through participation, the ethnographer is often surprised and even destabilized. To some extent, therefore, the value of full participation in this collagist ethnographic research lies in what it does to the mind of the ethnographer rather than how it contributes to his or her understanding of the experience of those he or she works with.

chapter 7
Sadomasochism and Bondage

One afternoon a few years ago, I was leaving Bloomingdale's department store when a tall white man stepped out of a cab holding a whip in one hand and what looked like a rope or chain in the other. Immediately following him from the cab was a Black man wearing ragged cut-off jeans, with a metal collar around his neck attached to the chain. He was barefoot. The white man said something to effect of "hold on, nigger" as the Black man was led through the crowd. The white man was dressed in a plantation-style, antebellum South outfit—white hat, string tie, and white shoes.

I thought, "They are obviously shooting a movie." I, along with many others—crowded together on Lexington Avenue—all expected to hear "lights, camera, action" at any moment. After all, this is New York, where movies are shot all the time. We watched the scene unfold. Surely cameras would reveal themselves momentarily. But no "action" was heard, and this white man and what looked like his slave moved through the throng, heading toward Fifty-Eighth Street. A larger crowd gathered as it became obvious this was not a movie but a real-life "event," as my colleague Robin Wagner-Pacifici would use the term: "Events are central to the ways we experience life, both individually and collectively."[1] The crowd grew nasty, shouting at the white man in the white hat and cursing at the spectacle. The man and the crowd began to be physically pushed and cajoled; eventually, the two of them hailed a cab and departed.

What had I witnessed? Was this a situation where two people had decided to leave a dark S/M dungeon and venture into public to live out an eighteenth-century fantasy? This is New York, and the occasional bubble from the underground does come to the surface every now and then. But is that all it was? I could say this was about race, power, pleasure, and privilege. It could certainly have been a kind of degradation ceremony taking place in the public square. To be honest, I'm not sure what it was all about, but I can say it was seen by a lot of people. Somebody knows what it was about. Others saw it too. Perhaps someone will let me know.

In our modern-day life, there are many ceremonies that help define us and our bodies in the city. We have degradation ceremonies writ large, as millions of our fellow citizens are housed in jails and prisons and asylums in the United States. We have shaming ceremonies, such as the "slut shaming" directed at a woman or a girl on a subway platform, in a bodega, or on a dark corner of a city block. In all of these situations, people suffer a "personal defacement" and "identity stripping." These acts need not be deliberate. They can be the result of mistakes or misjudgments. Nevertheless, they might feel like a form of punishment for those on the receiving end.

Then there are other situations where these same ceremonies are acted out in deliberate scenes, the result of patience, planning, intention, and desire. Those scenes might take place in sexual locations in the city, but of course, they may not. No location better exemplifies the play element in culture than the S/M scene in the city underground, where these personal shaming ceremonies are enacted.

The next set of notes about safe sex come from a different group of professionals. I head off to the Till Eulenspiegel Society, named for Till Eulenspiegel, the peasant hero of the oldest German chapbook in prose. A historical figure of the fourteenth century, Till Eulenspiegel appears in literature as a scapegoat clown and prankster of rustic simplicity whose practical jokes are aimed at craftsmen, innkeepers, nobles, and the clergy. He personifies Low German humor. The anonymous collection of farcical tales in which he figures first appeared about 1840 and was soon translated into High German, Dutch, English, and French.

WILLIAMS FIELD NOTES:
GENE FRANKEL THEATER (1995)

I walked up to the theater and see a few people crowded around outside. I stopped at the front office, paid the entrance fee, noticed some very friendly people, a man and a woman laughing as they read one of the fliers. Everyone looked like any other person I might meet on the street that night: young and old, people in suits, a couple in dinner attire, some in jeans, several in black leather. Most were white, with maybe a handful of Blacks in the crowd. I noticed one Hispanic-looking man, but no Asians. As a reporter/sociologist, there are times when I can openly take notes, though I don't often do that in front of people. Here I notice several people in the room writing or scribbling notes. The three most notable people I saw included a couple handcuffed together, both in black leather, and a white-haired older man with the largest septum ring I have ever seen. I sat next to a man who introduced himself as Dave; he was visiting the theater for the first time and had a lot to say. "In the last couple of years I have learned to approach my sexuality as an open question that I will never be able to answer completely," he tells me. He said he was not from any of the local colleges but opined: "I've been exposed to many things by my own choice and through circumstances beyond my own control. I've explored in my actions, in books, in my dealings with other people. I'm somewhat familiar with S/M, but I was apprehensive about attending this meeting. I know you don't have to go to college to learn everything."

Dave tells me he's from the Midwest and trying to find a place for himself in the big city. He wanted to do some graduate work, if given the opportunity. "I wouldn't mind being an adjunct at the City University Queens campus." This fisting event is the first he has attended. He's hesitant to attend gay events, he says, because they make him nervous, so he decided to try the Eulenspiegel session. "I was afraid that I might be completely unaffected, and at the same time I was afraid that I might be completely repulsed by what I was going to witness. And what might follow could qualify as the strangest experience of my life . . . so far."

He said the man with the septum ring looked like he could be Santa at a mall during Christmas. "I'm counting about one hundred people here, since this is a tiny theater. Every seat seems to be taken, plus people are sitting on the floor and standing against the walls." I never learned if the people sitting on the floor were submissive (slaves), just couldn't find a place to sit, or both. There was one man sitting in lotus position with a rubber mask on; he did not move, just looked straight ahead. "I just kept thinking to myself how awful it would be if I became ill. I never thought of myself as squeamish until the day I watched someone having Norplant [a hormonal implant] put in their arm. I passed out, and I was terrified that could happen again, so I'm gonna prop myself against the wall and brace myself."

CONTACT: JASON, TILL EULENSPIEGEL SOCIETY (1995)

Jason, a twenty-six-year-old white male, sits with his arms folded, speaking with a slight lisp. He is a short man with an impeccable sense of style. He and I discuss the latest fashion; he tells me how excited he is to be part of this. He jokes and says he would be happy to attend all the events listed on the flier outside.

At 7:35 some friends and I entered the anteroom of the small theater in 24 Bond Street. As I learned from a flyer, the Till Eulenspiegel Society defines itself as "a not-for-profit organization which promotes sexual liberation for all adults, but especially for people who enjoy consensual S/M." I think there is more comprehensive information about the TES's creed that can be learned from the flyer. The "Anal & Vaginal Fisting" meeting was one of several events organized by the TES to inform its members about all kinds of S/M practices. The meetings usually consist of a practical demonstration and a group discussion. On Tuesdays and Wednesdays, the TES's meetings are located at 24 Bond Street. Whereas "Tuesday meetings are usually on topics of general interest, Wednesdays are for special interest groups."

Since we were nonmembers, we had to pay $5; members pay $3. After I paid, I picked up two TES flyers and entered the (fifty-meter-by-fifteen-meter) theater. I then sat on one of the red turn-up seats typical of many theaters. As I neither wanted to sit in the center of the upcoming event nor deprive myself of the possibility to leave easily, I chose a seat in the back, on the aisle. Sitting there, I began to observe my surroundings.

The theater was about to get full. People were either sitting on the installed seat rows in the back or on folding chairs, which were placed in front of those. Many of the folding chairs were arranged around an upholstered lying table that had just been set up by Peter and Elena (who were the performers, as it turned out later) in the center of the room. After the lying table had been set up, towels were spread out on it. It was obvious that these were preparations for the practical part of the event.

And therefore so many people, especially the TES members (as it turned out later), were sitting in front of the theater rows to gain a better view. While more and more people were arriving I eyed the theater itself. On the ceiling ventilators were spinning around; neon tubes and spotlights were installed. Beside this, all kinds of cables and pipes were running along the ceiling. The walls of the theater were paneled with big black-and-white paintings. The motifs of these paintings were jesters and fools in various settings.

I don't know if the TES chose this theater specifically, but it actually is a perfect setting for a society that calls itself "Till Eulenspiegel." Till Eulenspiegel is known in Germany for having fooled others all the time in his life. Translated, Eulenspiegel means "owl mirror." Eulenspiegel's specialty was to fool people by showing them their own foolishness. As this is more or less what I know about Till Eulenspiegel, I cannot immediately see the link between him and S/M.

I then drew my attention to the audience of the meeting. No one looked really freaky; most of the people were what one might regard as mainstream. That is, some in the audience were dressed in evening suits and gowns as if they were coming to see a real theatrical performance. Only a few were dressed in black leather, quite contrary to my expectations. Some women were dressed absolutely mainstream, except for a small leather chain at their ankle (by doing that, maybe indicating discreetly their membership in the TES). Most of the audience was dressed casually (with jeans and pullovers) and could not be distinguished from the group I was with. So except for the few who were dressed in leather, this meeting could have been a gathering for a poetry reading.

Another thing that has to be mentioned is the age of the audience. The people were I guess predominantly between thirty-five and fifty. Those who were younger were friends, members, or other curious newcomers. When the event started shortly after eight o'clock, the theater was filled with about eighty to a hundred people. Although many more folding chairs were set up, lots of people had to stand. And many others had to sit behind the lying table, which meant that they also had a bad view.

At ten past eight (I guess) a chairwoman of the TES asked for the audience's attention. Introducing the TES, she mentioned that this society, which is the oldest of its kind, would have its twenty-fifth anniversary soon. After she had received the applause that fact demanded, she introduced the chairman of the spanking group (a well-dressed man in a suit) and other revered members with special positions. Following the announcement of the next event on the eighteenth ("Dominant Woman/Submissive Men—Sensuality and Sex Play in the Dominant/Submissive Relationship"), all TES members were asked to raise their hands, and subsequently two of them were picked out to explain their reason for membership. First a man answered and explained that he appreciates the various benefits he has as a member, which were reduced admission to the meetings, subscription to the quarterly magazine *Prometheus*, and other kinds of discounts. Basically, he mentioned all the benefits listed on the TES flyer I was given.

The second was a woman. She pointed out that even though she already did fisting, there was always some additional information to learn about. And, moreover, she stated that the TES provided its members with information about how to properly engage in S/M mentally as well as physically.

Finally Peter and Elena, the performers of the vaginal fisting, were introduced, with a request for applause. Peter was wearing black leather trousers, a white shirt, and a leather vest. I guess he was in his early fifties. Elena, a fairly corpulent and warm-hearted looking woman, was wearing a colorful dress. With her long dark hair, her double chin, and a smile on her face, she made a sympathetic impression. Then the event started. Elena took off her dress, pulling it away over her head. There she was without underwear, only wearing a "sexy top" and net stockings.

Now one could see the full scale of her body. Her belly was hanging down and looked as if she had some kind of a natural life belt. The girth of her thighs was also quite imposing. Whereas some of my fellow mates seemed to be disgusted by this body, it (quite to the contrary of my own expectation) didn't disgust me. After Elena had undressed herself, she lay down on the lying table, her genitalia facing the audience. At the same time, Peter was addressing some introductory words to the audience. He pointed out that Elena would emit very intensive sounds and that those who felt they were not prepared or couldn't stand such an event should leave now, but not during the performance.

Peter then turned to Elena and connected the leather anklets (or sling at her ankle joint) with the leather bracelets Elena had put on before. Thus Elena was now lying on her back, with bent straddled legs, since her left/right ankle joint was bound together with her left/right wrist. Before starting the actual warming-up phase of the fisting, Peter explained the "ground rules" of fisting. He points out that the use of (latex) gloves is one of the most important things. Even though he and Elena were monogamous (I guess the two were a couple), he always wore plastic gloves simply to prevent any possible germ infection.

And despite the fact one was wearing gloves, hands should always be washed before.

Another reason for wearing gloves was that in such tight and sensitive bodily areas as Elena's vagina, even small hairs could cause abrasion. Moreover, he stated that fingernails should be cut. Though he heard of women who did fisting with long fingernails, he didn't know how this could work. Peter also mentioned the limiting factors of fisting, which were the pelvic bone of the woman as well as the fister's fist size.

As he explicitly pointed out, the relative elasticity of the vagina was not a constraint. Finally Peter indicated how deep his arm would be in Elena and stressed that the thumb had to be encompassed by the fingers, not jut from the fist. After the basics of fisting were reported, the lights went off. Only Elena and Peter remained in the limelight. Peter then said something like "I'll warm her up now," took his S/M latex whip, and began to whip her pierced vagina (which had two rings) as well as the inner sides of her thighs for the next three to five minutes.

He didn't whip too hard, but also not too soft; I guess for Elena it was a kind of pleasant pain. Peter commented while whipping her that she especially loved to be whipped on the insides of her thighs. When Elena seemed to be "preheated," Peter stopped the whipping and put on a yellow latex glove. He then made the glove slippery by putting some lubricant (which special name I have forgotten) on it and entered Elena with one finger. This was still a sort of preparatory phase, that is, widening Elena by entering her step by step first with one, then two, three, and four fingers.

Although the actual fisting hadn't started yet, Elena seemed to be pretty excited already. Her joy was not to be doubted: she was squeaking and moaning with pleasure. Finally Elena seemed wide enough for Peter to enter her with his whole fist. Now the actual fisting began. Peter's fist was moving back and forth, varying in speed as well as in the strength of the strikes. Another fisting technique he applied was turning his wrist back and forth. To the delight of the audience Peter's fisting turned out to be hard work. Working on Elena for about fifteen to twenty minutes was sudorific. Peter had to take a break in order to wipe away the sweat on his forehead, which led to laughter in the audience.

Until that time I had basically focused my attention on Peter, but then I started to concentrate on Elena's reactions. Alternately either smacking sounds caused by the fisting or Elena's groaning and yelling was to be heard. In waves the sounds of pleasure became louder and more passionate, if not to say ecstatic. Elena was beside herself. The closer Elena came to her sexual peak, the louder her whimpering, groaning, and yelling was. And whenever one of her many orgasms arrived, she pushed her abdomen up toward Peter. Another thing I realized was that Elena was clenching her fists during the whole event, which might have been due to her sexual tension.

Another thing that was interesting to observe was the role play between Peter and Elena that went on throughout the whole event. Peter was the master and Elena was the slave. Elena's satisfaction seemed fully dependent on him. Whether Peter really was in control of Elena's pleasure remains speculation, but at least this was the impression fostered by their role play. Here are some examples of their communication. Repeatedly Peter asked Elena something like: "Do you want to come, Elena?" and she would reply, "Yes master, please." Or Peter would say, "Do you like that, Elena?" and she would reply, "I love it." The closer Elena came to her sexual peak, the louder her whimpering, groaning, and yelling was.

At another time he asked Elena: "Do you see what I am doing?" This was a rhetorical question because Elena was lying on her back and of course couldn't see what Peter was doing. Elena said, "No," and Peter replied, for the audience's amusement, "Why not?" At this point, Peter's double role in the whole event became particularly obvious. On the one hand he was interacting with Elena, that is, he was her real sexual satisfier. On the other hand, he was the entertainer and fisting teacher for the audience.

While he was fisting her, he seemed not at all sexually excited. He was applying a technique to Elena with which he instrumentally satisfied her. It of course would have been difficult for him to take the role of the explaining teacher if he had been as involved as Elena was. Elena was in a sexual rage and hardly could have interacted with the audience. So Peter was Elena's sexual partner, but not vice versa. By commenting on his action, he acted as a teacher and dissociated himself from her. (An example for this is Peter's comment: "She is holding back, she is shy today.")

Toward the end, Peter interrupted his fisting for a second, and a woman helped him put another glove on his left hand. Then he turned back to Elena and began to satisfy her vaginally and anally simultaneously (anally with one finger, vaginally again with the fist). Shortly before Elena's big and final orgasm, Peter announced that with it she would push out his fist, and it was so. (Whether Elena really had a big final orgasm and if that one really pushed out the fist is hard to tell, especially as I am no expert on the realness of orgasms.)

At this point I would like to add what happened around Peter and Elena. While they were in action, a photographer (he was fully dressed in leather, so I guess he was doing it in the name of the TES) was taking close-up pictures of the act. Something else that happened was that the audience [members] who were sitting at Elena's head, thus not seeing what was going on, went from time to time to the other end of the lying table to take a closer look.

In the break between the vaginal and anal fisting, I left the event. I had seen a lot, and my head was full of stuff for the field notes. The whole event was, from my point of view, a mixture between a gynecology lecture and an appendectomy in an operating theater. The reason for this impression was the action and comments of Peter. As mentioned before, he didn't seem to be sexually excited: his actions were very instrumental, and so were his comments. Elena was an object upon which he had to do this and that and then one could predict the almost mechanical reaction. On the other hand, it was hard to believe that somebody could really be in such a sexual rage and so carried away as Elena seemingly was.

Her sounds were so extraordinary that I sometimes thought she was delivering a baby. So it was not clear for me if her behavior was real, if she had that many orgasms, as claimed. At least some part of her reactions could have been only an act. But maybe if one identified oneself with Elena and only concentrated on her, then the experience could have been a different one. For me the instrumental work of Peter was the strongest impression and thus dominated my mind.

All in all it was a weird experience, one not easy to fully grasp. Such a mainstream environment, a theater atmosphere, no less with people as if they had gathered for poetry. But then this event, and all of this, appeared very unreal to me, like a strange dream. I neither found it disgusting nor exciting. It simply left a lot of thoughts and questions in my head.

CONTACT: BRIDGETTE, TILL EULENSPIEGEL SOCIETY (1995)

Bridgette is now twenty-eight, married, and living at home for the first time in her life. Her braces over white teeth looked odd combined with the nose piercing in her right nostril. Her first question to me when we met was whether her husband could join her when visiting locations in the city.

The meeting started with a woman announcing upcoming events and explaining the event for this meeting. She then called out and introduced a man she said was Master Peter. He was dressed in leather pants, a leather vest, and a white billowy blouse that had a nineteenth-century style. He placed a collar around his submissive's (slave's) neck and then cuffs on her wrists and ankles. Then she took off her dress and got on a massage table. Master Peter linked the cuffs from her wrists to the ones on her ankles. He also explained why he used the cuffs: usually Helena (the slave) is secured into her sling and cannot move around too much. Besides, she's into bondage. He took out a nylon whip (it's washable), which he also uses on his other ladies, and proceeded to whip her on the inside of her thighs, which were already grayish from repeated whipping in that area and her crotch. Then he put on his latex gloves and placed two of his fingers in her vagina.

During his actions he was sure to tell us exactly what he was doing, how he was doing it, and what it felt like to him. He was rubbing her G-spot and massaged her vagina until three fingers fit comfortably in. He continued and placed his fourth finger in. Helena was not the quiet type and moaned and almost cooed as he continued to work on her vagina and massage her clitoris. Then finally he slid his thumb inside within the grip of his fingers and pushed until his wrist was well inside the mouth of her vagina. He moved his hand in and out, side to side and up and down. At one point she was about to come, and he told her that she could not come until he said so, and he made her hold it; then he counted down from five to one and she came. He exerted complete control over her orgasms, which were so powerful that her sound of delight resounded through the entire theater. He had to brace her body on the table so that she wouldn't convulse off of it.

She came about five or six times. I lost count because I thought I was going to pass out—not so much from the activity as from the heat in the place. There were moments when something would happen and the audience would laugh, including the slave. And everyone clapped when the "show" was over. At one point, Helena raised up her head and stared right into Master Peter's eyes, and I realized that they do share a very definite connection. I think that was about the same time that he also inserted two fingers into her rectum. He never really explained if that was something she liked, if it stimulated her more, or if it was even a regular part of fisting with Helena.

Master Peter said that fisting was the closest you could come to having someone's soul inside of you and that he could feel her heartbeat. He was very gentle with her when it was all over. He allowed her to rest and covered her with a blanket after he uncuffed her. But he still didn't take the collar off. There was a short break following the first fisting, and I took the opportunity to discuss how unbelievable his control over her was. It was so complete.

Then Morgan came out with her red sequined baseball hat and a red dress. She brought out her slave Tangerine, a man with a chain running from the head of his penis to both of his nipples. Occasionally she attaches a leash to this chain when they go out in public. He was wearing a black nylon hood, a G-string, stockings with holes, and spiked high heels. Later we learned that he had earplugs as well. She said it made her hot to make a man into her little girl.

She said they had no real safe word. All he had to say was "no." She caressed him sensually and removed his G-string. She smeared lube all over his anal area and on his penis. She talked about how hot this was for her, and she worked slowly on his anus as Tangerine lay on his back with his legs up. Her entire hand was inside him within a matter of minutes.

She said it felt as though his body was pulling her hand inside. She worked and worked, explaining that she didn't actually make a fist. She explained what she felt and that she didn't pound into him the way that maybe gay men might like. She then explained the way she moved her hand while she was inside of him. Then she removed her hand and turned Tangerine over into a doggy stance: only his elbows were down, as was his head. She proceeded to enter him again.

His moans were quiet, and he never moved. He also never came. Morgan explained that in the six months that they'd been working up to this he's never come during fisting. When she finished her demonstration, she placed a butt plug in his ass and kept it there until the show was over and Tangerine was led away. Then questions were taken. The importance and technique of enemas was discussed. Morgan said that enemas were not necessary for fisting, particularly if you're into scat, but she prefers them. She suggested that people talk to their doctors about how often they can be performed and that when performing them to only use water. Then, some books were suggested, and Master Peter said Helena had one, too.

There were a few things that I had problems with. First, I thought that the rule in S/M play was to use a safe word, yet Morgan and Tangerine had none.

And was it necessary that Tangerine be made up as a woman? Why couldn't he be made a man and still be her slave? Or why did she feel that turning him into her little slut was the ultimate display of her power? Following the event, I discussed the fisting with others, and they all seemed to be saying that the persons involved—the fistees—were made into the receptacles for someone's fist and became nonpersons.

At first I agreed with them, but I no longer do. The first and simplest reason why the fistees seemed to be receptacles was because the emphasis in the demonstration was on the penetration of their bodies with fists. But because we were sitting as far away as possible from the stage and at an angle, the lighting and our situation enhanced the idea of fistee as receptacle. In addition to that, the fistees spoke little or not at all. But does this mean that within their respective relationships Elena and Tangerine are merely receptacles? And if they are, does that mean that they did not allow themselves to become receptacles for the use of their masters? And this is when my questions about S/M come in.

First of all, where does S/M begin? What constitutes S/M play? Is it biting, whipping, burning, controlling, binding? I know it can be all of those things and more, and some people derive a great deal of pleasure from it. The only part that really disturbed me was the dominance and submission part, especially where the roles are fixed. How can a person give themselves so totally to another person, like O in *The Story of O*? Can she really be considered a person, much less a sane and stable person? Her body, her existence, her life belongs to someone else. Is that healthy? Is that part of S/M, and is it a significant part of someone on the fringes?

And is it a way of life, as it is for O, or is it a part of S/M play that switches on and off according to the partners' moods? Because as a woman, I think a woman would find it very easy to find a master willing to dominate her without her having to wear chains around her neck and have orgasms when he tells you to. I understand playing, but making such play a permanent part of our life? You've got to be kidding.

As to whether or not the fisting aroused me, the answer is yes. But I also started to feel as if I shouldn't be watching, that there was something truly bizarre about all of us in the theater staring at such a private act, but at the same time, it was like watching a medical procedure on the Discovery Channel. I think that the fact that these people were real and in front of me and not removed by a camera or the curtain of my imagination as in a book made me at times more uncomfortable than anything else.

CONTACT: JEANA, TILL EULENSPIEGEL SOCIETY (1995)

Jeana, a bubbly personality, turned twenty-three this week and was celebrating her birthday. Her interest is strictly educational: "I want to learn as much as I can about sex because I have been very sex deprived." She smiles a broad smile and hands me notes from the last TES event.

I can honestly say that I have never in my mere, but somewhat eventful, twenty-three years of life seen anything like what I saw that night at the Gene Frankel Theater. I didn't know what to expect from this event, although I will admit that I had been anxiously awaiting its arrival. It was something interesting to have in my appointment book: "No, I can't go to a Student Union meeting on Tuesday, I have a vaginal and anal fist-fucking event to attend. Perhaps Wednesday?" However big a kick I got out of shocking people with using the phrase "fist fucking . . . it's for my research project," I couldn't even begin to imagine what such a thing was or what would actually occur.

The Gene Frankel Theater is located on a somewhat quaint and trendy East Village street linking the shopping areas of Broadway to a section of Bowery that has just recently become gentrified. Several new upscale restaurants have opened along this area filled with large warehouses. Right next door to the small theater is the Elephant & Castle Café, and across the street is a Barnes and Noble. The sign for the theater is wooden and quaint. Flowers and other suburban touches decorate the outside, which make it look like it belongs in Pennsylvania Dutch Country rather than the East Village.

As I approached the theater a young, rather attractive man was walking in front of me. He was wearing black jeans, a faded pinkish T-shirt with a local East Village bar logo, and a leather jacket. Only because I was looking for signs of other guests of tonight's performance did I wonder if he too was going to the theater. Sure enough, he was. Outside there were several other older men and women standing around talking. They looked like everyone else in New York, meaning only that they looked like no one else in the country.

One man, approximately in his forties, was wearing a white pirate shirt, baggy leather pants, leather boots, and a leather vest. He was talking with a woman, also in her forties, who was wearing a simple floral-print dress and thick leather bracelets around her wrists with two steel rings coming out from the center of the leather band. They were talking to a man in his fifties wearing a brown jacket, wide polyester brown tie, and a pink shirt and carrying an old leather briefcase. He had the look of an elementary school principal from New Jersey.

I couldn't help but think that they made for unlikely conversationalists. The man wearing the leather pants with his graying ponytail seemed like someone whom you would see getting off his Harley over on East Third Street outside the Hells Angels space. I thought that the principal man is just the kind of guy they would beat up just for fun over there, back in the days when the Hells Angels were notorious for random acts of aggression. Yet here they were, engrossed in conversation.

As I entered, I could barely make my way through the door. I actually had to show my ID, which was humiliating, but they were gracious enough to make one of their own members in line behind me also show her ID just to make it look like policy. They seemed to get a big kick out it. As you walk in, there's a table to your right, which resembles the table that would be set up at a high school dance. They had a little lock box.

They politely asked me for the $5 that it costs to enter, being sure to point out that if you become a member it's cheaper. I was handed the schedule of upcoming Eulenspiegel events and told about the special offer of *Prometheus* magazine for members. A young man in his thirties wearing a black T-shirt with the sleeves cut off and longish hair asked me if I was here with "the class." I said no. He told me that they often had students come in and observe. "Lots of NYU students were just at an event last week," he told me. He asked me if I went to NYU, and I told him that I went to the City University of New York to do social research. He had always thought they were the same school (a common mistake).

In this front lobby, there are several posters of past performances at the Gene Frankel Theater. Along the wall on your left, there's autographed pictures of past performers. To see many of the stars of yesterday and today in unusual theatrical masks made me wonder if this would be some strange performance art thing. I could imagine bongo drums beating and strange laser lights flashing, while two silhouettes mimed fisting. I never could have imagined what I was about to see.

The atmosphere at the Eulenspiegel Society most closely resembles a Teamsters Union meeting. There was an "MC" of sorts. She was a large white woman with a thick Brooklyn drawl. She demanded that the group be attentive and launched them into a pitch she must have done many times before. "Who's here for the first time tonight? Don't be shy! Raise those hands! Let's give them a round of applause!" I was struck by the number of first-timers there were. I imagined the entire room would whip their heads around to the back five rows (where my friends sat) and exclaim, "FRESH MEAT!" No, we weren't the only ones who had launched themselves into the Eulenspiegel world at such an auspicious event. After a speech about special deals, complete with an introductory offer, the saleswoman sat down, and the show began.

I have never been fist fucked. I'll be quite blunt. I wouldn't necessarily think of it as strange, but it is when you consider that I'm a bisexual who primarily only dates girls. Fist fucking is supposed to be a mainstay of lesbian sex, and I never got the chance to do it. I was excited to learn about it. I could tell my new girlfriend wanted to do something like that, but I had no idea how to go about it. A demo is just what I needed.

Well, a demo is what I got. The first couple, Master Peter and Helena, were quite helpful in teaching the mechanics behind fisting. The master (I refuse to capitalize that) was quite clear in his explanation of what was to be done. He whipped her a few times on the inner thigh, where she had huge bruises that covered most of her rather enormous thigh. They were so broad that it seems that most of the class just thought they were shadows, but I contend they were bruises. He told us that she loves to be whipped right there. He uses a latex whip because it is easy to clean. Who would have known the practical uses of latex? It reminds me of a Tuscadero song called "Latex Dominatrix." The refrain says, "She's a latex dominatrix, / her bras are made by Playtex."

She did seem to like the whipping, but I was a little thrown off. I have such a hard time getting over the fact that (a) she was calling him master and (b) he was whipping her, a woman, another human being, while a packed audience of over one hundred people at least looked on. I know this is supposed to be accepted in the spectrum of PC (politically correct) values, and I'm not the sex police, but I couldn't help feeling my own desire to run down there, tie him up, and whip the shit out of him, while making him scream "master" to me. I'm the ultimate sexist. If a woman is humiliating a male, then that's fine, but if a male is in a position of such visible power over a woman, I want to change that.

This is the problem that I have in general with S&M. It's a game where people get hurt. I have grappled with this for weeks now, trying to get a handle on it. I understand that it's sexy, and I'll admit to enjoy being tied up, but when it's on display for a room full of people, I just wonder what the point is. I have been hearing this ongoing debate about S&M and feminism since the summer, and I'm more confused than ever. I had hoped to work out my own personal shit through writing these notes, but I can't. I'll come back to this issue later.

Tangerine was a male being dominated by a woman, Morgan. Even though I was more comfortable with this setup of woman dominatrix, I still felt so bad for Tangerine. He was wearing fishnet stockings, heels, a purple hood, a leash (which Morgan would attach to him as they walked around). I honestly couldn't even picture Tangerine as human. This seemed to be like an episode of *Deep Space 9*. I felt completely detached and numb. He didn't seem to enjoy it, and the whole thing became so bizarre. The only one who really seemed pleased was Master Pete (from the vaginal fist fucking), Helena (who incidentally came eight times during the fist-fucking demonstration), Morgan (who just seemed to like to humiliate her slave), and the guy taking pictures for *Prometheus* (which, by the way, you can buy for a mere $36.00 for twelve monthly issues delivered in black plastic right to your home). I think that although I won't be going to too many Eulenspiegel events, this is something that I will be writing about for some time.

I wish to reflect on the layering of the previous accounts: beyond the attention to separate details and focalization on different aspects of the evening, the most interesting aspects are the separate observations raised by the informants. I want the reader to reflect on what it means that several individuals experienced and thought such different things while watching the same performance.

The BDSM community possesses elements of a *play community* because it involves intimate contacts and the tendency for these contacts to become permanent, even after play stops. At its core, then, the BDSM community could be said to represent a need to come together as some kind of association of sorts, its members uniting in the idea of sharing something important, of mutually withdrawing from the rest of the world, and in rejecting the usual rules in favor of a more expressive, present-oriented lifestyle. Yet the boundaries of this community are in constant flux: the founding, closing, and reopening of clubs affected by changes in state laws, gentrification and the transformation of neighborhoods, and urban decay and flight are all classic phenomena in New York City and all factors that have shaped the durability of these contacts.

The idea of sex as play is certainly not new. I account for play in a more elaborate way by defining it according to the way the people in these BDSM clubs and sex venues do. Play is when one or more people take on a different identity during a scene, for instance, doctor-patient or supervisor-trainee. I draw from critical work on play from two scholars: Johan Huizinga and Roger Caillois. Huizinga saw play as embodying six characteristics: freedom, stepping out of reality, spatial and temporal boundaries, order, permanency, and secrecy. Caillois both honors and critiques Huizinga in some interesting ways. Specifically, Huizinga's argument that play is "unserious" disturbs Caillois, who sees play as joined with the serious. As a matter of fact, Caillois sees the serious as "indispensable to it."

In what follows, we will see a tension between these "serious" and "unserious" definitions of play, what emerges as a kind of *interplay* of experiencing, understanding, and misunderstanding. The Hellfire Club is the venue explored in the next vignette, which has moved from Manhattan's Meatpacking District to Brooklyn because of gentrification.

CONTACT: VANESSA, HELLFIRE CLUB (1995)

Vanessa, twenty-four, tall, and eager, wears glasses and speaks with a West Indian accent. She was one of two African women in the group who wanted to know about S/M rituals. She said Hellfire was "a refuge for the unsexy" and describes the club this way:

Walking down the stairs and through a doorway into the Hellfire Club makes the place feel secretive and shady. Those two elements heighten the activity Hellfire specializes in: S&M. After you descend into the club, you wander down a long, dimly lit hallway. There's a great swing to the left, which Bonnie [a friend] noted was full of spikes and a gynecologist chair with a light. There also was a bizarre little settee next to it consisting of a chair of sorts, a pair of bright yellow rain boots, an apple on table displaying leather strips, and a hard hat. I felt clueless as to what that was all about and really wanted to see someone use it.

The three main areas of attraction are the crucifix, the whipping post, and the center-stage table. These three places served as nodes, fixing the onlooker's attention on the activity taking place. Along one wall were couches, along another was an elevated dungeon and a table, along another was a table with mirrors behind it. The bar was stationed in the middle and served as a less spectacle-driven node. In the farthest corner from the initial entrance is the doorway leading to private dungeons.

Small rooms for patrons to wander into and do what they like. There also was a room off this entrance that held a Harley Davidson motorcycle as a particularly interesting prop. The lighting was great, sort of dim, but enough colored bulbs to mix in an ambient hue. The couches looked comfy and low to the ground. All the equipment available for the patrons' use looked safe and professional. The whipping post was wrapped in duct tape, and the crucifix had leather bondage gear. The music was quieter than most bars, loud enough so there isn't any dead silence but not so loud you couldn't talk.

After a while it got hot in the room, but I think that was because there were quite a few people there. Since no alcohol is served, nudity is allowed. Lots of people were smoking and drinking Pepsi. Since there was a good amount of floor space, there were a lot of cruising options.

The people in Hellfire were quite a variety: Baby Face, the bartender; John the construction worker from the Bronx; the naked guy talking to Margot who eventually asked to sniff her barstool; the first spanking couple; the man with the T-shirt saying something like "woman masseuse"; Evita with the strap-on big black dick; the exit sign beat-off guy; the fifth-grade teacher whipping the naked guy whipping what looked at first like a little boy but was actually a midget; the great-looking fifty-something couple at the crucifix;

the kneeling guy with Evita; a couple of drag queens; the table full of leather ladies, lots of guys in suits who looked over fifty; some regular Joes; and the coat-check guy. And there was the guy walking around with the butt plug inserted with a bow ribbon hanging low.

Most people just mingled and talked, occasionally going over to one part of the room, wherever the action was, to check it out. I liked the fact that some men started off dressed and eventually ended up walking around naked. I sat next to John (who said he was a construction worker) for at least forty-five minutes while he was beating off, and we had a very cool conversation.

I thought the atmosphere was friendly, and it was pretty communal. Lots of couples but lots of single people also. Most of the people were white, but there was some representation of Black folks. The male-to-female ratio was probably 60/40, and there was a strong representation in the patrons of the over-forty crowd. It was predominantly a heterosexual scene, but there were some lesbian couples.

There were a number of scenes I would like to talk about. Remember when I said the little settee at the beginning of my notes was just a display? Wrong. As I sat at the bar, I noticed John talking to a woman in a black garter belt, high-heel shoes, and bra, very pretty, with handcuffs on one wrist. John took her over to the settee and instructed her to put on the yellow rain boots and coat. He attached the handcuffs, put the apple in her mouth, and bent her over the table. He took the leather straps from the table, asking her which size she wanted, and after selecting the thinnest leather strip he pulled the coat over her head, so you could only see the side of her face with the apple, and began slowly to spank—no, whip—her ass until it was red.

There was no blood, but her ass was very, very red. At first she just grunted but after about ten minutes began to cry out louder and louder, flinching and distorting her ass, and he stopped and rubbed her ass with his hands. She turned to him and said, "Did I say stop?" At that he whipped her more until she said something like "meltdown" or "me down," which I assumed was her codeword to stop. She turned after taking the apple, now bitten, and kissed him passionately for a long time.

The crowd was very excited by this, and hard dicks were everywhere. Women were licking their lips, and I was sweating. I decided to keep my eyes on John the construction worker, as did a few others. Meanwhile, I went over to get a better view of another spanking about to take place. A male top and a female bottom were using the table as a prop for their spanking session. Lots of squealing and shouting of "Daddy!" could be heard. So I wandered over to the bar to get a better view and sat down next to a guy beating off.

I started talking to John again, and he asked me if I was here for a class or something. I don't know why, maybe because I was young or looked out of place. I told him yes but that I had been here before for a Barbara Nitke [a famous photographer] show. He asked me if I liked this kind of stuff, and I said yes. We talked for a while about how comfortable Hellfire was to hang out in. He felt it was more real; there weren't so many games here as in straight bars. He had found Hellfire when he had a blind date and thought it was fantastic that he could beat off and watch all sorts of scenes take place.

He said he was a "rock-hard rod" the entire evening. We also had a conversation about his ex-girlfriend. As a couple they employed less-than-conventional techniques, which included exploration in role playing and multiple-partner sex. It's funny that here I was talking to a construction worker who had a tremendously open mind about the varieties of fucking and getting fucked, who would occasionally add in how bankrupt his coworkers were when it came to sex ("For most of 'em, it's like going from point A to point B. Ha! How boring!"), when the horrors of construction workers' comments are constantly cited as a typical example of sexual harassment. Throughout the conversation he would either beat off or get out his lube tube. He said it was cool that I wasn't grossed out by his solo dick dance. Eventually he wanted me to tell him what I do when I have sex, so I did. He seemed to enjoy it. He also asked me a number of times if I would go in the back with him, but I had to refuse that request. I just didn't feel like anonymous sex that night. John and I actually had a lot in common when it came to what kind of sex we like, and it was cool hanging out with him while he beat off.

Meanwhile, the spanking couple eventually moved to one of the couches, where other men were invited to spank her. After about an hour or so, the woman got a full body massage from the older gentleman wearing the "woman masseuse" shirt. Another good scene was the elegant fiftyish couple at the crucifix. It was refreshing to see a female top with a female bottom. The top had on a fabulous red dress. She looked just like my fifth-grade teacher. The bottom had a leather miniskirt and a leather corset.

A lot of very loving whipping took place, the top very sensitive to the bottom's needs, even stopping and realigning her so as not to damage the bottom's leather. It really seemed like every one wielding a whip had technique. No novices tonight. There was a strategically placed mirror right across from the crucifix near the exit sign. I was sitting on the elevated area near the dungeon and was able to watch the top's back while she whipped. It was an interesting angle from which to watch.

The pauses in the whippings are really important. It gives the bottom a chance for anticipation and the top for control. Unlike John the construction worker and the gorgeous redhead. But I should caution because I think that's what she wanted. He was just accommodating her. Anyway, with this couple the whipping was very rhythmic. A lot of touching going on too. The sensitivity quotient was probably high.

Another scene worth watching was Evita challenging any man to beat the length of her strap-on. This was a variation, with a twist, of the big-dick contest held every Tuesday night at the club. Everyone was gathered around the center spanking table watching the shanks get laid down. A few tried, hoping to win a free night at Hellfire, but Miss Evita defended her title. There was one guy that I was sure could beat her. He had been beating off under the exit sign earlier in the evening and I swear his dick was as big as a small child's arm.

He either wasn't around or just didn't feel like challenging Evita's title. Evita's outfit was outta sight. Leather bikini top with chainmail over it, tight short-shorts, fishnets, boots, and a HUGE strap-on dildo. I believe she was working because a number of times I saw her hanging with some guy, then abruptly turning away, walking to the back dungeons with the guy sort of tagging along. Evita did a lot of cruising and mingling. One guy knelt down and kissed her dildo, which she swung away from him. I was into watching it.

Another whipping was with a male top and female bottom. I didn't watch too much, but the man had a style. Between the whippings he would touch the woman, and eventually he stripped her down to a G-string. They ended their scene with him hugging her, and I thought that was pretty nice. The whole scene was very social. People talking and moving around. There definitely was a place and role for voyeurs. Of course, there were different types of voyeurs. Some were beating off, others just coming closer to get a better look.

My friends thought the most interesting part was the guys in the suits. As one said, "They must have lied to their wives, said they were working late, and

ran over here so they could walk around naked and have people look at them."
He found the whippings and the spankings kind of boring because they were
public acts. Mostly, I found the place really comfortable. I think it was because
people were talking with each other and it was okay to turn someone's advances
down without getting shunned.

Hellfire is a place where public and private become one and the same. Masturbating in public is usually considered a crime, but here there is no fear of
punishment. Being naked in public is usually considered illegal, but here it's
a very natural thing. Sexual touches between partners are displayed out in the
open. Sexual games are the object of many interactions and promoted as the
norm. Spectacle is part and parcel of the evening.

When one watches a whipping, there is the possibility of multiple positions.
Having the whipping post and the crucifix in prominent places in the club,
with mirrors flanking all sides, promoting the expectation that people will
watch and move around for different views, creates an atmosphere where people can watch in multiple ways. You may be going to watch out of curiosity or
out of excitement. One could be watching knowing someone else is watching
you watching. Being in a crowd is social; one is always in relation to the comments and actions of those around you in an intense way. Not only are spectators' positions variable, but what you can choose to watch is pretty wide
open because of the physical setting in which acts take place. Mirrors allow
you all sorts of options. Different angles on the action are available without
people repositioning themselves. A spectator can concentrate on particular
actions or particular contact points between the top and bottom. Watching
just the face of the bottom or, say, just the whip hand of the top will give you
a different scene entirely.

Of course, the dangers of a spectator atmosphere can manifest in a
type of desensitization and overlooking the nuances of what may be going
on. Also, if you get a b-rate act, you have to sit through it. Also, if there
aren't a lot of people there some night, how would it affect the act and its
spectators? Even though the club has a very public feel to the space it creates, it is also quite private. It costs a lot of money to get in if you are a
male, and not all types of sexual acts are allowed. Even though the physical setting allows people to be social, it offers the option of "private" places
to go and hang out. And there is always the option to just hang out by
yourself and beat off.

In what category do the patrons of Hellfire place the club in relation to other activities in their lives? There were a lot of gentlemen over the age of fifty at the club. Do most treat it as a secret? Do most bring people with them? How familiar are the people in Hellfire with one another? What exactly goes on in the back room? What kinds of tricks are turned in Hellfire? What activities are offshoots of the club? Do any of the patrons go to Paddles? What are the differences between places like Hellfire, Paddles, and the Vault? How do the acts feel about the spectators? How do the acts feel during different stages of their act? All in all, going to Hellfire spurs a lot of questions in my mind.

Is there a representation of the fantasy of the dominatrix that is more than an unconscious reaffirmation of the identification of the phallus with sexual agency? I believe that it can be found in the explicit presentation of the production of the fantasy of the dominatrix itself.[2]

At one point, I was sitting next to and underneath a large, sparkling American flag. I find this "decoration" rather amusing. Is this flag on the wall to amuse individuals in this space? What is its meaning, if any? As I examine the red and white glowing stripes and the white stars, I conclude that the owners of this club are making a statement with this flag. Maybe the owners are claiming that S/M is as American, whatever this word means, as the symbol of this flag. When one thinks about America, one may think about baseball, the colors of the flag, and apple pie. According to this American symbol in this environment, maybe one also needs to think about S/M.

Feeling out of place, I decide to walk around and explore this space. Walking around the center bar, I pick up my pace when I feel an older white man reach toward me. Unaware of his intentions, I continue exploring the club. On the far side of the main room, a television screen shows a man spanking a woman. I find this interesting, since it appears that the men in this setting are searching for women to dominate them.

The women who work at Hellfire are extremely professional. They wear black leather outfits with whips hanging from their belts. Initially, I expected these women to embody the role of a dominatrix only while they are beating a man. While watching an act, I overhear a man address a dominatrix. She looks at him and states, "Until you properly address me, I will not talk to you. Now get away from me." This job does not begin or end with the whipping and spanking of men. This is a complicated role that these women act out perfectly.

The woman with the large, strap-on dildo is whipping a middle-aged, white man. While many spectators crowd around, the man stands at a large, chair-like structure with his legs spread and his back to the woman and a mirrored wall. The man is completely naked except for the white, cotton briefs around his ankles. While she whips this man, one can see that she knows exactly what she is doing. The loud, sharp sounds of the whip hitting the man's back inspires a young, white man to converse with me.

While holding his pants and his belt, this man appears anxious, and it seems that he is next in line to take the older man's place. He says, "That sounds like it hurts." I shake my head and say, "No, I don't think so." I can tell by the look on his face that he is surprised by my response. After a few moments pass, I inform him that I am only joking and that, in fact, it does sound painful. At this point, I am still fixated on this woman whipping the man in front of the mirrors. She pours hot wax from a candle onto his back and shoulders. By the expressions on his face, one can see that this man is in pain.

Are these also expressions of pleasure? Can one differentiate between expressions of pain and pleasure in an S/M club? The dominatrix whips his penis with quick, light strokes. I notice that his penis remains limp. Does this indicate that he is not aroused by this situation? As I watch this display, a naked, hairy man rubs against my back twice. As he rubs against me, he gently touches my shoulder and makes it look as though he is merely walking by. He may need to get through the crowd of people, but I know that he may also have an agenda. At this point, a man who approached me earlier in the night asks if I speak Hebrew or Arabic. I tell him that I do not and quickly walk away. He approaches me and asks me to shake his hand. I say "no" and walk away.

I leave this area of the club to witness the "big-dick contest." The contest is extremely playful and amusing. The woman announcing the event tries everything to get the men involved, but only a few enter the contest. It is interesting that the men in Hellfire are shy about entering this competition even though these men are either naked or have their pants undone with penis in hand. Why do these men put their penises back into their pants as soon as a contest is announced? The fact that the yardstick in this contest is a large dildo may have something to do with this sudden change in behavior. Do these men think that once the contest is over the audience will not judge their penis size? I find it difficult to define the atmosphere this evening. It is definitely sexual, but I do not feel that it is either homosexual or heterosexual. This is interesting, since I do not see any overt manifestation of homosexuality while in this space. The atmosphere is sexual given the open expressions of sexuality evident in every corner and space of this room. The blatant openness of this setting may account for my inability to define this sexual atmosphere.

The actors in this setting are predominately white males and females. For the majority of my visit, one of the few African American men in this club sits near the hot-wax room jerking off. Why are the actors in this environment predominately white? How does this connect, if at all, to the ways that S/M desire is manufactured? The individuals in the three S/M locations I visited are markedly similar. This may speak to the ways in which this form of desire is manufactured.

Before leaving this scene, I notice a feeling of desperation in the air. The night is wearing thin, and numerous men search the rooms for some action. Over the course of ten minutes, three different men motion for me to lean down and talk to them as they remain seated. One man asks if he could grab my butt, and another man inquires if I am "into domination." With every motion and inquiry, I feel a power struggle taking place on this stage.

This is a result of the persistence and manipulation evident in these actions and my attempts at avoidance. The feeling of struggle may also be the result of the power differentials playing out in the different areas of this club.

These notes help us understand how the "fantasy bank" concept might be applied to some but certainly not all members of the scene, because many are getting their "kicks," or sexual gratification, immediately. But people use experiences of others to enhance their own sex lives by "banking" those experiences through smell, touch, or keepsakes, for later recall. This helps them keep sexual experiences close at hand by remembering sexual actions and behavior and to exploit from memory and aides-memoire.

Our next body of field notes comes from Club Edelweiss and Paddles in Times Square. We begin with the notes recorded at Paddles, a twenty-year-old S/M club in Manhattan where blood is drawn by caning.

CONTACT: BEBE, CUTTING AND PIERCING WORKSHOP, PADDLES (2003)

Bebe, twenty-something, has a series of fascinating tattoos, most of which are hidden, except one on her left cheek. She is a serious-looking woman but has a quick smile and a mysterious gaze that at first is hard to read, but once in conversation she is affable and engaging. Her humorous personality soon becomes infectious.

I felt queasy and faint, closing my eyes to avoid reading any more of the handout that rested in my lap, covered with words describing skin layers, needle varieties, and the health hazards of cutting. What if I had just fainted right here? Maybe choosing the cutting and piercing workshop was the wrong choice for someone as queasy about blood as I am. I always had this problem while watching any sort of bleeding or needle poking; even the description or reading about it was enough to make me feel faint.

I could practically make myself faint on demand by thinking such thoughts. But I knew it would pass, and it did. The workshop was a regular Friday evening meeting for the group DomSubFriends, which meets here for a variety of panel topics appealing to the S&M scene in New York City, including taking care of one's body as a social activity. Now that other dungeons in the city have been closed, Paddles is the last remaining club/dungeon for folks to practice their whipping, restraining, and caning skills. There are rumors that Hellfire will reemerge downtown in a new location in two months and that even the apparently notoriously seedy Vault may reopen. So it was perfectly natural for this organization to hold its weekly meetings at such a location.

A nondescript door descends into the basement where the club is located off Twenty-Sixth Street. Immediately upon entry I was glancing around at the older white men, who returned my curious gaze. But suddenly a friend (I call him Victor) grabs my attention and leads me to a seat as if this was a Broadway performance and I had an upscale ticket. He came back to me and introduced himself. He was the founder of the DomSubFriends group and provided background information and asked how I had come to be here. He led me straight to a row of chairs near the front, in a wing slightly hidden next to the stage. Once seated, after taking the handout and signing the e-mail list, I glanced around the room.

The attendees did not surprise me: middle-aged white folks, mostly "straight" looking, a few wearing leather. A woman in a leather dress showing off her enormous cleavage, a gay man in a leather vest, and a transvestite made up the more "dressed up" or "eccentric" portion of the crowd. There was one middle-aged black woman seated in front of me, and, later on, two black men arrived. That was the entire racial diversity of the club. Gender was divided fairly evenly, filling the three sections of seats in the club.

When the doors officially opened at 10 p.m., the chairs would be moved to the side, and the space would open for play. Once this transition happened, however, the gender diversity would sharply decline and become predominantly male, even with the biased door cover: men $30 and women $5.

A professional dominatrix and nurse gave the presentation about piercing, cutting, and needle S&M play. The distributed handout covered the more intricate details of skin layers, injury risks, lists of places to buy or dispose of used needles, and an anatomy chart with directions on where not to cut the body. The lecture turned into more of a nursing seminar as the presenter covered anatomy details in a lengthy manner; the content contrasted with the surrounding black walls, black lights, photographs of naked women, and bondage gear scattered about. On the mini-stage were two rods with handcuffs hanging from them; in the corner was a rack on which someone could be strapped down and whipped.

Eventually a volunteer was called on stage, and the needle play was demonstrated. The volunteer took off her shirt and bra, showing off her more recent scarification acquisitions before getting started. The presenter began weaving needles in two rows down the volunteer's back, five in each row, barely tucked through the skin. Once the needles were inserted, she laced a ribbon through them, constructing a corset of sorts. The entire time she continued giving sanitation tips, and the audience members asked the volunteer about her feelings.

The volunteer described how the experience of having needles inserted in her skin provided an endorphin rush that she said "was better than any drugs she could buy on the street." It was thrill, excitement, a rush that she said made her feel high as a kite. I found that fascinating: a divergent perspective on needles, piercing, and cutting, something actually sought out instead of merely tolerated.

I had a vague connection to piercing and cutting concepts through my own immersion into tattooing and knew this would be a point of relation with the crowd, yet our demarcating lines varied tremendously. I didn't mind getting tattooed but sat through it more for the end product, although I did actually enjoy the experience. But the thought of piercing with a needle going all the way through made me feel faint. It was not something that I would seek out but merely tolerate for the prize of a certain hoop through a body part. But the volunteer was expressing that it wasn't the end product of piercing or permanent needle marks but the temporal experience and endorphin rush that was desired.

Once the workshop was completed, the club was officially open. Victor then proceeded to give me the tour. He introduced me to most of the people in the club, maybe twenty people. It was like being at a wedding or some tightly knit inner circle into which I was being recruited.

I was thankful for the warm reception and was immediately put at ease. During the tour, Victor told me about the S&M scene in NYC (the closing of Hellfire pushed its crowd here), the history of Paddles (in business for twenty years), and the events that take place here and with the DomSubFriends group (lectures, private parties). Off the main room in which the lecture was given, now cleared of chairs, there was also a bar that sold soda called the "whips and licks bar," with a few booths and barstools, mostly unoccupied. Maybe twelve people remained in the club.

Off toward the entrance of the bar was another room with different nooks and crannies, each of which had some instrument of torture or restraint. The black walls sported hoops to which someone could be tied, a rope net, a restraining chair, bed, wrist restraints hanging from a wall, and so on. People sat around indifferently, talking about their whips as easily as they talked about the recent warm weather and the ensuing thaw.

Victor, the gracious host, passed me on to other people, and I soon became partnered up with Michael for the evening. He and I talked about the S&M scene in an interview-type conversation. He was quiet and reserved, which matched the mood I was in, although I felt quite content and comfortable. I was one of the younger people in the room and one of few women. I wore a short-sleeve shirt so as to show off my tattoos, which I figured would be an appropriate conversation-starter in this particular context.

It worked perfectly. Victor was once a professor at a university in Europe; Michael had a PhD and was a computer analyst. We talked about work life as easily as we switched to sexual fantasy conversations. They were eager to talk about the community and about media misperceptions.

Victor argued that the S&M community didn't have "losers." Instead, it consisted of professionals, because one has to have some sort of social status in order to question normative sexual behaviors and fantasies. The people I talked to tried to tease out what my draw and particular fetishes were, and I awkwardly attempted to sort through possible fantasies that were S&M oriented. I was a novice and delighted in that position, because soon enough I would be immersed into the scene in a more knowing way.

I was open for exploration and unbiased judgment. I was a switch, not a top or a bottom. I could as easily be whipped as tie someone up. My particular role and interest would find me through experience. It was odd to be talking with strangers about sexual fantasies, what in S&M turned me on, and how I wanted to play. This was a conversation I barely had with lovers.

I also enjoyed the nonalcoholic environment. I was accustomed to hiding my insecurities behind a veil of liquor, a trait from which I was slowly trying to be liberated. Therefore my delicate sobriety wasn't shattered on this night. Michael is into rope restraint. He described in detail the ways that patterns could be made with the rope: restrictions with loose ropes easily removed, tension points of the design, that the action would be of short duration.

The sound of rhythmic spanking emerged from the other room and drew our attention from the conversation and the looped bondage/fetish movies playing on the two monitors in the bar area. We both grabbed our jackets and made our way into the next room, finding a seat on the bench from which we could observe both spanking scenes.

A shirtless man stood against the wall as a large white woman pounded on his back with something resembling a rubber mallet. Two other women sat at a nearby table, drinking soda and watching that scene. To our right a man was bent over a woman's lap; his bare ass was being spanked monotonously. Men sat against the wall in shadows, perhaps watching another scene just out of my view around the corner.

Everyone remembered my name, but I remembered very few, only the ones that were significant to this visit and the one I found attractive, a reminder of an ex-lover. Most of the people were middle-aged men, maybe two or three women. But now more men were milling around, old white men, a frat-boy type, a Black guy, a good-looking young couple, the volunteer for the needle work. Michael led me to a back room with more elaborate setups, a whipping post, two bondage chairs, a bondage bed, and the topper, an ornate rotating board on which people could be strapped to and rotated upside down.

Michael was politely asking if I would like to hop on, and I was certainly interested in getting tied into each and every one of the pieces, but since no one had really been playing at that point, I declined. He began asking if I'd like to be tied up, but there was no rope in the joint, and that was his shtick. I said I'd be willing but that we should perhaps keep something for the next time as well.

Later on in the evening, the best scene was performed by "the ballerina," as Victor called her. A crowd had gathered around a woman in a schoolgirl uniform (the fetish of the owner that would get the ladies in for free). She was amazing with the whip, swinging it around with such speed that it whispered through the air before it smacked its object, the white ass of a man facing the wall, wearing nothing but his black socks. He remained mute as his ass was performatively slapped by the woman.

Victor, Michael, and their posse were getting ready to leave, and I felt that I should also, although I could have stayed and watched the scenes for hours. Victor pointed to the restraints on the stage and said, "Now soon I want to see you up there, then I'll say 'there she goes.'" I replied with affirmative enthusiasm, "I would love to." As I left, my new acquaintances invited me back for more, exchanged e-mail addresses, and bid me a good evening. While this act of drawing blood is done in the spirit of play, it is serious because the act can raise rather troubling consequences. As W. I. Thomas noted: "if the situation is real it is real in its consequences."

Bebe continues her account after visiting another venue.

As I walked into the lobby of the TES building, there was no one behind the desk, and I walked swiftly into the basement where the meeting for the youth (under thirty-five) group was having their monthly meeting. Tonight's feature: knife play with Andreas. I found a seat in the back row and noted that, indeed, this group was younger than last week's meeting, more attractive and familiar with one another. The audience soon filed into the six rows of metallic chairs. The facilitator—Tower, as he introduced himself—listed off several upcoming events of future meetings and the TES festival in mid-May: a weekend of workshops, vendors, twenty-four-hour access to Paddles, and private parties.

Then Andreas introduced himself and his knives. Andreas is a white man, 240 pounds (as it came up), maybe five foot ten, with short brown hair. He was into erotic knife play and studying Philippine martial arts. On the table next to him was an array of many knives, ranging from small brass-knuckle thrust knives to swords and bone-chilling curved daggers. He talked about safety issues around knife play, how to run a knife along someone's body and not accidentally slice them, the difference between a thrusting and a slashing knife, and how knife play is all about building up fear instead of pain. Then his girlfriend Elizabeth arrived and quickly changed in the back room— emerging in black lace panties and a black sleeveless shirt.

The couple was very loving and sweet to each other, calling each other "honey" and "sweetie." He used her body as an example of the ways that a blade could run across skin, the reaction it provoked (she was squirmy and squealy), and how to switch the knife over to the dull side when it was out of the submissive's sight. He cut her shirt off with a curved knife, while holding her close. After each demonstration with the vast array of knives, he would give her a kiss on the forehead or a hug.

Andreas's discussion was short and sweet. There was a brief Q&A about safety, mostly, or questions about more basic S&M issues such as building trust or "after-care with the submissive."

During the break, I took off. After the break would be a more informal "circle," where people can discuss either related workshop issues or other general S&M themes. I regretted taking off, knowing that the more informal sessions are most likely where the more intimate and interesting information is disclosed, besides offering a more intimate introduction to the audience members.

chapter 8
Orgies and Swinger Events

The orgiast is not in search of a powerfully unique self; rather the orgiast seeks to belong to a unique class of persons whose collective ecstasy is greater than the happiness of any individual or of an entire society.

—Karl Toepfer, *Theater, Aristocracy, Pornocracy: The Orgy Calculus*

From these contradictory practices, at once debasing yet stimulating, even pleasurable, we might begin to see the activities in the Soft City as urban ceremonials. These urban ceremonials are ostensibly spaces where a partitioning takes place, a passage of transformation or absorption; they are windows into an altogether different world that encompasses the city, saturates it, but never quite punctures its surface. Van Gennep provides the frame for this abstract leap when he states:

I have tried to assemble here all the ceremonial patterns which accompany a passage from one situation to another or from one cosmic or social world to another. Because of the importance of these transitions, I think it legitimate to single out rites of passage as a special category, which under further analysis may be subdivided into rites of separation, transition rites, and rites of incorporation. These three subcategories are not developed to the same extent by all peoples or in every ceremonial pattern. Rites of separation are prominent in funeral ceremonies, rites of incorporation at marriages. Transition rites may play an important part, for instance, in pregnancy, betrothal, and initiation; or they may be reduced to a minimum in adoption, in the delivery of a second child, in remarriage, or in the passage from the second to the third age group.[1]

The question is, then: What interpretation can we give to, or what significance do we see in, these rites today? What symbols can we witness in these spaces, these acts that accurately or adequately represent our postmodern lives? Public sex acts, sex club rituals . . . these rites of passage are breaking, challenging, and bearing witness to public behaviors where the body is clearly a site of struggle, where significance and meaning become contested. Yet as we have seen in the accounts so far, these rites remain experiential, never quite condensing into the knowledge that would yield power. In the Soft City, when does experience become understanding?

This chapter will discuss how these rites of passage—of separation, transition, and incorporation—apply to many of the individuals we have encountered thus far: the club goers, peep-show enthusiasts, S/M players, all strangers in the night, be they engaging in orgiastic performances or just people hanging out with other people. There is a kind of marriage in the Soft City between these separate spaces— the sex clubs, the fetish party, the S/M event, the burlesque show—in the sense that people are coming together to bond for a night with strangers, to engage in fun, frivolity, sex, and other types of adventures. It is marriage on the fly, Las Vegas style, caught-in-the-act, spur-of-the-moment-type of betrothal. What people desire is not just sexual pleasure but to become involved in collective expression.

WILLIAMS FIELD NOTES: THE VAULT, GREENWICH VILLAGE (1998)

It was the middle of the semester, a few hours after class ended, when I attended the Vault. To my surprise, I see a former escort/model whose wedding I attended and who met her husband in my "Sex and the City" class; she is strapped to a Berkeley bench being hot waxed and whipped. Her husband is considered a master in the S/M scene, but I was unaware she was a player, too. The candle had only a slight odor, as if I had anosmia. But the other aromas— sweat, leather, the funk of perfumes, colognes—overwhelmed me.

People were now gathered around the bench; one tall, stiletto-stacked woman with a black leather outfit and a whip in her back pocket stood watching, while on both sides of her, men on their knees looked up at her like puppy dogs waiting for scraps, not saying a word, just hoping to be recognized via a beating.

A few slow grunts could be heard, and they got louder. The groans became more insistent—a crescendo, a patterned whisper, a cacophony, a sing-song—as the whip replaced the hot wax and the crowd got bigger and bigger; it was as if the odors got louder as the crowd swelled.

Gloria, the former escort/model, was reaching orgasm, and the circle jerkers, men from New Jersey and local areas who stand around masturbating, stood back from the crowd now—so that no ejaculate would hit anyone. Nobody I could see "shot a load," but there was a general release in the room: a big sigh went out as Gloria got off the bench after being wiped of wax, hugged by her husband, and applauded by the crowd. The room smelled only slightly musty now, though several jerkers were still holding their erect dicks along the edge of the room, and two stood erect near the bar as women sat down for nonalcoholic drinks.

I waited to see if Gloria would come over after the session. She didn't, so I went to the back to see what was happening there. As I went near the back, I saw a jail cell. Inside the cell was a white male standing with his dick out and a woman on the other side stroking him. She pulled on his dick; he looked pleased, but she stopped as soon as she started, and he got erect, then waited till he begged her to start again. She did.

At that moment I saw two apprentices who looked at me, smiled, and nodded, but they didn't come over to say anything. This was typical behavior, though I was accustomed to the anonymity factor: most people didn't want to acknowledge being on the scene in too public a way. I don't know why exactly, something to do with shame on the one hand, and just being cool, on the other. International flaneurs, I might add, were more open to these sexual explorations than Americans, but there was not a lot of talk in class about how to interact in these venues. Just act "normally," one German student said to me.

I'm not sure what it meant to "act normal" to them. As I recall, many students would acknowledge me by just smiling, but some students, when we saw each other, would readily greet me and say hello, even chat. I noticed that it depended on the venue. In topless bars, for example, we would often talk more openly, but as the venues got more raunchy or sexual, we would not say much to each other; this was the case here, near the jail cell.

The woman was now sucking the guy's dick through the bars. A crowd gathered. I say "crowd" because there were often gatherings of ten or more, clusters of men and women surrounding a particular scene. Yet it is interesting how this crowd would migrate: depending on what was going on, a crowd would develop based on the action nearest to them, and as one scene reached climax, another scene would develop, gain the attention of the particular crowd, and so on.

I rarely saw any of the men ejaculate, though many could be seen holding their dicks and stroking them long enough to have come. Perhaps they had already come, or maybe they suffered from priapism. I don't know, but I do know the crowd at the jail cell was intense, as the man was clearly on the verge of coming. The girl on her knees anticipated his climax and was working feverishly to make him come, and he did. This was a first for me. I waited to see how this act would be cleaned up.

The ejaculate shot partly onto her shoulder and the rest onto the bars and the floor. The guy, a smallish man in his thirties, sat down in the cage. Someone handed him a paper towel. I was waiting to hear a person in charge emerge to say he couldn't do what he did, but nobody came around, and the crowd slowly dispersed. As I walked back over to my spot at the bar, I saw Gloria with her husband talking to the woman who I thought was the manager (she was the one who had reduced my students' admission fee).

What could be more public than a public orgy? Though I had never gone to one, I had heard stories from people who attend these events. I began to think of reasons why people would go there. What comes to mind mostly is to engage and be with others, to share with others, including to "school or teach" others in the rules of the game, perhaps even to instruct newcomers. People often may want to meet new people and share the meaning of their world with others, whether they are friends and fellow players or strangers.

What people want is not just sexual pleasure but to become involved in collective expression, or in the "action." Van Gennep would argue that this rite is one of aggregation: to find this rite, to engage in this rite, is to find action, to move on to the public arena, onto the stage, to not only become part of the scene but to *be* the scene. What this suggests is that this "action-seeking behavior" is pleasurable because being present where others are engaged in intense action is stimulating to all concerned. We can see this aggregation in the gathering of a crowd, but I am attempting to capture something broader than that: aggregation seems ever-present, a potential that only has to be initiated by someone to become realized. It would seem that, on the surface, any group of individuals has this potential to aggregate. Yet we know that this potential is not always realized.

CONTACT: LOIS, A TOUCH OF CLASS (2006)

Lois is a tiny, talkative young woman. Even wearing high heels, she looks barely five feet tall. She prefers to be called "Lo," the shortened version of her name, and is quick to wink and smile when something pleases her. She writes in her notes:

We walked to the front of the room and saw the group of four young Latinos who had been dancing it up earlier in the night. They were paired in distinct heterosexual couples with a few feet between each set of them. The woman in the brightly colored mini-dress had it hiked over her hips, and her boyfriend was fucking her from behind with his pants around his ankles. He held both her hips with his hands and methodically pumped away behind her. I was impressed most by how their heights matched so well that they could align themselves to have sex in that position. Next to them, in the darkest corner, were their two friends. I couldn't see how they were doing it, but I could hear the movement of two bodies together, with the faint rhythm of skin slapping together and small squishing noises from the meeting of wet places. I slowly traveled back to the far end of the center bench, looking at the sex all around us, and stepping carefully through the bodies seeking space for their pleasures.

When we reached the end of the sex island, we established a place for ourselves to stand and have a look around. We had our backs to the staircase and watched as the two couples in front of us had sex. Both women were lying back on the bench with their legs spread wide and the heels of their matching red, spiked shoes bobbing in the air over their men's shoulders. Both men had only the fronts of their pants pulled down to engage in intercourse, and the one nearest me was so close I could have reached out and put my hand on his arm. Instead I ran over in my mind the unusual, repetitive urge I had to touch one of the women's high-heeled shoes.

This night I was flooded with absurd images of what would be inappropriate in this space. The room was strangely silent for how much activity took place inside its walls. I wondered if people would stop what they were doing if my man and I had any of our conversations above the hushed whispers we used to talk back and forth.

Would we be asked to leave? If I laughed out loud just once, for all the times, for different reasons, that I stopped myself from doing so. Would I get scolding stares fired at me and be approached by one of the monitors? I noticed again what seemed to be the total absence of any detectable climax from the guests who so eagerly engaged in this public sex. Anything white or light glowed with a greenish-yellow tinge, and I kept searching for a visible sign of ejaculation.

The audible hints that some women gave seemed to fit a cycle of waves of sexual excitement that escalated and ebbed but never peaked. I questioned whether my images of female orgasm had been too deluded by popularized, exaggerated versions of women screaming in ecstasy and dramatically performing the sometimes-elusive female orgasm. It's quite possible these women were having quiet, relaxed orgasms or that the men were having orgasms but not experiencing ejaculation.

I had touched several benches when my man and I would walk past a vacant spot. They always felt dry. I was also surprised by the absence of sex odors. There were at least forty people engaged in some kind of sexual activity when the fourth floor was full, yet I did not detect any of the pungent aromas of female or male genitals, which continued to surprise me as I watched many variations of foreplay, oral, and penetrative sex. There was something strangely sterile about the whole floor that seemed almost in opposition to its dedicated use.

Why do people hide when engaging in public sex? In large part, this narrative is about public, not private, sex, though as Lo's notes suggest, people want to be private in public. It is this sense of quiet that suggests privacy despite the "public" nature of the goings on. The sociologist Georg Simmel argued that the fascination with secrecy is because it "seduces by the tension between the necessity to conceal the stigma and the desire to confess it."[2] I could interpret his meaning several ways; for one, secrecy is an individual phenomenon, and the sharing of a secret makes interaction between the sharers (keepers of the secret) the most important facet of their lives. He also suggests that secrecy is seen as a feared stigma, one that fosters a clear-cut identity as well as a close-knit community. This secrecy fosters a sense of an elite, chosen people, granting them a status that Simmel described as the "aristocratizing principle." By this he argues: "The stigmatization of the surrounding, hostile society is used in a kind of martyrdom of the elect, breeding a heightened sense of both superiority and unjust persecution. There is a high degree of association with other members. A related effect of aristocratizing is equality among members."[3]

And though the orgy is a "secret" event, it is never a strong assertion of any notion of "privacy." "The orgy scene may be defined as the presentation of a *collective* act focusing on excess—be it of sex, of food, or of language—and on confusion: mingling of bodies, hybrid foods (such as fish and fowl), blurring of the line between natural and artificial decor. At one and the same time, orgy connotes the hybrid, repetition, and equivalence, and constitutes a scene."[4]

CONTACT: MISSY, OLANA'S HOUSE (2005)

Missy has a strong, husky voice that reaches out and grabs you as she speaks. I sit at my desk. We are talking about another sex scene, and Missy is being "debriefed," as it were. She reads part of her notes and stops to talk about the scene intermittently. She tells me tonight is one of her partner's sex events, or "sensual soirees," at Olana's House. The owner likes to create safe environments, regulate sensual freedom. Power games take place, but without pain. S/M sex games are more tease then real at her parties. Olana is more interested in a creative process of establishing community, safe playgrounds where fashion, arts, and imagination intertwine with sexual desire—a type of interactive play where patrons are required to contribute to the atmosphere, not simply consume.

The owner's brother was in charge of certain tasks tonight—specifically, making sure the expensive furniture, silk rugs, pricey paintings, and imported Indian artwork were not harmed. He was also told to avoid having too many people in the whirlpool at the same time. When we speak of rules and regulations in such settings, no one has more rules and regulations than Olana. The scene Missy describes is a swinging party at Olana's House, whose strict etiquette, specific themes, and rules of order make it difficult for invitees to keep up. Missy, as events partner, has intimate knowledge of these procedures, all of which require each couple to bring a piece of art. There is no specific definition about what the term "art" should entail, but if nothing is brought, there are consequences. I knew people who attended another of Olana's parties, one in which the upper floors were "foreplay bar areas," with downstairs for full nudity. Clothes were optional in the upstairs bar area, but if one wanted to participate in the activities downstairs, you had to take off your clothes, down to your underwear, and then enter. I elected to remain upstairs.

8.1 Night at the Pyramid, 101 Avenue A, East Village, mid-1990s.

The guard showed arrivals lockers where clothes could be kept. I asked where Missy was and was told she was seated in the coat-check area in charge of making sure patrons have the artwork they were supposed to bring and to remind people to remove their shoes. Thick silk carpets cover the entire lower level of the spa, and all clients received paper slippers before they hit the stairs.

Missy's notes and running commentary describe in greater detail the rules of engagement:

It is the Eat In theme—Paris, masks + artwork a must. It can be anything from cheap depictions of Paris to collage, self-inspirations, photographs, you know, anything artsy. Whoever doesn't bring an artwork is punished—stripped down to their underwear immediately after their arrival. Oh, forget about spanking. They love spanking; nobody would even bother bringing an artwork at all. But taking their clothes off as soon as they arrive—that's something nobody likes to do.

Do you know out of thirty couples, only one didn't bring an artwork, and that one couple had to take off their clothes as soon as they walked in the door? I didn't expect such resistance to it. Both of them tried to soften the dominating Olana with different excuses: they were late, the commute was too long, they didn't have time, blah, blah, blah. Olana just stood there, half-naked, with her arms on her hips, in a position of power, and wasn't hearing it; it reminded me of a school teacher trying to reestablish order in the class when children wouldn't stop talking. The couple had to take off their clothes, and I could tell they were very uncomfortable. Olana was waiting to make sure it was done thoroughly. "All down till your undies. You too!" she was saying to the woman, who had asked if she could at least keep the sweater.

People attending her sex parties never read all the instructions, because if they did, when they get to the scene they wouldn't be so resistant. For example, one part of the instructions says every one should take off their shoes. No exceptions. Well, I didn't realize the extent of the importance of taking off shoes until that night; it's because of the expensive rugs.

The majority of women refuse to take off their stilettos; the small coat-check area is already overcrowded with couples and noisy with complaints. There are at least two women at the time that stubbornly refuse to go down-stairs without their powerful sex symbols, "high-heeled shoes." I was convinced that every woman would be relieved to walk without pain on soft silk, but I was wrong. This created a different kind of "social trouble" brewing that night. Not just the carnivalesque variety such as drunken behavior, solicitation, cruising.

One woman, Natasha, a known dominatrix, said she would never take her shoes off because her boots are part of her main costume for the night! She arrived with a thirtyish man who avoided eye contact, constantly looking downcast and, in addition, was not properly attired for the event. "I am not taking the shoes off!" Natasha yelled. She was wearing a red corset tightened so hard to make her waist look so tiny. I wondered how she got the air to yell at me. She was very aggressive. I assumed she took some drugs but couldn't figure out which; it was certainly nothing calming. My gaze was aimed at her dominatrix boots, black and shiny, high platforms that reached high to the black lace up to the playful finish on her corset. The heel was at least fourteen inches. She spread her legs, standing now in a dominating position, trying to get "yes you can" out of me.

A new couple was there: a man looking exactly like Sylvester Stallone, his facial expression was the face of Rocky. His wife was a brunette with gentle facial features, a perfect opposite of his face. The man wore a tailcoat, and his shirt was too tight. The woman was relieved to get rid of her shoes, but her husband was not so happy. I turned around and just snipped at Natasha to take off her boots or to leave. I guess she didn't expect that, and she quietly took them off, left them in the middle of the room, and barefoot with her nose up, like a queen, went downstairs, her partner for the night following her silently.

I went to the lower level, where the living room, considered the central space, was located; there, two divans filled with bodies moved rhythmically. I tried to count them. I could see ten bodies intertwined like snakes, but there were more bodies in the middle; I could not count them all. I see more hands, then asses, touching, teasing, moving from body to body. It was already after two in the morning. The party was in full swing. I missed the foreplay. Sometimes there is no foreplay, and people just jump right into it. I often saw people chatting, with drinks, all dressed up one minute, then but a few minutes later already naked and having sex.

I stayed in a central room to see how this ball would unravel and when. I hoped that nobody would ask for their bag or a coat, but all the patrons were too busy for that. There are five smaller rooms where sensual massage therapists were working on couples or single people. One therapist was teaching a man how to give sensual massage to his partner. The man is instructed to mount his partner, who is lying on her back, and to massage her nipples with aromatic oil, which he does, gently, moving his hands in a circular motion. She lies with her eyes closed and her mouth slightly open. Her face has the expression of calm and joy. The therapist is moving the man's hands lower to the woman's stomach and then lower to her pubic area. The man had an erection now, and the therapist was pouring oil over his hands to massage the man's buttocks from behind.

A woman on the massage table moans louder and louder. I assume that she is having an orgasm, but her moans do not stop. The New Age sound of Persian song and African drums gives rhythm to the moving bodies. The male singing, a sound from the desert, rises up and down, and so does the woman's moan from massage table. The masseur moves to instruct and massage another couple; the couple he has just visited is now deeply engaged in sex.

It must be almost half an hour, and the moving bodies are still interconnected, still moving, searching, watching, and engaging. I can see only part of activities there; the rest is hidden by darkness and by other bodies. People from other rooms gather around to watch. The crowd is always where the most orgasms are heard or sensed. There are always couples that are not engaging with others, some who are just watching, and some who are in threesomes, but there is always a creation of a tight ball of bodies, and they become a center of other activities. Everyone starts gravitating toward that point. The temperature rises. I could smell the sex, the sweat, the odor of bodies, the aroma of different juices, all so intense that I have to run upstairs to catch some air.

I feel dizzy as well. That is what I always feel when I stand long enough in the room packed with people having sex. I always thought that is due to the lack of air, but a few times when I invited my colleagues from the university, they too complained, even in rooms with more regulated air conditioning, to have felt a very strange dizziness, as if their drinks had a drug of some kind. Could it be that even if we don't feel aroused consciously, the amount of hormones, the pheromones in the air, induce a chain reaction and move the hormone levels of the spectators?

When I go back to go downstairs, I see that the whirlpool is overcrowded, and too much water has spilled. The mountain of bodies is still moving; I think the whirlpool crowd got bigger and the smells stronger.

One man fell asleep while getting a massage. And his partner was trying to wake him up: "Get up, Jorge, we have to go! Oh! Wake up you stupid man. I told you not to drink that much." The man was snoring and wouldn't move a muscle. A security guard heard and rushed to help the woman. In order to wake him they decided to slap his face lightly, but nothing worked. Olana suggested that we leave him there to sleep but later made it clear that the place had to be empty for the cleaning lady. I thought she could help and tried other methods for waking the man: shaking him, yelling at him, massaging his hands and putting aromatic oil on his forehead—nothing worked. His girlfriend, sitting desperately to the side, needed to be at work in a few hours.

Meanwhile, an argument ensued between the Stallone lookalike and his wife: "So why you didn't join us?" Stallone's wife was rushing upstairs, mad with him, and I followed them. "You were doing your thing and I wanted to go to the sauna; you didn't want to."

"We were to be together tonight," she was pushing him back.

"Yes but, honey, you had your thing, I didn't want to go to the whirlpool—you did!"

The woman suddenly stopped. "You don't like me anymore, is that it?"

"No, that is not true, baby. You know I like you. I always like you."

They wanted their coats, but the discussion went on for some time; it went on after they put their clothes on—instead of costumes, they both had on sweatshirts and sweatpants, sneakers, and vests. Her hair, still wet from the whirlpool, her face covered with tears.

"You think I am not cute anymore."

"No, I think you were cute tonight; I didn't know what you wanted me to do, that's it."

This party had a few conflicts. The fighting couple. The man who was asleep—they woke him up under a cold shower, finally. I watched him and his girlfriend leave at about five in the morning. The upset Natasha, who claimed the stars were not right for a sex party tonight—but Olana and fifty other patrons didn't complain. The relaxing whirlpool and amazing sensual massage was described to me by one sexy redheaded woman as a "glorious experience" and by one German singer who came from Frankfurt as *toll*, which means "awesome" or "extraordinary."

Oversaturated with body smells and tired of moving heavy bags and walking up and down the stairs, I longed for a long shower and sleep.

CONTACT: LALA, A TOUCH OF CLASS (2000)

Lala is twenty-seven, with an engaging smile, dimples, and a well-proportioned physique. She obviously has taken good care of her body and mentioned this at our first meeting.

I was conflicted, as I wondered whether choosing to dress to fit in would also make it more likely that my man and I would engage in some kind of sex. I was also honest enough with myself to know I was conflicted by the arousing effects the third floor had on me the last time.

I like my body. I train it and take care of it, and I wanted to see it flashing easy peeks of itself in the mirror mounted across the front of the DJ stand. I didn't need to try on more than one outfit when I dressed that night. I chose the black lace garter belt and stockings I had only worn twice before—most women's realities prove how impractical these poorly functioning costumes are—a matching black lace pushup bra, a short black skirt, and a fitted black suede, button-down blouse. The boots I took out of the top of my closet hugged my muscular calves and defined my thighs by boosting my body into an alignment of display with their block heels.

As my man (Joe) and I got ready to get in the car, he teasingly asked me, "Is that skirt for easy lifting?" I wasn't sure what to say, because the truth of my desire made the answer a definite "yes," while the lines I drew for maintaining some objectivity in my study and the integrity of our relationship made me lie with flirtation and say "no."

We pulled up to the club at 12:30 a.m. It seemed almost routine after having been there only once before. I wasn't nervous at all; I felt like I knew what to expect, and I trusted myself and my partner. We were greeted by a different doorman and walked over to pay our $65 and check our coats. We paused on our way up the stairs to the second floor to be frisked. The doorman stopped for a moment to finger what I knew was the money clip and accompanying bulge in his front left pocket. Once again I was neither physically patted down nor questioned. If we had wanted to carry anything illegal, all we needed to do is pack it in on me.

We turned into the second-floor bar, hoping that we wouldn't see the group of "regulars" we did last time and be monopolized by their initiating intentions. We moved over to the bar; neither of us saw anyone who looked familiar. The bartender and the guests were all new faces, and we overheard people talking about how it was "dead" that night because none of the "regulars" were there. To me it seemed packed. I didn't know what "dead" or "pretty empty" meant because I had just gotten there. I imagined it meant the third floor would be slow, because the second level had about the same number of people as I remembered from my last visit, and the fourth floor wasn't open yet.

My man ordered a scotch on the rocks with a lemon wedge, and I declined his offer of water. We were quiet as I listened in to what the people around us were saying. The bartender was a woman this time; she was the same lady who had been working the register the last time we came. She talked endlessly as she served drinks and kept returning to visit a very slim woman in a tight, zebra-print top and a black miniskirt with slits up both thighs.

I was not uncomfortable making eye contact with the other guests, and I surveyed the room several times. Both of the men on my right had wedding bands; there was a couple on the other side of the bar who wore wedding rings, and the two women who joined the men on my right flashed ring fingers heavy with diamonds. The assumption among the older and more professional-seeming couples was that other couples were married just as they were. Even with my fingers bare of any ceremonial symbols it was assumed more than once that Joe and I were married.

We ordered another drink and started a conversation with the bartender. She told us she had been tending bar for over four years and how much she preferred working up here to being down at the register, where she would just say over and over, "Thank you, enjoy your night." She had long blond hair and wore a two-piece designer leather outfit. The skirt was short, and the tightness bulged over her belly where she was a little overweight.

The top displayed her generous breasts in a décolletage with thin straps that crossed in the back and supported their weight. I gleaned more information by listening in on her open and frequent conversations with customers. She was a Jewish girl who had an Italian Catholic ex-boyfriend with whom she was still friends. She said they were awful together because she would just say "Fuck you," but he was looking for some little girl who would sit at his feet and say "Whatever you want, baby." She was adamant that she wasn't that girl. It was a little after one in the morning, and I told Joe I was ready to go upstairs as soon as he was, because I was in the mood to dance.

We had not been approached by any individual or couples before we headed up to the third floor. I had heard the music out on the street when Joe was getting the car valet parked, and I didn't remember it had been that way the last time we came. I did have the memory of the effect the club level had on me in this atmosphere. As I walked up the stairs my body reminded me with moistening and subtle quivers that it liked it up here. As my head crested the landing, I could see that the area all around the third-floor bar was crowded.

I couldn't imagine why the bar area would be so packed if the space beyond it was so open. I didn't assume that the people from the floor below were liars, so I started to wonder where all the people could have come from that were packing the club level. I realized many people must come straight to the third floor without stopping at the second, and I would have had no way of seeing them from the level below. It requires taking a right turn through a doorway to enter the spaces of the second and third floors, so people in each space are not fully aware of the comings and goings of others. I told Joe I wanted to move up to the front, where we had been before. We maneuvered and pushed through the heat of the pulsing crowd toward the DJ booth in the front.

The two-tops were broken up and not all pushed together like the "regulars" had had them. The crowd was collectively younger. Instead of most couples being in their thirties and forties, most were in their twenties and thirties. There was a similar mix of people of color with an even representation of Latino and mixed-race people, and not as many African Americans.

Neither time did it seem like white couples were the majority on the club level, whereas on the second floor they definitely were. I spotted the DJ, who was up to his same tricks: dancing in his jockstrap, fondling himself, and performing different acrobatics behind his stand. Joe moved into a chair to nearly the same space he had sat before. He was to the side of the DJ booth, with his chair facing out for a view of the crowd and me. I stood leaning against the back of a chair, with my body open to the dance floor, about ten feet from him. Joe and I were separated by one table and a group of Latinos who appeared to be in their twenties, dancing and having a good time.

The women were petite, with small breasts and big high heels. One had on a loud, brightly colored mini-dress that slipped up over the curve of her ass when she danced low. The other had on a two-piece outfit with a V-angle-cut skirt that rode up high on one hip, exposing her whole leg. She only came away from watching herself in the mirror to dance with her girlfriend or tease her boyfriend, who sat in a chair immediately to my right. As she watched herself dance, she'd set her heeled feet wide and open her legs to flash the little white panties under her skirt. Her pussy was shaved, which was apparent because her underwear gaped on one side as she'd rhythmically spread her legs, making her hairless vulva visible for brief moments.

We'd dance all night: by ourselves, in a group, and partnered with each other. Joe joined me, and at first we danced together while we talked and looked around. The DJ changed his spin, and we started the standing foreplay in which those on the dance floor engage. I moved in and out of his space, so close that I brushed my face against his crotch as I grabbed his thighs and danced low to the ground, then back out to slither a circle around my own private turn-ons that clamor in lover's heads but their partners never know. We turned to face the mirror to be reflexive voyeurs. I had my back pressed in tight to him as he danced behind me, and I squared the heels of my boots to spread my legs before the DJ and his magic mirror.

My legs are like pistons, and I used them to drive my hips to each side while pushing my ass out and rubbing it against his crotch in between. My hands moved up and down on the insides of my thighs as I rubbed them together and shot them back apart with the driving beat. During my show, my underwear had become visible where the clips of my garter belt held fast to the top of each stocking, and on my deepest hardest thrusts a peek of black satin at the crotch of my panties revealed itself. I fit Joe's dick on a track between the crack of my behind and rode it around as we continued to move.

A couple had been advancing into our space, and I thought it was because they were starting to get it on and weren't completely aware of their direction. We didn't move, but I didn't push them away from continuing toward us. The woman was facing her partner, and her back was to me, as first her long black hair brushed against my shoulder and chest, and then she moved her ass against the front of me. I didn't even notice the man she was with, who was on the other side of her, as I looked over my shoulder at Joe for confirmation that this was okay. He just grinned and kept moving, so we coordinated the rhythm of our train to include two more. I had still not even seen this woman's face as I allowed her to reach around and put her hands on me.

It was like two blind people meeting, she and I, back to front. I touched the outsides of her arms as if to say, "Nice to meet you," and sent my hands down her sides to her hips. This unusual introduction seemed to go well because she turned around, and upon meeting face to face I smiled with a combination of the outrageous and the aroused and said, "Hi."

She had beautiful light brown skin and a flawless smile. She returned the simplicity of my greeting, and the wordlessness of our meeting turned into the silence of our agreement. The woman's partner reached around and began to massage her breasts over the thin material of her tight black top. He pushed her closer toward me, and I didn't back away. Instead, I arched my back and thrust my body toward hers as Joe's hands came from behind me to grab my chest.

This man, whose face I did not even see, pushed down the woman's top and bared her breasts to me as he rubbed them more intently, squeezing toward her nipples. Joe's hands went to move inside my blouse, and I sped things along by unbuttoning most of my shirt. The increasing lack of restraint and the total engagement of restraint were simultaneous and in direct conflict. I was past aroused; I wanted to take off my clothes, remain blind to the other man, fuck Joe all the ways I like best, and have the added stimulation of this woman just for me. My fantasy bank was spilling out onto the dance floor among the contrary contents of other people's heads.

I was touching this strange woman's breasts as she and Joe pulled my chest out over the cups of my bra and stimulated them, all while we continued some sort of rhythmic movement that felt almost like a mockery of dance. We had become the most outrageous event on the third floor. When a second woman came over, I recognized the three of them as the group that had been having so much fun dancing together earlier.

From outside the links of our groping train, this woman moved between the other lady and me and began to caress her friend's chest as she leaned in to take one of my nipples in her mouth. She ran her tongue over her lips when she pulled back, and I slowly moved my mouth down to the woman's breast in front of me. I was hot, too hot. I was glad I had decided to wear panties, and they were wet with my excitement as I rubbed against this stranger's leg.

The sexual fog in my head was getting more potent and dense. I didn't want to be the fool who tried to figure out what she'd done the day after, and I didn't snap back to clarity until I saw Joe's hand on the breast of the woman in front of me. I wasn't angry, I wasn't jealous, and it didn't make me want to shut this whole thing down. It reminded me to check in with him and reconfigure this writhing arrangement.

I turned around and faced Joe directly. When I turned around the other woman must have also, because we were soon back to back, with our asses bumping and sliding against each other's. Joe's eyes had the first glaze of arousal. He was sweating; his lips were parted, and he didn't say a word. I didn't either. We started to kiss, deep and hard. I felt the hands of the woman still pressed tightly behind me move over and around my ass, down the outsides of my thighs, and between my legs to search for my clit. Joe's hands ran into hers; he asked me if she was touching my pussy.

I told him she was as I licked the sweat from around his mouth, nibbled on his lips, and he grabbed my face to lock me into an urgent kiss. I reached behind me, clutched this woman's ass, and moved my hands down to feel the tops of her thigh-high stockings. My hands met hers between her own legs, and I quickly figured out she was unsnapping the crotch of her underwear. I felt the coarse softness that is the unique contradiction of black pubic hair and moved my finger to the wet spot of her arousal. I only stimulated the outside of her vulva and stopped when the years of having my sexual response trained for one person overwhelmed me with longing for the man who was right in front of me.

I moved my hand out from between this woman's legs to reach for Joe. I wrapped one hand behind his neck with my fingers rooted in his wild hair, pulled his mouth to mine, and grabbed his erection with my other hand. He was turned on, and his hands were forceful, the way I like them best. We touched against each other's bodies while we made out in front of anyone who cared to see, and he moved his hand between my legs to do what time and intimacy had taught him to do so well.

He pushed my panties to the side, and his fingers cupped my pussy lips and clit. We continued to make out as I shifted my pelvis to align his fingers with my vagina so I could get the penetration I was craving. I fucked his hand right there on the dance floor. I wasn't sure if the other couple was behind us anymore, and I only looked around once to see what the reactions of the people around us were. The group of Black people I had seen earlier was still in the same area, and it seemed like their slow dance had ceased completely to look at the spectacle we had made of ourselves.

To have people looking at me like I'd gone too far in a swingers club was a surprise, but that is what their expressions hinted. I looked over Joe's other shoulder, never stopping the finger fuck we had going on, and saw a mixed-race couple staring at us. These looks were different than the ones passed so freely over sexually engaged bodies on the fourth floor. In a surreal moment in my head I could hear people saying, "Excuse me but this is the third floor, you can't do that here." At that same time, the woman whom I had been using, as she had been using me, said, "We're dying from the heat and are going down to the bar to cool off and get a drink. We'll see you later." The combination of intrusions on my fantasy romp was enough to make me disengage myself from Joe's hand and begin to straighten up my clothes.

This involved getting my crotch back into my panties and under my skirt and putting my breasts back in my bra and buttoning them into my blouse. I watched as the sex haze in Joe's eyes cleared; he looked around, reoriented himself, and told me that he was going to go get a drink, too. He asked me if I wanted anything, and I told him that I was fine. I thought I wanted to keep dancing, but the context of what had happened shifted so quickly everything seemed unreal. The idea of figuratively standing with "two feet firmly on the ground" made me want to laugh, as the muscles in my legs were rubbery from the combination of physical demands I had placed on them and the feeling that the height of my awareness was now in my pelvis.

I danced around distractedly for part of a song. My experience had altered my frame of reference, and I looked around at the other guests, expecting another scene to escalate to the point mine had so easily reached. I began to make my way through the other people on the dance floor and was looking for Joe at the bar. He smiled when he saw me coming and asked if I had changed my mind. I told him I had, created a space for myself with the bar at my back and Joe close in front, and told him I'd love a bottled water. I wanted to regroup. I felt out of sorts, not as if anything was wrong, just the distinct awareness that I had allowed things to become different.

Whatever might be in Pandora's box, I knew I had been picking at the lock and could open it up if I wanted. My thoughts were interrupted when I noticed Anita, the owner, heading for Joe with some look of intent. She touched the outside of his arm and said, "Excuse me, this must be your first time here." He and I looked at each other rather smugly; we were not first-timers but still only on our second visit. She continued as if reading a script: "This must be your first time; otherwise you'd know that jeans are not allowed." Joe clarified that his pants may look like denim in the club lights but were indeed not.

He fondled the material and extended it toward her, as if to invite her to have a feel and prove it to herself.

When Joe and I entered the second-floor space it was close to two in the morning, the big fourth-floor opening time. We had seated ourselves at a two-top table along the wall when we looked over toward the bar and saw our "friends" from the dance floor. We all smiled at one another as if we knew each other, when we had not even spoken a dozen words among all five of us. The woman with whom I'd been dancing smiled a wide inviting grin, waved for us to come over, and said, "Please, come join us."

We walked the short distance over to their table, and the lady began to make introductions before we were even seated. She looked very attractive and somewhat cute in her eagerness, sitting there being so proper and going through the formalities. I smiled as I thought to myself that this woman and I have had each other's breasts in our mouths and hands in each other's skirts, and here we are going to revert to formalities for comfort.

She motioned to the man who sat at her left and said, "This is Luis. He's my boyfriend. My name is Luisette, and my other friend will be right back." I extended my hand to Luisette first, smiled wryly, and said, "My name is Lala. It's nice to finally meet you." The four of us had just begun talking when the other woman in their threesome returned. Luisette introduced her to Joe and me, saying, "This is Marcela." Luisette presented Marcela to us affectionately and held her with one arm around her back and both hands draped fondly over her shoulders. I had not seen Luisette or Luis make any contact between each other. Luis sat back looking sort of proud, as I thought to myself how much the two women gave the impression he was a third wheel.

Luisette and Marcela continued to be affectionate with each other: hugging, touching hands, brushing each other's hair, and looking into each other's eyes like they knew something the rest of us didn't—including Luis. Meanwhile, Luis spoke proudly of introducing Luisette to swingers clubs and repeated what I had heard others say on my first visit: "I initiated it the first time, but she wasn't too into it, but once she got here she really liked it, and now she's the one who wants to keep coming back." Luisette tossed her full, long dark hair to the side, looked at Luis, and told us how the first time Luis told her about clubs "like these" she didn't even know such places existed, and they had a huge fight because she felt insecure. She said the first swingers club they went to was down by where they lived in New Jersey. It's called Club

USA, and she said they don't go there anymore because the clubs up in New York are so much better.

Luisette and Luis had a distinct set of rules for agreed-upon behavior when they first started going to swing clubs. There was to be no kissing on the mouth and no sexual intercourse with others. They didn't say exactly how long they honored this arrangement, but Luis quickly became talkative and told us about the first night they disregarded their agreement. Luisette blurted out that she was really drunk that night, and Luis said, "Yeah, I was pretty drunk that night too." Luis went on at length about how good looking the woman in the couple they swapped with was and how she just had that "heat" that some women have. He said, "Ya know, some women just have that heat. They're just all about sex. They're so hot, and they've got that heat where you can just tell." Luisette was quiet for the first time, and she tilted her head to one side as she listened to Luis tell us how this woman had just grabbed his face on the dance floor and started kissing him on the mouth. He went into detail about how they were all just so turned on that when this woman started kissing him, nobody said no. I wondered who exactly "nobody" was and noticed that Luisette was still not saying anything. Luis said this woman wanted them all to go upstairs and that all four of them agreed to go up to the fourth floor together.

He said when they went upstairs, all four of them were fooling around, and each couple was mostly focused on their own partner, until the man in the other couple asked Luis if he wanted to fuck his wife. It was not clear how the transition was made, and there was no mention of Luisette initiating anything that happened, but Luis told how the other man was equally interested in having sex with Luisette, so they all swapped. After a brief pause in the storytelling I asked Luisette and Luis if either of them in any way regretted what they had done, either later that night, the next day, or any time after.

They both said no, and each looked sincere when they said it. Luis continued by saying, "We still don't have sex with other people, except for that once." I wondered how long that would last. I figured until some woman's "heat" was just too hot for Luis and her man was equally as hot to swap for Luisette. They both laughed and reaffirmed they have no regrets, admitted that all their rules had gone out the window, and maintained that they still weren't going to have sex with others.

After Luis and Luisette had finished their disclosure they looked at Joe and me as if it were our turn to bare some personal information about ourselves.

Our big admission was that we don't swap. I wondered how much the first impressions we'd given on the dance floor made our statement seem unbelievable, or at least malleable. I continued by saying I really wouldn't be happy sharing Joe in that way and that it would create a lot of problems for me given that we are very happy the way we are. In my head I could very vividly picture my imagined reaction to Joe responding to another woman's passionate kiss.

I felt a sour heat in my stomach and wanted to twist off his lips and punch him in the face. I didn't want to continue down that path in my imagination, but when I centered myself back on the present, I noticed there was a lull in the conversation. When Luisette started talking again, it was as if a shift in mood had taken place. There were a few awkward moments when it seemed like our rejection of their lifestyle had prompted them to defend it, and they each made a few justifications before we simply reverted to small talk.

While we were talking, Marcela alternated between a feigned look of boredom and being physically affectionate with Luisette. There seemed to be a certain antagonism between her and Luis, and she took opportunities to question him whenever she could, as if challenging his very presence. Outside the context of any conversation we were having, she said to Luis, "Where are you sleeping tonight? I hope you're not getting in the middle again." At one point in our conversation she placed her hand on my thigh and began to run her fingers up and down toward my crotch.

I placed my hand on top of hers to stop her motion and moved my chair closer to Joe's side of the table. I had an acute sense that her place in a threesome with Luisette and Luis neither satisfied her nor provided her any sense of security. She was operating with no exclusive relationship as a reference point, and Luisette seemed to meet her halfway because of the alienation I detected in her own arrangement. Luis seemed to just sit above it all, both feeling proud and looking foolish. At times the two women would ignore him, spite him with the tenderness they showed only for each other, and laugh while he sat apart from their intimacy. Yet he was smug, and why not? He was a man who simultaneously had both open and consensual sexual access to two successful, attractive women.

Luis bragged about how he can "always spot a player" and how he knew Marcela would be into a threesome with Luisette and him. He said that when Luisette introduced them and Marcela kissed him on the cheek, he could just tell. It was that "heat" where you can just tell that some women are all about it. I wondered if a woman who turned Luis down could still be that "hot" or if his use of this concept only applied to women who were sexually interested in him.

Joe and I headed up to the fourth floor about fifteen minutes after our three "friends" had. We went up to the landing before the final staircase where an elegant man was acting as a greeter/bouncer for the sex floor. There was a door plainly marked with a sign that read "Private." I asked, "Excuse me, but what goes on behind that door marked private?" He smiled almost teasingly and said, "I can't tell you. It's private." I took the bait and pressed for an answer. "Is it something fun for special guests that I'd want to know about, or is it just office space where very ordinary things happen in an extraordinary place?" He kept the same Cheshire grin on his face and just said, "I can't tell you what goes on in there." I let it go at that point, mostly because I suspected the room was just office space and he was teasing me.

I walked ahead of Joe up to the brief landing on the fourth floor where the lights abruptly switch to dim black light, and there is a sudden silence that is so quiet it seems out of context with the sex by which I am totally surrounded each time I mount the final step to this place. My eyes adjusted quickly, and so did I, because after only one prior visit, I mingled among all these people's sex like I belonged there. Joe and I surveyed the room and walked to our right toward the front end of the back-to-back benches that define the center of the space.

We heard a whispered "hi" and saw Luisette, Luis, and Marcela getting into their sex. Luis was standing between the two women, and each of them was sitting on the bench in front of him. Both ladies were scooted down and back, leaning on their elbows with their asses pushed to the edge of the bench. Their legs were spread with their knees bent up toward their chests, and Luis was rubbing their pussies and fingering them while they leaned in toward each other to kiss and fondle each other's breasts. Luis looked over at us and asked if we wanted them to make room. I said no thanks and told him we were just watching. He shrugged and good-naturedly told us, "Your loss."

The couple with them was giggling. The other man nudged his partner and said, "Go on, baby. Lick her pussy. See if that gets her up." I watched as this young lady bent over her friend's hip, pushed her skirt up to expose her vulva, and bent down to take a few laps at her pussy. She stood up, still looking amused, and announced the result of her efforts, "Naw, man. She ain't gettin' up. We gonna have to carry the bitch outta here." Neither Joe nor I were amused by this scene. Joe stepped in closer to the woman's husband and told him, "Look, if you're having trouble getting her up, I can help you carry her. You might need another guy to help carry that dead weight." The man shrugged off the offer and insisted he could get her up. He repeated that this happens with her a lot, to which Joe asked what kind of drugs she's on. The blacked-out woman's husband said, "Oh no, man, she ain't on no drugs. She just drinks too much now and then."

The episode came to a close when the group's pushing, nudging, and cajoling got the woman up enough to be helped to her feet by the three of them and assisted down the stairs. I wondered for what transgressions the monitors who watched this level were supposed to be alert. This group's scene played out facing one of the monitors, who stood not more than ten feet in front of them.

It was about three in the morning, and we were ready to leave. We agreed we had both had enough and wanted to go home. Joe asked me if I wanted to fool around at all, to which I replied without ambivalence, "No." We made our way the short distance to the stairs and headed down. We said goodbye to the elegant man who was still at his post and continued our descent. Upon coming through the door to the third floor, we saw that the dance floor was empty and the DJ was casually standing by the bar having a bottled water. He bid us a good night and smiled as if we were old friends. Joe and I traveled down the single flight of stairs that took us past the second floor and delivered us to the landing of the first level. We then collected our coats and left.

As I look at this narrative, I see a few common elements: the rites of aggregation, incorporation, and the fact of belonging. We can find in common the pleasures and the feelings amplified by the fact of belonging to a larger community. In the case of orgies, the matter seems to be about putting pleasure first, treating it as a principle of belonging: collective pleasure and collective ecstasies provide an added value that improves the intercourse and forms something more complete than private sex, as if it were important for individuals to draw from some sensual part of themselves and to share it with others.

8.2 Paddles at Leather World. New York City.

This is because the need to explore and learn more about our sexuality is not driven by some abstract force or some necessities of good health and feeling but rather by the essential intensification of pleasures. What solidifies these bonds is sharing something by, paradoxically, withdrawing from the parts of the world that reject the usual rules. Although the matter of the gratification from belonging to

a larger community is a vastly studied issue, its application to the orgiastic setting anticipates exciting ideas.

I believe that more study of these forms of belonging and affiliation is necessary. The affiliation found in partaking in practices that deviate and challenge
common rules can be uplifting, as underlined in the chapters on sadomasochism.
But if an individual's libido and sexual appetite drive him or her toward these
unconventional practices, how much is will and how much is desire? Maybe desire
is more a psychoanalytic question than a sociological or ethnographical one, but,
as these social scenes attest, is there any difference?

I would like to suggest that the psychoanalytic or libidinal aspect is always
sociological and ethnographic in aspect, too. I believe the complication being
offered here is that the psychoanalytic is often treated as foundational to whatever forms of socialization take place for the individual during and beyond
adolescence. Yet this seems to suggest that there's something to tracing these
practices and spaces, something fundamentally sociological, that explains the
boundaries/borders between will and desire in a way psychoanalysis doesn't
quite account for.

Can one really choose the object of his or her desire? Maybe there is no choice
in breaking the rules; maybe participants consciously highlight their belonging
to these groups to justify the impulses of their desires, like the man who says in
Bebe's notes at the Paddle Club that one has to have a certain education to challenge normatively established sexual patterns. This view could also be fortified
by the gradual expulsion of all sorts of sex clubs from the city as a consequence
of gentrification, for instance, as it is expressed by the relocation of topless
bars and other venues from Times Square and other places to the periphery of
the city.

The sociologist Talcott Parsons paid scant attention to the social importance
of sex, but he did elaborate on what he called "erotic gratifications."

Erotic gratifications here specifically involve certain types of somatic stimu-
lations and processes. Hence in the erotic aspect of the relationship the bodies of the parties have particular significance. The first aspect, then, of the
expressive symbolism is the organization of the erotically significant features
of the body of each around the "genital" level of oral gratification. This means
a certain symbolic priority of genital intercourse over other possibilities of
mutual gratification; rather generally these are the standards of taste with

respect to the expressions of this relative to other elements of the total erotic complex.[5]

The antagonistic or conflictual nature of heterosexual desire also was recognized by Enlightenment thinkers such as Hobbes, who writes: "Every man has a right to everything, even to one another's body, and the exclusivity of mating to lead to an ever present potential for conflict."[6]

chapter 9

Lesbian and Gay Spaces

I n a sense this chapter is about the "mainstreaming" of homosexuality, start-ing in the 1990s and continuing today, and the formation of specific areas of the city that have a kind of concentrated power—wealth, cultural cachet—aligned specifically with gay and lesbian communities. There is a conservative element here, as the deviant behaviors and practices mentioned in the previous chapters, which appear more fluid, take on a more definitive, concrete character. Beyond my own notes, the venues I chose for my contacts include the Rambles, a secluded area of greenery in Central Park; the Cock, a bar for gay men, located in the East Village; Crazy Nanny's in Greenwich Village; and Henrietta Hudson, whose website describes it as a "Bar & Girl" for lesbian rocker girls and brainy dykes, also located in the West Village.

CONTACT: FRIDA, CRAZY NANNY'S AND MEOW MIX (2003)

Frida is thirty-two and tells me "darkness serves a special purpose." When I inquire what that might be, she says, "To make life grand." Eager to explore the city, she is full of energy but wonders if there will be lipstick lesbians in the place where she will conduct her observations.[1] Her notes are presented after one of her excursions:

> The general atmosphere of the lesbian bars is completely different from their male counterparts. Venues I visited: Crazy Nanny and Meow Mix. While the gay bars are sexually charged, the lesbian bars projected a very friendly,

sisterly atmosphere. You do not simply hook up with someone. You do not go to the bar in search of love and sex only. You are here to bond, to enjoy the companionship of fellow females, and to have a good time. I visited two lesbian bars; my school friend C, who is a lesbian, recommended Crazy Nanny and Meow Mix, and so I visited both. Both bars are similar in style. They are not the glamorous, lipstick type of bars, but the dive-like dyke bars (C is a dyke). Although the clientele are predominantly dykes, I still see a lot of femmes, all dressed up and having fun with their dyke partners.

Crazy Nanny is on the corner of Leroy Street and Seventh Avenue South. It is a dyke bar with predominantly Latino and Black patrons. Though mostly women visited the bar, I spotted a couple of gay men among the patrons. The moment I stepped inside with my straight girlfriends, we knew that we were different. Maybe I really have this totally straight look, but apart from some friendly smiles from the women in the bar, we mostly talked to ourselves. My friends were "freaking out"; they were at once afraid of being picked up by women and also feeling very uncomfortable because they were different.

On the other hand, I felt pretty comfortable. I did not really care if someone approached me, although I knew the chances were slim. Curiously enough, I would rather be picked up by a female in a lesbian bar than be picked up by a seventy-year-old guy in a regular bar (an actual experience). I am straight, but I don't mind female friendship. I am not so sure about actually sleeping with a woman, but I would not mind a bit of cuddling, if need be.

Crazy Nanny's is a two-level establishment. The bar area is situated in the entrance area. There is a pool table at the back, and the bathrooms are at the far end. The second floor was closed on the evening of our visit; it usually opens only on the weekends for dance parties. There is a jukebox by the stairs to the second floor, and there are two overhead TV sets tuned to sports channels (the TV was showing an American football match). The music in the bar is mostly pop tunes, usually sung by female singers.

The walls of the bar are painted in dark orange, and the lighting is dim. There are three heart-shaped red light outlines hanging from the ceiling, reminding the patrons that this is a women's bar. In the back of the room, a few butch dykes were playing pool. There seemed to be a competition in progress. Several couples were sitting cozily around the bar area, chatting and gently canoodling. Some of the dykes really looked masculine, and I was

9.1 Lesbian couple at local club.

amused to find that they were actually acting more like men than the two male patrons in the bar. No doubt they were gay.

My friend needed the bathroom and walked toward the back. On her way, she asked directions, and in turn was asked politely if she needed an "escort." My friend declined. Meanwhile, I headed toward the bar and ordered beer for all of us. The bartender, a very cheerful Latino woman, only gave me the drinks after she made me promise to have a good time.

We were soon informed that Wednesday night is always karaoke night. We decided to stay for a while and participate. I was not entirely aware until this moment that most of the patrons were regulars. The host addressed them by their names, calling out who was going to sing which song, and the patrons happily shouted pleasantries over the loud background music. The host sang the first song. One of the regular patrons sang the next one. Then my friend sang the third. When she approached the karaoke stand, the host asked her if she had done karaoke before. She lied and said no. Then she told the host the truth, which was simply that she had not visited this venue before. A patron sitting close by told her that since she was a double virgin, she had to "pop her cherry."

Apparently, my friend had not heard the term before and asked what it meant. The dyke, no doubt amused by having a straight virginal girl in the venue, explained to her with much laughing that "popping the cherry" means "losing one's virginity," that is, breaking the hymen. Since they were only going to perform this "ceremony" metaphorically, my friend popped a cherry into her mouth.

By the time the fourth patron was on stage, a person, who I really could not say was male or female, sat on the stairs and began to touch himself/herself all over, while dancing to the beat. It seemed that he/she is a regular, though he/she was considered "wacky." This person proceeded to sing (he/she sang spectacularly badly), when a butch from the pool table came up and joined in. Soon, they were doing some "pseudo-humping" on stage. He/she was in ecstasy. Little did he/she realize that the butch had stuck a half-burning cigarette in his/her hair. She must probably be quite fed up with the person, who apparently enjoyed showing off too much. Although a bit dangerous, I found this rather funny.

After ending this episode, Frida headed to the next location a few weeks later:

About two weeks later, I went with my friends to Meow Mix. From the information I read in the *Sexy New York City* guide, Meow Mix is quite a dive bar. I could vaguely imagine what the bar would be, judging from the location. Meow Mix is on East Houston Street and Suffolk Street, on the far, far eastern side of New York City. It was very quiet walking outside on the street, but when we opened the wooden door, it was completely different atmosphere.

We were required to pay a cover charge. R, my straight, male friend, was very concerned about not being able to get into the bar. But, accompanied by two girls, he had no problem getting in. The bar is small, very dark, and the ceiling is low. There is a stage to the left of the bar. Someone had just had a retirement party there, and there were still some of the decorations left. The bathrooms have no locks, and on the walls are some pictures and graffiti, as well as love notes written by smitten patrons. The music is predominantly country-western. I realized later that this is a symbol of toughness, since there are a lot of dykes in the bar. The overhead TV was again tuned to sports channels, and there was a basketball match on show the evening we were there.

In contrast to the late twenties to early forties clientele at Crazy Nanny's, the majority of the girls at Meow Mix were between twenty and twenty-five. These very young girls seemed to be friends, and they were no doubt regulars of the bar. Apparently there was a birthday celebration going on. One of the bartenders, who was dressed in a skirt, carried a lot of gifts and a big bouquet of flowers. A lot of regular patrons went up to her and gave her smooches. Similar scenes were often observed at other locations, for example, the Hellfire Club. They seemed to be very happy and enjoying themselves very much. The dress code is mixed. We see some "construction workers," some "butch," and a few "femmes."

There was a fair amount of leather and punk people too. Most of the girls there are white, and the majority of them are lesbians. The atmosphere was not very sexual; in fact, it was very sisterly, very cozy, friendly. The bar has an atmosphere of a hangout, and everyone seemed to be chatting and enjoying a good time. As straight people, no one seemed to be paying particular attention to us. Perhaps our ages were also over the default age group. However, we did not feel unwelcomed. The conversations around us were very casual, from everyday life happenings to friendly gossips. We noticed that there was a straight couple inside the bar at some point, and they seemed to be at lost. We did not know if they realized they were in a lesbian bar.

We hung out in the bar for about an hour, totally enjoying the friendly atmosphere and having fun watching the young girls bond. They have their

9.2 Bisexual activists play at the Hellfire Club in the old Meatpacking District, New York City, c. 1993. From the hellfirepress.com archive.

own community language, and people seemed to be arriving at the bar and then immediately locating their own group. There were more and more people arriving at the bar around eleven; the small place was crowded. However, the atmosphere was never unpleasant, and we agreed that anyone would feel comfortable and welcome here.

Unlike gay bars, lesbian bars are really much less sexually charged. In Crazy Nanny's, there was a high level of humor, fun, and sisterly love. In Meow Mix, young energy and girlish love made the dive bar look very cute. The concept of love for young men and women really determined the atmosphere of each venue. Often, a space itself does not necessarily indicate anything, but with the reaction of the people in mind, it turns into a different place. In addition, Frida thought that perhaps women enjoyed more emotional connection. Therefore, at these lesbian bars, the sexual energy is superseded by an urge to connect emotionally. Thus, gender plays a very important role in determining the nature, the atmosphere, and the consequences of such venues and the events held there.

CONTACT: KAROL, COCK (2003)

Karol is tall, skinny, with braided hair. She is thirty years old, and although she has lived in the city for a few years, she has not been to any sex-related clubs.

The Cock was my first ethnographic experience in the field. I was feeling very nervous, and I didn't want to do it on my own. Because the Cock is a gay bar, I decided to invite two of my gay friends, Bee and Cee [pseudonyms], who would help me not only enter the place but also give me feedback on their own experience. Jenny, a close friend of ours, joined the group.

The day that we decided to go, the Cock was celebrating its anniversary, and they were having a Big Dick Contest. We were told to arrive at the place before 11 p.m. if we wanted to have a good spot to watch the contest. So we went to have dinner at a restaurant nearby and at 10:30 decided to walk and look for the place. The Cock is supposed to be a very famous gay bar, and having no experience whatsoever in the field, I was expecting to find a big sign, lights, people outside, etc. But the place looked very different. From the outside it seemed like a closed store, no windows, no lights, and just a small neon sign that said: The Cock. We knocked at the door, and a man dressed in a jaguar-printed leotard with a blonde Afro wig opened it. He said: "Ten dollars each." We paid and went in. He immediately closed the door.

The place was dark and simple. Blue and white veils were hanging from the ceiling, and just a few blue lights were illuminating the space. No chairs, no tables, no stage. I was thinking at that moment: Is there really going to be a contest here? Because it seemed that nothing was going on. At that moment the place was almost empty: there were just a few guys drinking at the bar, one or two were dancing, and few more were talking. My friend Bee started dancing on his own, and Cee, Jenny, and I decided to walk around. At the back of the bar there was this other room that was separated from the front room just by a plastic curtain. There was nobody in there. It was an empty space, with no windows or light, just a dark room. We had no idea what that room was all about.

Around half an hour later, more and more people started to arrive. I saw some of my other friends—all women—waiting on line to hang their coats. An hour later, the place was packed. Men, men, and men. Young men, older men, cute, slim, well-built, beautiful men. There were also some older guys, in their forties, maybe in their fifties, not so cute, not so well built, and most of them by themselves. We decided to sit down on what seemed to be a dais. Bee had disappeared. He went to the back room and stayed there. A lot of men were going in and out of that room. We still didn't know what was going in there, and I wanted to find out. I asked Cee if he would go in with me, but the contest was about to begin and I also wanted to see that. I forgot about the back room for a while.

One of the men who was going to perform asked us if we could move because he was going to start the show. We stood up, but we managed to stay close. The contest started. Two guys came out. One was dancing standing on the bar, and the other one on the dais. We were very close to the second performer. He was young, light skinned, dark hair, slim, and well built. He came out almost naked, just with a little towel around his waist, but the minute he started dancing he took it off. I couldn't believe what I was seeing! He had the most huge dick I had ever seen in my life! Ten inches? Eleven inches? I do not know, but it was huge.

While he was dancing, he was touching his body and masturbating at the same time. There was another man, dressed with black leather pants and a white T-shirt, who was standing near him, just looking. Suddenly he approached him and started sucking his dick. I don't know how he managed to suck all that dick into his mouth, but he did it. A few minutes later, the performer had a complete erection, and the guy then stopped. He went into a small room behind the dancing area and we didn't see him again.

The performer continued to dance, and other men approached him. Some said a few words to him—I couldn't hear what—and others touched him: his arms, his chest, his dick, his ass, everything. He seemed very comfortable, he was smiling all the time, talking with a soft, friendly voice to the guys that were getting close to him, as if he knew them.

It was getting harder to move. Cee started walking in front of me, and we went in. The second we crossed the plastic curtain I felt a completely different energy. It was very hard to see, but you didn't need to see to feel what was going on in there. I stood close to the left wall and observed. Around thirty, maybe forty men, were inside. With no subtlety at all they were touching each other, sucking each other's dicks, fucking each other. I couldn't hear a single word; I could just feel their breathing, their sweating. It was very hot, and there was no ventilation whatsoever. It was getting harder for me to breathe because of the lack of air, but I wanted to stay.

I saw two young women sitting in a corner. There were completely naked, and one had a dildo in her hand. They were kissing, touching, licking each other. I found it so bizarre to see two lesbians in that environment, but they seemed so excited that I found it attractive. A few men were standing just like I was, observing. I couldn't take my eyes off one who was masturbating while looking at the other men. I was feeling so aroused. Should I be enjoying this? Well . . . Why not? But . . . why am I enjoying it? I was feeling so weird and guilty but at the same time liking it so much.

About ten minutes later I saw Cee again; he had finally found Bee. We came out of the room and joined Jenny, who was still enjoying the contest. The performers had switched and at the dais there was now a black, tall, incredibly built young man. He was holding his dick up with a belt, and on his head he had a miner light. He did not let anybody touch him. He was dancing but not interacting with the audience. I could tell he was not having fun at all. Bee was having the time of his life. I was stunned to see how he could touch everybody with so much confidence.

He was just touching dicks and telling me how they felt. "This is big!" "This is well . . . okay!" "No, this is too small!" "Like this." And then, he started telling me to touch. I couldn't do it, but for him was completely natural; he did not have any inhibitions what so ever. Bee was not the only one. Most of the guys in the place had the same approach. They didn't need to talk. They were there not to socialize but to fuck. And that is exactly what they were doing. Touching and fucking. That is it. For Cee, the experience was different. He was observing everything with distance and didn't participate like the rest. At one point he said to me: "This is like an addiction, and I'm glad I'm out of it."

After three hours in the place we were tired and decided it was time to leave. We took a cab and went home.

In reflecting on these accounts, I'm reminded about our method, ethnography, this art of narrating. I see my various contacts not just as storytellers but as seers. They are reality checkers, impartial examiners of the social worlds we feast on; we are appraisers of the facts underlying a particular matter as observers and participants. "The stories we tell are grounded in others, in something that we, as individuals, do not make up, even though we transform it, on the basis of our own experience."[2] The voices of Vanessa, Bebe, Karol, and others are observing from afar and participating from inside, from within. It is an art and a scientific practice. It involves intellectual knowledge and sensual experience. It is about us; it is about the people we work with, those we like and those we don't. It makes us and them, together, the object of an enduring and often peculiar inquiry that dwells on human experience.

The focus of the remainder of this chapter is on, I hesitate to say, "perverse" places where sex acts occur that are not deemed "right," good, conventional, or healthy. More specifically, I concentrate on how bodies are perceived, used, abused, examined, exalted, prized, degraded, enhanced, reinvented, reconfigured, and glorified in those spaces. I am interested in the architectural dimensions shaping "perverse" behavior—bars, parks, toilets, dungeons, glory holes, for example—and in the roles these places make possible, roles where body parts are exposed for titillation without knowing who or what will be used to titillate those body parts.

While we begin the chapter in one of New York's known gay cruising spaces, the Ramble of Central Park—in the majority of this chapter I am focusing on a more recent phenomenon: how these spaces are managed, discovered, and mediated by technology. The Grindr app figures here as something that sits between the Hard City and Soft City, a kind of middleman or gateway for accessing parts of the city that were previously reachable by word of mouth only. I am seeing something like a shift in the narrative of this manuscript from the fluidity engendered by the Soft City and its disappearance in more contemporary, "hard" aspects of technological mediation, gentrification, and consolidation of social cachet. The areas tracked in the last two chapters are no longer on the fringe or secret but "open secrets": they are the product of the knowledge of (queer) communities that have organized and created spaces and even apps that serve as maps that help newcomers and veterans alike navigate what was once much less visible.

CONTACT: JAMES, CRUISING THE RAMBLE (1995)

As a member of a CUNY team of ten researchers, I, along with the sociologist William Kornblum, conducted a study in 1987–1988 for the Central Park Conservancy. I visited the Rambles, a small, thirty-six acre area of the 840-acre park, using a cartography/ethnography approach, mapping out sections of the park and noting the behaviors associated with each area. Our many visits to the park included areas that were never completely explored (*atlas obscura*). The Rambles, being one such area, remains uncharted terrain for sociologists. The following notes describe a revealing encounter in the Rambles.

Here the reader is introduced to the issues of investment and the conduct of businesses, both legitimate and illegitimate, along the street. I present some of the many social worlds that converge in the sex zones in the city. The ecology of populations in space and time and the way the major population groups perceive these areas are primary concerns. I am able to describe most of the characteristic patterns of behavior and group interaction along these sex corridors, lesbian strolls, and the nearby "gayborhoods" from pedestrian counts, survey questionnaires, and hours of observation and participation in the life of these zones.

James is twenty-seven, a white male with an easy disposition. His notes involve an encounter with one of the passersby at a location in the heavily wooded Rambles:

At the north rim of the lake the path comes to a fork with one end continuing north, while the other veers east. At the fork is a mounted sign that reads "RAMBLES." According to my map, the Rambles is approx. 1 square mile, whose boundaries are indicated by 4 main streets. On the west is West Dr., the north is an extension of 79th St., the east is East Dr., and the south is an extension of 72nd St. The Lake, as it is labeled on the map, lines the west end of the Rambles.

As I venture into this area, I'm immediately aware of an increasing density of trees and brush that line the path. The tall branches and thick green brush create a feeling of isolation and enclosure from the rest of the park. It's as if I've stepped outside the chattering chaos of the mainstream and entered into a dark, mystical "otherworld" reminiscent of a Sherwood Forest from the tales of Robin Hood.

It's almost paradoxical how each of my "6" senses are aroused and come to a conscious forefront as I leave the bombardment of random energy and enter into more subtle stimuli. It's the scream of silence that has my ears ringing. It's the cast of shadows that scintillate my eyes. As I venture further down the main trail something catches my attention. It's not something I see or hear but rather the absence of some element I might expect to find in a park. Since veering east on the path into the Rambles I haven't seen the smiles or heard the laughter of any children.

There are no children at all in this area. Another interesting dynamic in the population of this area, of all the couples I now see sitting on benches or walking together holding hands, nearly everyone is with same-sex partners. Even more interesting to me is the ratio of male couples to female couples. After walking about a mile I've seen both male and female couples.

Toward the east end of the Rambles I see an empty bench and decide to sit down awhile, jot down some notes, and continue my observations from a stationary position. As I scan the area I notice that I am not the only man sitting alone on a bench. Just like the trails outside the Rambles, benches lie about every twenty feet. On the four different benches I can see from where I sit, three are occupied by single men only, while on the other is a male/male couple. At the moment, this doesn't strike me as particularly significant. However, I will soon enough learn the symbolism of this subtle gesture.

I'm not sitting down more than two or three minutes when a young (mid-twenties) man in tight blue jeans, worker boots, and a tight gray tank top walks past me. As he walks by, he is staring directly into my eyes. Feeling uncomfortable, I do what I think is appropriate and say, "What's up?" Without saying a word, he continues walking past me. I watch him to see what he's about. He walks twenty feet and sits down on a bench by himself. The most striking thing about this guy to me is not the way he is behaving but rather what he is wearing.

I have on a sweatshirt and sock hat, while this guy is wearing a tank top. The sun is hidden behind a veil of thick gray clouds, and this guy is dressed like he is impervious to the cold. I look away from him for a few minutes to write some more notes when I notice, from the corner of my eye, someone sitting about three feet away from me on this bench. I glance up for a moment to see this same man in the gray tank top burning holes in the side of my head with his eyes. Unsure of how I should respond, I go on writing in my journal, pretending not to notice him. I do, however, note the time on my watch: 4:40 p.m.

After exactly ten minutes of staring at me, this man gets up slowly and walks away. I look up momentarily and catch him looking back at me. My senses told me that he clearly wanted something from me, but I was unwilling, at this point, to engage in any interaction with him that would allow me to find out exactly what it was he wanted. I was honestly unsure of my feelings at this point because the idea of another man possibly making sexual advances toward me is an experience that is new to me.

Parts of me want to tell this guy to "fuck off" and not be bothered, other parts are curious to see how far he is willing to go to pursue me, and even other parts are actually afraid of how far he may be willing to go to pursue me. Feeling more comfortable on my feet and on the move, I wander southeast back toward the lake. In my wanderings I have no destination in mind, so I begin to take random, less-traveled paths that lead into the foliage and toward the water's edge. It is on these thin, windy paths that I notice the residues of some kind of clandestine activities that must take place in this area.

Everywhere I look are used condoms and opened condom wrappers scattered along the ground on the paths and in the bushes. Suddenly I hear a rustling behind a bush about five feet to my left. I feel my heart stop. Is it a big rat? Is it a couple of big rats? Slowly I approach the bush to investigate the sounds I'm hearing. Maybe I shouldn't, but my curiosity is piqued. Perhaps the trail of clues I followed to this point should have made me more prepared for what I was about to find. Behind the bush was an older man (fifties or sixties) wearing nothing more than bikini underwear and locked in an intimate embrace with a younger man (perhaps in his twenties), who at this point was still fully clothed.

The nature of what they were engaged in appeared obvious in my mind, so I definitely didn't want to further encroach on what I felt should be a private moment (whether my presence would have been welcome or not). So I continued down the trail.

The time now is five o'clock, and I find myself standing on the banks of the lake, looking out at a boathouse dock. "I'm coming down. Are you going to catch me?" I hear a voice squeal from up on the bank. Unsure if I'm the object of this question, I pretend to ignore it. The voice continues on, "Well, here I come anyway!" At this point, I look up and see a six-foot-tall, bald, skinny, white man in a dark sweat suit and rollerblades come rolling down the embankment right at me.

"So how's your story coming?" he asks.

I'm totally taken aback by the question, "What are you talking about?"

"I saw you writing in that little book. Are you writing a story or a play or something?"

"Oh you saw me, huh? Well, I'm just kind of checking out the scene and writing some notes. I'm not exactly sure what I want to do with them."

"So in other words, mind my own business."

"Naw, it's not like that. I just really don't exactly know how I want to use these notes. Maybe I will put them together and write a story, or maybe I'll write a play. Maybe you could be the main character."

"That could be interesting . . . are you here cruising?"

"What does that mean?" I asked, feeling a bit naive.

"Are you cruising for a man? That is what this place is here for," he responded in a frank, matter-of-fact tone.

Further playing the role of the naive observer, I asked, "Is that what you are here for?"

"Hell yes! Want to show me something?"

Trying to retain my composure in this situation was a formidable task, but I remained calm.

"Nah, but maybe you could tell me some things about this area, anyway."

"If you are here to talk or for a relationship this is the wrong place, because people come here to *fuck* and to have fun."

The directness of his language and the bold way he spoke of sex made me feel somewhat violated and uncomfortable. "When you say 'place,' are you talking about the Rambles in general or what?"

"Well the Rambles is a big area, more specifically this peninsula. When my friends say they are going to the Rambles, they are talking about coming to this peninsula to fuck."

"So, how do you know to come here? How do you know that this is a place to do that versus some other place in the park?"

"Just look at the signs."

"Like what kind of signs?"

"Single men sitting alone or cruising the same trails over and over by themselves."

"So, how would you let someone know that you wanted to have sex with them?" I asked, almost scared to hear the answer.

"Just do this!" He leaned back and grabbed his crotch. "Or just stare him in the eye and touch yourself somewhere, or even touch him."

"So, if I was sitting on a bench by myself and another man came and sat next to me and just stared at me for ten minutes straight, I could take that to mean he wants to have sex with me?"

"Of course, that's him making his move, and then it's your turn to respond if you're interested. So, are you sure you're not interested?" he said, as he flashed me what I assume was supposed to be a seductive smile.

"Well, hey, I want to thank you for talking to me. I definitely think you could be good material for a story. Maybe I'll see you here again sometime."

"I sure hope so. I'm here all the time. Now that it's getting dark I better get busy finding myself another man."

Despite the need or the desire to know the other, the stranger, it becomes impossible to know everyone—there are just too many people to know. So how can my contacts and I know the people we meet more intimately, without access to their biographical information? I thought one way was to glean information by gazing at them—to closely observe their appearance. But the interplay of gazes and glances involves a wealth of rules to be observed and transgressed, and this visual aspect of city sexuality is no more vividly exemplified than at places like the Cock or the Rambles scene.

The "gaze" theories drew their inspiration partly from "cruising" and how powerful the look/gaze might be if applied correctly. In a class I taught years later, I would advise my students on how to draw from and tap into this language of gazing and glancing. I discussed this in the context of a typology developed around the gaze. I argued there were three types of gazes noted so far in our research. They included "the casual gaze," which is to look and then quickly look away. The second is "the truncated stare gaze," a look of longer duration than the first but not as long as the third, which is "the obsessional gaze," in which the looker not only stares for a longer time but begins to imagine themselves in the position of the person being watched. That is, they imagine themselves either being the top or bottom in an S/M scene or the penetrated or penetrator in a live sexual outercourse event or intercourse situation.

These notes are invaluable for a number of reasons, including that they show how sex work has evolved so quickly over the past few decades. But what is most interesting is how new technology feeds into the way sex is done. This is certainly true of gay sex, particularly the Grindr phenomenon, which I believe was the template for future het/cishet apps like Tinder. In an interesting way, then, the literal mapping of queer desire—the creation of technology to organize and form sexual connections with others—was formative to the development of the same for heterosexual desire.

Dean, an ambitious young scholar from the gayborhood, provided me with an account of how the Grindr app works:

Well, you just have an app which allows you to tap into a person who lives in your area where you happen to be and you can find a person you are looking for by getting the information you want; black, white, Asian, tall, short, whatever you want. Then you tell the person where you are located, what street, bar, corner, or whatever, and you go to see that person. That's how it works, but you could be anywhere: a bathroom, bar, store, whatever and meet up with the person you want to have sex with. The picture you see is from the neck down. Sometimes people will say they don't want Black or they don't want white boys or they want little API [Asian/Pacific Islander, transgender variant] or something like that. And you hook up with that person.

In the past chapters, I consider what kinds of societal messages about sexually active homo/queer/cisgender and heterosexual women and men are revealed and constructed by the architecture of sex clubs and other spaces. Erving Goffman recognized the import of spatial or space dynamics, and throughout his work we see the connection between space, power, and knowledge. At the same time, the politics of space is always sexual, as one voyeur put it, even if space is central to the mechanisms of the erasure of sexuality. I began to see "perverse" spaces as Goffmanian "stages" where the action or performance happens both at the front and back stage. "Successful performances are when individuals demonstrate their conviction that what is enacted is the real reality" while sustaining a viable "front," Goffman writes. This "front comprises stage props and appropriate facial expressions and role attitudes. Successful performances are staged not by individuals but by teams, who share both risk and discreditable information in a manner comparable to that of a secret society."[3] I am reminded of Dwight McBride when he writes about Blatino genres:

> Generally speaking, in the all-black genre and in the blatino genre, black men are represented as "trade": men with hard bodies and hard personalities to match them, men from or tied to ghetto or street life one way or another, men possessing exceptionally large penises (with few exceptions for the rare black bottom man—the passive sexual partner in sexual intercourse), and, more often than not, men as sexual predators or aggressors. Both the all-black genre and the blatino genre provide prurient consumers a glimpse into the fetishistic world of racial blackness.[4]

CONTACT: DEAN, URGE (2006)

Dean is half Filipino/Chinese, a very funny human being, quick-tongued and well dressed. He is what is called a "clothes horse," but he laughed at that description and said he would rather be called a "super twinkie." He speaks with a lisp and considers himself a "bohemian Queen with exaggerated gestures." But for Dean to pretend to be anything but himself suggests that "the sacred constructions of silence are futile exercises in denial. We will not go away with our issues of sexuality. We are coming home."[5] He said he has been "out" since he was two. He turned twenty-four last year. He writes:

> Gay bars are always different from straight bars because sex is so much more up front. The reason for this is that guys in general are straightforward in terms of sexuality, and when guys use their "dicks" to do their thinking, everything becomes sexual, and this situation explodes when the bar is full of guys. In places like Urge and the Cock, the only way to attract a crowd is to use "sex" and hot male bodies. These are just commonsense theories. Others believe men are trained to be "active" when it comes to pursuing sex.
>
> Guys tend to be more up front with their desires, while women are traditionally trained to be a bit more reserved. Put another way, men think about sex first, while women think about a relationship first. Of course, this is not all men or all women but I would say most gay men think this way. That is how magazines portray the cultural standards. Look at the mainstream men

and women magazines, and their topics tell the story. *GQ* teaches men how to approach a woman, while *Cosmopolitan* sets up questionnaires on how to tell if your partner is interested in just sex or a real relationship.

Regardless, gay bars are straightforward with their publicity—sex, drag queens, and naked men, and there is no doubt that the popularity of "Urge" plays on these factors, and "Ass Wednesday" is second to Splash's "Men on Men" evening.

According to its website, Urge is a "spacious and friendly East Village lounge with huge two-tier center bar, comfy nooks to frolic in, nightly DJs, cut bartenders, plasma televisions, go-go boys, game shows, drag performances." The description is pretty accurate, and they contain all these elements, and tonight's mission is to check out one of its most popular contests, and I indeed went to two different showings, so this field note is a combination of both occasions. So what is "Ass Wednesday"? Ass Wednesday is "a hilarious show where the greatest ass wins $100 cash and $75 worth of drinks and games." Well, the cash is not that attractive, but it is a good fun show to get the crowd rowdy and change this typically quiet midweek into a crowded space.

I arrived at "Urge" around midnight, because not much usually took place earlier, and I did not want to be wasted before the show. A couple of friends had already arrived at the place, after a very frustrated cab ride to Urge, as it is located in a very difficult location, Second Avenue and Second Street. (There is also a not-so-convenient subway stop a couple of blocks away.) Located in the so-called "sleazy" bar row, next to the famous Cock, the success of Urge is based on a number of factors.

First, Urge is designed to cater to a classier crowd, the so-called Chelsea crowd, who has more money to spend, and second, Urge aims for the hipper and the so-called yuppie crowd, and everything is trendier—plasma TV and nicer sofas, silver-coated furniture, and most importantly, Cock is situated next door and has a different kind of reputation, even after the major "clean-up" efforts and a change of location, as both the gangs and police are attacking the bar back and front.

Urge needs to differentiate from its main competitor and people who want cheaper drinks and hookups will go next door. It may also be a reflection of the so-called normalization of gay desires or even a "hetero-sexualization," or simply a following of the mainstream society, in which sex continues to push into private spaces and desire of gay men to not be seen as hypersexual.

Of course, the tension lies in the determination of what is too much sex and what is too little. The entrance of Urge is actually very low key, with only a very simple neon sign of the four-letter-word URGE. Second Avenue is really quiet at midweek, with only a few folks smoking outdoors. The doorman does not even check my ID and give us a friendly smile.

Once you enter and pass through a curtain, you enter a very different space. There is a large lounging area with a few comfortable seating areas with small drinking tables with candles. That area is usually reserved for couples who have either just met or are long-time things. They are usually less in the looking mode but staring into each other's eyes. The color of burgundy decorates most of the walls, along with pictures of various naked men, who I assume were the go-go boys featured in the lounge.

This is more artistic nude male photography, very reserved poses, and no penis is shown. The focus seems to be on the ass, and the male bodies featured there are different from the twinks depicted at Pieces [another bar]; they are the more muscled, Chelsea type. They are also a bit older than the barely legal twinks and are in their twenties and early thirties. After passing the sofa area, one reaches the so-called two-tiered bar. The bar is basically a rectangular structure, with half of it raised up a level toward the left side. The design is interesting because the folks in the raised level can basically stare down onto the guys in the lower level, and that creates an interesting visual aspect. There is almost a feeling that the guys in the lower level are being checked out and that the guys in the upper level will approach you if they want to. Of course in the upper level, it provides a better view of the stage and also the really comfortable sofa area up front.

Then I noticed an average-looking white man with a cute beard sitting alone on the side of the lower bar, and he started first on the frontal seating area and then slowly moved to the bar, once he saw an opening. He quietly sipped his vodka cranberry, and while in contrast, there was a rowdy group of white men in their thirties in the raised level about three seats from this guy. Those men had been quite loud throughout the evening. I called them the "rowdy blonde group." One of them had shoulder-length blonde hair wearing a linen shirt, along with a couple of his friends in T-shirts and short hair. They were drinking, and then they noticed this guy quietly looking around.

Then this blonde guy just looked at him, and signaled him to join them, and said, "Hi honey, what is your name?" This shy guy of course responded, walked up to their level, and began their brief chats. The majority of the patrons in Urge is undoubtedly white, Chelsea/East Village types with some money to spend, dressed mostly preppy: a jacket with a polo T-shirt or T-shirt and a pair of brand-name jeans. There are a few folks in their suits and ties, who came straight after work, and the corporate type (that I am strangely attracted to).

In terms of people of color, there are a few black men, who are also Chelsea types and a bit more feminine or bohemian. There are also a few Chelsea-type gym bunnies, as well as a few Asians in the crowd. Asian patrons are commonly found in all these gay spaces, sleazy or not, but interestingly, they are not always on the stage or employed as workers, whether as go-go boys or bartenders, except in gay Asian bars. Women patrons are similar to other bars, mostly so-called fag hags, and there are usually three to four of them every evening. They seem to be at ease with the bar and have tons of fun.

There are two bartenders: Frankie and Juan. Frankie is a white guy with a beard; he wears a very casual T-shirt and does not serve our area. Juan, on the other hand, is a very handsome Latino guy. Despite his shorter height, his face is just beautiful, with a pair of big brown eyes and very nicely cropped hair. His body is a bit stocky from the biceps bulging in his arms, and since he is a friend of Jesse, the bartender at Pieces, we get some attention from him and at least some stronger drinks.

Throughout the evening, there are two go-go boys working, and they take shifts. On a busy night, both bartenders will be working at the same time, but only on the weekends. The two go-go boys are both Latino on this particular evening, and they are both very chiseled with a wide chest and a perfect six-pack. They emphasize their ass by wearing the tiniest bikini thongs available. One of them made a very strong impression because he did not just walk around the bar shaking his ass but actually laid on the bar and moved his ass toward the patron's face. Of course, his acrobatic skill is amazing because he does not have much space to maneuver and basically has to move his legs without hitting your face, and therefore he wore knee pads.

However, some folks find this "ass in your face" too aggressive and almost too vulgar. One of the guys was chatting with his friend; they were laughing but all of a sudden there is this ass in their faces, and both give out a yucky look. "That is a bit too much, honey! You are so cute, but excuse me, we are talking!" Then when the go-go boy moves away, they said, "Okay, that is a turn off more than a turn on. Shoving his ass to my face definitely will not get my singles."

But then as the go-go boy moved toward an older couple sitting next to me, they took notice of his rounded ass and gave him a single, asking, "What is your name, honey?" Of course, as most white people think it is appropriate to ask whenever they met a person of color, this white-haired white guy gave him a dirty look and put his hand toward his and asked, "Where are you from?" The go-go boy told him that he was from one of the Central American countries and then continued to shake his ass in front. However, I have to credit to this particular go-go boy for his creative technique and flexibility. Once again, go-go boys are definitely in demand in New York City. Away from the bar is another front area with more comfortable sofas and wider drink tables. Plasma televisions are hidden underneath the glass table tops, and different videos are played at those televisions. There is also a main projector screen in front of the stage, as well as on the right side of the bar and a few other locations.

On the main projector, music videos are shown and, on the bar, a softcore promotional video for Chi Chi La Rue's Love and Raw Internet Live Show. Chi Chi La Rue is the king/queen of the gay porn industry and a famous drag queen/gay porn director; she produces hundreds of videos, and no one in the gay circuit does not know her and watch her videos. However, on those hidden televisions at the sofa area, hardcore pornography films are shown after midnight. Yes, they did not cut out anything.

There is no law banning bars from playing triple XXX videos, but most bars won't do it because that really attracts cruising, which will get them into troubles with the authorities and will create a different reputation for their bars. Despite being hidden, Urge definitely has a very strong sexual content. There are about five and six sets of sofas with a good view of the stage. Thankfully our big group of friends has already occupied one of these sofa areas, and at this time, the Divine Gusty Winds made an announcement from the bar, "Hi bitches, welcome to Ass Wednesday, and the show will begin in a few more moments."

"So far we only have three contestants, and you know I like to divide my boys into pairs so I can lick two asses at the same time. Hi honey, what's your name? You are very cute, and I know you want to join the contest. Right? I swear I will be nice. Don't worry! No one will see your penis, which I am sure will be a decent size. Okay anyway, folks, I still need one more contestant, and the winner can take home $100 cash."

The MC is the Divine Gusty Winds, and she is typically a drag queen. She is a big gal and wears a giant wig. She is extremely witty—and also mean. She wears exaggerated makeup and a low-cut dress. She begins the show with her typical monologue and tries to get a fourth contestant. She then looks to see who in the crowd she can tease. Her first target is "Nathan," a straight guy sitting in the front. "Hi, cute boy, how are you, and what is your name?" Because it is almost impossible to hear what the guy says, we only get the information from Gusty Winds. "Oh your name is Nathan, and do you want to join our contest? What . . . you are straight? Honey, what are you doing in a gay bar? Oh, your friends are gay and are you sure? You are sure that you don't want it up your ass or some tight ass to fuck? What? Okay, what are you drinking? Oh, Stella—then you *are* straight! But have you ever been orally serviced by a clown? I can give you a blow job in the bathroom later." Then Gusty Winds notices a lady. "Hi, sweetheart, what are you doing in a gay bar? Are you sure your boyfriend is straight? What is your name? Meghan? Morgan? Does not matter, anyway, I will forget it later! What? Are there any other women in the bar? Are you a lesbian? Well, not really honey, unless you count me as one of them. I certainly have the breasts and the makeup, and if you don't count . . ."

It is interesting how Gusty Winds divides the contestants. Both groups contain one white guy and one black guy. The first contestant is an African American male, Sean, who has a very slim build, but his ass is very firm and rounded, which is no surprise because he is a modern dancer. The second contestant, Josh, is white. After more raunchy jokes directed both at the contestants and the straight people in the crowd singled out earlier, Gusty Winds asks, "Who likes Sean's ass better?" and then "Who likes Josh's ass better?" The result was predictable. Josh wins the first round, as he showed off lots of skin and was not shy. He was also cuter and more masculine.

The third contestant is Kevin, a computer technician. Unlike Josh, Kevin is a shy and tense on stage. Gusty asks him to take off his shirt, but he chooses to keep it on. I think that really lowers his chances to win, and then he drops his pants and shows a pair of pale ass cheeks. The crowd is not particularly impressed. Then there is the last contestant, Patrick. He is a bit on the feminine side with a slim physique; he is cuter than Sean, but his body is not as sculpted. In this pair, Patrick won by a landslide.

The final round is between Josh and Patrick, and once again, Gusty Winds asks both of them to take off their shirts. Patrick reveals a decent but not as sculpted body (even compared to Sean). However, the focus is on the "ass." They both drop their pants, and the reaction of the crowd is actually quite interesting. In some way, Josh seemed to win by a clear margin, but then Gusty Winds just said, "Something is not right here. Let do this again!" Gusty Winds definitely has the power to change the result, which brings me to an interesting question. Do their races have anything to do with results? Does Patrick lose more votes because of his slightly effeminate trait or because he is Black? Gusty Winds's reaction caught me off guard: she obviously thought that both asses looked good, and Patrick's was more firm and rounded.

The ultimate question is: Does race matter when it comes to beauty? The two black men really do not follow that Hollywood ideal of beefy muscled men, and they are rather slim (despite toned and firm), compared to the two white men. Or is this not about race but simply a manifestation of the classic question in the gay world: Is being effeminate considered a lower breed? Reading my notes, I notice that I differentiate between masculine and effeminate gay men, and I will be candid: I like more macho-looking men, at least not sissies. Perhaps I consider myself more as a bottom and lack a strong, secured figure, and, therefore, my attraction leans toward a stronger masculine person, but at the same time, I want someone who is also sensitive, and this top/bottom, masculine/feminine label really bothers me.

There is a trend that a gay man just wants to meet an average person, not overly macho and not overly feminine, and perhaps to try to beat the stereotypes that gay men are like women. However, that sentiment also reveals the hostility towards sissy or effeminate men. Somehow the sexist notion appears here—feminine traits seem to equal being weak. From the thirties on, some gay men blame the drag queens and fairies (gays) as giving homosexuality a bad name and thereby causing the police raids and repressions.

The third reason is the simple fact that Josh has a really hot body and a somewhat outgoing and confident appeal. He knows what he is doing and makes the crowd really like him. Nevertheless, I feel that race and level of effeminacy have something to do with the crowd's reaction. Gusty Winds seems to feel that the crowd had not given appropriate appreciation to Patrick. Or perhaps Gusty wants both contestants to feel good about the whole experience.

At the end of this accidental black-versus-white contest, the races break even. I still can't help feel that a bit of racial dynamics are playing out here. Finally, Gusty Winds decides she will split the prize equally between the two contestants. Each get $50, and, interestingly, Josh gives Patrick a kiss on the cheek and a big hug.

The evening pretty much ended after the show. It was a weeknight, so the venue died down a bit. The go-go boy was back at the bar dancing for a few folks, who were still interested, but the front sofa area cleared out quickly. Gusty Winds did a final number, another classic song, and then passed around her bucket for tips. Most people gave her something. I like Gusty Winds better than Vodka Stingers at Pieces, but nothing beats Paulina and the Japanese bitch at Lucky Cheng.

Of course, as a "fattie," my problem with the lounge is with some of the more unwelcome looks I get in the bar, but New York has nothing as bad as the situation in Hong Kong and in gay Asian bars, where I am judged head to toe. One thing is certain: gay male bodies are under lots of scrutiny, and it is surprising that relatively few authors have written about it and the standard of beauty within the gay world. Ass Wednesdays provide a good platform to observe what bodies are really desirable these days. We are still stuck with Brad Pitt and the Hollywood type—white, tall, masculine, broad and firm chest, six pack, a small waist, tree-trunk thighs, and a pair of legs showing off your strong calves. The ideal weight is getting lower, but you are still expected to retain some muscles. Of course, gay men are held to nothing as extreme as the ideal female bodies—thin waist, big breasts, and firm and round buttocks— but the ideal gay male body is also getting harder to achieve. It is hard to gain much muscle while retaining a decent waist size.

Of course, men still have more freedom, and even within the gay world, there are different body types—bears (big hairy men), twinks (young skinny boys), All-American types (Brad Pitt), and muscle men (really built)—but everyone seems to have to adopt a particular body type in order to be accepted. The Chelsea Boy body is difficult to maintain and requires lots of gym time. I suddenly realize that more things need to be written about body images among gay men and how they are also under constant pressure to lose weight and to go to the gym.

Finally, I want to clarify that Urge is not a sex venue, and not every evening is like Ass Wednesday. There are go-go boys every evening, but only after midnight, so the lounge itself can be a place to chill out normally. Ass Wednesdays just provide another reason to sell the lounge on a typically slow night and to get the crowd more cheery and more willing to buy drinks. But Ass Wednesdays are somehow closer to real life in some way, by reflecting desires in a more spontaneous form—something that is not carefully planned and also less intense. Of course, one can argue that some of these contestants may want to show off their heavily gym-trained bodies, but at least when they shake their ass, they are not aiming to get tips from people.

They are also mostly gay and not "gay for pay." Sex can be really "sexy" and a major "turn on" without complete nudity. Everyday sexuality doesn't need to be that extreme. I actually recommend Urge's Ass Wednesdays as a beginning activity to check out the gay circuits and to get a different feeling or perhaps a less professional, but more amateur, fun.

We'll return to the question raised in the previous field note: do Ass Wednesdays make Urge a bit "perverse"? The event sells nearly naked bodies and uses sex to sell alcohol, but compared to Pieces, it is a bit less perverse in a sense, as the nakedness is definitely controlled. The Jell-O shot wrestling at Pieces, by contrast, turns a regular neighborhood bar into a very sexually charged space.

CONTACT: PAUL, PIECES (2006)

Paul is twenty-six, a short and stocky light-skinned Black man who speaks slowly and with a measured, professional cadence, as if he's worked in radio or television. What makes a space "perverse"? Is it the secrecy? The explicit sex? The nudity? The privileging of dominance and submission? The sense of human rationality going out of control? Or simply the permission to let desire take over all our other senses?

Pieces is not a strip joint or a go-go-boy venues but a neighborhood bar located in Greenwich Village. It is in its fourteenth year and describes itself on its website thus: "Start with a friendly atmosphere, hot sexxxxy staff, lots of 'B' lights and decorations, current and classic music, big drinks for cheap prices mixed by the best bartenders and add the most fabulous clientele in NYC and you've got Pieces!" Paul says:

> What is great about Pieces is its casualness and the friendly bartenders, and this bar is definitely different from the competitive and intense clubbing scenes in Chelsea. Normally, this place is just a chill-out space with not much to write about, but tonight, it is the Spring Fling evening, which is to celebrate the beginning of spring and an imagined return to the fraternity house and college days. The majority of the clientele is in their middle ages, and those fraternity days are long gone, so the arrival of spring is an excuse to return to those days and imagine a better version of it.

Will these explicit sexual elements transform this normal bar space into a "perverse" space, in the spirit of Spring Break (in which America's youth indulges in excessive alcohol, drugs, and sex in warm tropical places)? Paul continues:

> Unlike normal times, nobody was smoking outside Pieces, as it was raining dogs and cats, but it also reflected the smaller crowd today. I was a bit worried about the last-minute cancellation of the Spring Fling, but thankfully, things continued, but just on "gay standard time" (9 p.m. = 11 p.m.).
>
> As I entered the bar hurriedly around 10 p.m., not much was happening in the bar. Not even all the stools are occupied, and the bartenders, Jesse and Roy, were chatting among themselves. Pieces is not really a huge place, and its décor remains very basic, and indeed not much to discuss. The walls were dark, and only some dimmed neon lights and a few Christmas lights surrounded the side, and the reflection from the TV showing a COLT [a famous pornography video brand] promotional video added a few shades of lights. Dimmed lighting is almost a universal theme among bars and clubs, and the effect is to add a particular mysterious visage to each person, perhaps to create a more secretive identity among patrons or simply to make a person look more attractive. It also reiterates the theme of "secrecy" in a perverse space.
>
> Pieces is a very simple bar. You will immediately see a small front lounge area, and on the left-hand side, the main focus, a long bar with the typical showcase of liquor bottles and bar stools. Most of the clients mingle in that area, especially the single ones. The bartenders stand behind the bar all night

long, and then further down, there is a serving area connected to the bar for the waiter.

At the end of the bar is an ATM and a games machine, which features puzzles, matching, slingo, and all those simple computer games that cost additional money. Further back is the DJ booth, followed by the back entrance. On the right side after the main entrance is a security guard station and a coatroom leading to staircases heading to downstairs office and storage. Then there is another main open area that features a really small stage, for two to three people at most, and then a pool table in front occupying the center area that can moved toward the side if there is a bigger show, like today. The bathroom is rather large, but its design prevents any backdoor and/or cruising activities. There are two urinals, which have a tall separator, and only one toilet stall. The door is always open, and the lights are dim but sufficient enough to discourage any public sex.

When I arrived around 10 p.m., it was pouring quite heavily, and the entrance was quite slippery. The security guy [Bobby] and the coat-check guy were chatting among themselves and did not even bother checking my ID. There are few clients in the stool area and a pretty loud table in the back area, close to the pool table. They have been here for a while, apparently. In general, the clients at Pieces are a bit older. The atmosphere was really a bit more cozy and relaxing, and not many people were wearing extremely flashy clothes. The average age is almost thirty-five to forty-five. There are a couple of older guys sitting in the bar and wandering around slowly. There is a guy that is obviously in his early sixties with a balding head, and the rest of his hair is white. He wears a sweater and a pair of trousers with a hat. He seems to do alright financially, as he keeps a very clean appearance, but the fact that he does not use the "complimentary" coat-check service and is carrying a Duane Reade bag around suggests that he is a bit on the frugal side.

He is also a bit on the heavy side, weight wise, but is obviously here for a drink and not to stare at the younger crowd. A man also in his late fifties or early sixties sat in the bar and wore all black. A few of his friends, in a similar age group, arrived, and they stayed throughout the evening. They had a few beers and chatted among themselves. They also did not bother to wander up toward the Jell-O wrestling pool later on. I did not think that they were uninterested in seeing the young guys wrestling, as they were pretty happy tipping the go-go boys later. Maybe it was just too much effort to move toward the center to see some amateur wrestling.

Another characteristic of Pieces that Paul noted was the diverse crowd:

There are always a number of African Americans and Asians mingled around. I have to say that the gay circuit is often heavily segregated, and I have only seen some Black guys in gay Asian bars before. Even in big-name venues like Splash and Cock, people of color do not appear much, not to mention the mingling that takes place therein. Here, unlike in those other spaces, Black, Asian, and some Latino clients actually will mingle with the mostly white bartenders and with the "loyal" customers.

Paul speaks about one of the regulars at the club, David:

David, a loyal customer, is a thirtysomething Asian man. He is pretty tall and big, as he used to do bodybuilding. He has spiky hair, and everyone at

9.3 Party at Limelight, on Sixth Avenue and Twentieth Street, 1990.
From the hellfirepress.com archive.

Pieces know him. If there is a "Mr. Congeniality" contest, David will win hands down. One of the co-owners was very fond of him, and the bartenders all give him free drinks. He is now back at school, so no longer comes every day, but every Tuesday, Friday, Saturday, and Sunday, David is always there at least during happy hour. Throughout the special event, he carried his digital camera around and took lots of pictures of the wrestling contest. He was almost like a staff person, but there were also times that I felt that he needed this place to reaffirm his presence.

As David and I were saying hello, a short and rather feminine guy, Tim, squeezed between us and interrupted our conversation. I found that to be rude, but Tim apparently had a little crush on David. Tim is African American and wore a black tank top with jeans. He did not look particularly muscular or toned, but I guess that increases his appeal. He has really short hair, Afro style, and was a bit drunk. "Hi David, how are you? You know I love you!" He gave him a big smile and then turned to me. We shook hands, and he said, "I hope you don't mind me interrupting, but I just love David." Later in the evening, Tim got into a fight with Jesse, the angry bartender. David told Tim, "Oh honey, don't piss off Jesse or he can beat you up in a second." Tim replied, "But I was not drunk." David then smiled and looked at him directly, "Yes, you are drunk and you know it."

Another of David's friends, Danny, is a pretty attractive guy considering the lower standard in Pieces. He is a typical American fellow in his early thirties, wearing a very causal T-shirt, jeans, and a backpack. He is hairy and sports a beard, which makes him look more mature and also more masculine. You cannot tell that he is gay if you see him in a regular setting. He is quite friendly. Later another white guy, a bit more clean cut and wearing a nice sweater and jeans, walked over to him and asked him if he [Danny] was a friend of so and so. Then they started a conversation: a neat example of how Pieces is really defined as a neighborhood bar. Of course, there is a little caveat that this guy definitely is interested in Danny somewhat, but in Pieces people are able to recognize one another and have interesting conversations, which the loud music in Splash, XL, or other gay clubs make impossible.

Throughout the evening, people will ask one another, "Are you getting into the pool?" Even the bartenders and waiters said no. Finally around 10:30 p.m., the DJ brought out a giant inflatable pool with a blowup monkey, lobster, and three beach balls. The television was already blasting the gay or guy version of *Girls Gone Wild*, of course, this time, *Boys Gone Wild*, featuring many unknown young boys baring their soft penises. It was a bit boring to see fraternity or college boys getting drunk and high and doing some not-so-interesting silly things. There are better jerk-off solo videos of straight fraternity boys. The bartenders were fully disgusted by it but played this video repeatedly nevertheless.

At 11 p.m., the drag queen/MC, Vodka Stinger, finally ascended from the downstairs dressing area, followed by two go-go boys, Joseph and Shawn. The first item of business is to announce the Jell-O wrestling contest and that today's flavor is lemon, and then the second urgent item is to find participants, which is difficult, because as a patron told me, "This place is not straight frat houses and it is different from girls wrestling, and gay men generally don't care about Spring Break." Sweetening the deal was a hundred-dollar grand prize, which is, given the neighborhood, not a significant amount of money.

Then of course, there is the introduction of the two go-go boys, who look like identical twinks. "Twinks" refers to boys who typically look very young and have really slim bodies. Vodka Stinger asked folks to buy them drinks and slip them money, as they will be dancing all night long.

As one of the go-go boys walked by, David immediately yelled out, "Hi Shawn, long time no see!" Shawn just waved back and moved along; crowd was quite large by now. David also added, "Well the rumor that I know most of the go-go boys in New York City is still wrong, and I know Shawn because he used to be a bartender at Pieces. Jesse was hired to replace him back then. I guess he was demoted from bartender to go-go boy now."

This brief conversation highlights, first, how gay bars develop a loyal following, like straight, lesbian, or transgender bars do; second, that people notice the coming and going of people and that most customers develop a real relationship with the bartenders, which is how loyal customers also feel obligated to pay more money. Third, the bartender actually needs to be quite a versatile position, and the main criterion is their attractiveness in gay bars. They can be a bartender one minute and then stripped to their underwear a minute later.

There are four bartenders in Pieces that rotate from day to day, and the ones present tonight are Jesse and Roy. Jesse is a white man obviously a bit younger than the main clientele. He has been in the bartender circuit for a while and has participated in various bartending competitions before. He is quite attractive. He is of average height and is slim. He is not quite a twink because he is not particularly feminine. He is also quite an angry young man and has had two major fights with customers. David said that he had anger-management issues, not uncommon among some young men.

Roy is a bit older than the average worker in Pieces and features bigger muscles, a beard, and a more masculine presence. There is a rumor about Roy's sexual orientation, and most people think he is straight. I don't know and honestly don't really care. He is a direct import from Ireland and is also quite slim. He has a very handsome and also hard face, that ex-army look. He is a quiet bartender and new to Pieces. He is even-tempered but has that "don't mess with me" or "don't make me angry" look.

Other staff members include Rafael, who is a runner waiter and also does all the undesirable tasks, like sweeping the floor after the contest. He is a skinny boy but quite tall. He wears a pretty revealing tank top and knows most of the clients well. Then there is DJ Jason, who is a bigger and hairier man, different from the slim types there. He always has a big grin on him, and he stays put in the DJ booth. The DJ booth is a room in the back, and yes, you can see the DJ spinning his records there, but most of the time, you only make out Jason's dark shadow. Sometimes Ricky, the co-owner, sits there. Despite Jason's claims that no sexual activities take place there, like with President Clinton, oral sex apparently also does not count as a sexual activity in the DJ booth. It is well known that Jason receives such services from a loyal patron in the back.

Shawn was an ex-bartender, but tonight he truly shines as an "out-of-control" go-go boy. First, he reluctantly joined the Jell-O wrestling contest, and second, he moved his hips like nobody before and really made the crowd move. Both Joseph and Shawn are scarily all-American twinky boys. Their first outfit involved a pair of boy-sized white underwear featuring some graphics, and then a pair of dark-rimmed glasses, as well as a collar (just the collar) of a schoolboy shirt with a tie.

Joseph wears a more traditional striped tie, and Shawn has this Disney tie around his neck. Their skin is extremely pale. Their small pink nipples really stand out, and both have a flat stomach but not much chest to talk about. They are almost hairless in their upper bodies and really look like fifteen-year-old schoolboys. The crowd was completely in an uproar as they watch these two young boys grinding each other.

I will argue that the hundred dollars of prize money is only little additional incentive, and most people who participate in these contests know what they are getting into and have a "show off" mentality. They are proud of their bodies and looks, and their primary goal is getting the attention and praise. Vodka Stinger was really good because she had already caught attention of this relatively cute fellow in the front of the lounge area. He was already somewhat drunk, and a few words of praise were enough for her to drag him to the backstage area.

The wrestling is really simple: four patrons divided into two teams. They wrestle in pairs, and then the winner moves on to the final round. The rules are no biting, no Jell-O outside of the pool (which is not working), and that since this contest is meant to be erotic, don't be too rough on each other. The crowd got worked up very quickly after the first match began. Both Auggie and Edward, the first two contestants, started out squeamish, but Vodka Stinger just walked into the pool. "Boys, just come on in and get it over with. I am getting my thousand-dollar shoes wet with Jell-O. You guys don't have any excuse."

The contestants were dressed only in white underwear, with a bit of padding in the frontal area. Auggie was already in a "sumo wrestling" position, like a big ape ready to take down his opponent. He made funny faces and knew what to do in order to please the crowd. Edward was a bit more reserved at first, as if unsure about what was happening. Then both immediately slipped and fell over. I kept screaming because it looked like it hurt to fall; the Jell-O was really slippery. Soon, their underwear was wet and their asses visible.

Edward was almost always under Auggie, as Auggie was the taller and stronger one. Then the first round was over after about a minute. The Jell-O was flying all over the place, and Vodka Stinger reiterated that this was not supposed to be a real wrestling match. "Make it more sensual, okay boys?" The second round was a less fierce and more erotic. Soon Auggie was under Edward, and Edward pretended to be riding Auggie, and Auggie played along by moaning.

Soon Auggie was in the doggie position, and the crowd was really cheering on. I really don't know what the criteria for determining the winner was. The second round ended soon, and then the second pair appeared. The second match was between Johan, a big guy whose day job was as a director of sales, and Shawn, the go-go boy. Shawn had been pushed into this wrestling match last minute. He was removing his collar and taking off his socks and shoes.

The fragrance of the lemon started to permeate the place, which mixed well with the popular vodka and gin drinks at the bar. Johan and Shawn were definitely more aggressive, with Shawn very determined to resist Johan's massive attack. They immediately rolled into the mess and got their hair all wet; then Johan tried to pull Shawn's underwear down. Honestly it did not make much difference, as they were transparent pretty much once they hit the Jell-O. The pool was slippery, and Johan's slightly large build played to his disadvantage. They tried to sex it up at the end, and it was interesting to see that Johan spotted a hard-on. Shawn retained his cool, and the winners for the first round were Auggie and Shawn—not surprisingly the cuter ones. But the runners up got $20 each as a consolation prize. Better than nothing, but not enough for anyone to get in that nasty pool.

The final match between Auggie and Shawn was more interesting, as the sexual tension was quite high. Auggie was at first caught off guard by Shawn's aggressiveness. He had not watched the second match between Johan and Shawn, but Shawn's slightly smaller frame did not play to his advantage, as Auggie was definitely more flexible. After Shawn was under Auggie's control, the "fucking" motions returned, and both contestants actually got turned on. The shapes of their erect penises began to show through their padded underwear.

The blond boyfriend definitely saw that, and his facial expression was one of disgust. The second round began with more erotic energy in the air, but the rhythm was interrupted when Johan surprisingly came back out and jumped into the pool. That was a truly disgusting scene: three nearly naked men rolling around in a pool of lemon Jell-O. Vodka Stinger just said, "Oh my, oh my! Never did I see such hot men-to-men action here!" The judge finally announced Auggie the winner. Ricky, the co-owner, slipped five twenty-dollar bills into Auggie's underwear, which was still full of Jell-O.

Was I sexually turned on during the evening? I was a little bit turned on at first, when I spotted the ties, and during the final showdown between Auggie and Shawn, but nothing serious. Definitely not when I slipped a bill down Joseph's briefs! However, the key question remains: Does this wrestling transform Pieces into a slightly more perverse space?

The definition of "perverse" is still too broadly defined, and it is up to an individual's perspective to determine its exact coordinates. For a middle-American white person, Pieces is definitely a very queer space, and nothing is normal about the bar—except, perhaps, that the alcohol is the same whether in Billings, Montana, or Greenwich Village, New York. Yet from a gay perspective, Pieces is actually quite a non-perverse space. Yes, there are softcore pornography videos being played on the bar's TVs, and there are some secret blowjobs or hand jobs taking place. But the question raised in the preceding notes concerning the perversity of Pieces brings us closer to acknowledging its more conservative, conformist aspects. Paul reflects on this:

Nevertheless, the bar is pretty sexually undercharged, and at least the bartenders sort of keep their shirts on, unlike other clubs. (Just a side note, I later found out that bars can show hardcore XXX videos if they want to, but most bars and clubs don't because that send a signal that guys can fool around openly. When a triple XXX feature is shown, the bartenders literally had to stop guys from openly having sex, which is still illegal in the United States.)

Nevertheless, this wrestling contest is actually very erotic, more so than I have anticipated. Jell-O is slimy, but seeing men rolling around nearly naked can be quite a turn on. The public display of sex seems to add more perversity to the normally neighborhood-style bar. Moreover, the actors really got into the act, and their pretend sexual acts actually created an interesting effect. Yes, people were laughing and cheering on, but combining slimy Jell-O with interesting-looking guys is really perverse. There are explicit elements of sex, nakedness, and secrecy (sort of, as they happened in the back, and only loyal customers knew about this event in advance, but you can glean more information from the bar's website), and those normally reserved guys really went all out. Even Johan, our director of sales, all of a sudden jumped in between Shawn and Auggie.

That creates a comical effect and sort of lessens the sexual tensions, but at the same time, they are completely blown out of their minds. Of course, all those actors know that they are in a showy mode and proud to show their bodies in one way or the other. Auggie did not stay for the next contest because soon there was a big fight going on between his blond boyfriend and himself. It was clear that his boyfriend was not pleased with him rolling around with so many boys in the first place, and then the "erect" penis really bothered him, when he rolled around with Shawn, who was sort of attractive and did not resist Auggie's advances. After Auggie got cleaned up and changed, they stormed off.

Johan and his boyfriend seemed to be fine, but both of them followed them out. It was an interesting scene afterward. So what is fueling the fight here? Maybe it is natural to be mad if your boyfriend makes out with another guy in public. Likewise, two men rolling together would definitely create some tension, not to mention pretending to have sex. Maybe it is also the public display of his body, and Shawn did try to take off Auggie's underwear and vice versa. Perversity also crosses borders, and this Jell-O wrestling just crossed that border slightly.

Ricky is super-hot and a recent additional co-owner of Pieces, according to David. He joined the family about a year or so ago and is quite fond of David. Ricky is white, not so tall, and always has a big grin on his face. He pretty much smiles at every patron, and nobody minds, because Ricky is very handsome. His face is somewhat angular and has a very Eastern European look. His body, hugging a long-sleeve T-shirt, covers a pair of muscled arms and a very chiseled chest.

The final event was the hula-hoop event, and once again, there were not many contestants. Few had the thin waist to hula-hoop well, and some of the older patrons had passed their prime for doing these kinds of exercises. Therefore, it was show time for Ricky. The contest was relatively simple: you lost an item of clothing if you dropped the hoop. So it was practically a slow stripping show. I will add "stripping" to the element of creating perversity or at least increasing sexual attractiveness.

A naked body does not produce the fully eroticized effect if they just appear naked, but Ricky stripped piece by piece, sexual tensions immediately rose in the air, and things started to get interesting. Even a relatively average looking person can add eroticized energy into the air. Edward, Ricky's competitor, no longer created the effect on everyone because he had previously wrestled, but the moment Ricky took off the shirt, there was almost a riot in the room. His shy smile made him even more adorable.

His upper body was a beauty, not to mention the six-pack. Not an ounce of fat in this body, and every inch muscle. His hula-ing hip movements really showed off the asset hidden beneath his tight jeans. God knows what was hidden there—and it did not take long to find out. Ricky was definitely prepared: he was wearing a pair of tight animal-print swimming trunks.

It was not a Speedo but a square swimming trunk. The crowd was really worked up despite the persistent rain outside. Ricky is definitely a super hunk, and I don't think I can ever stop fantasizing about him. This Spring Fling evening was definitely a success.

Referencing George Chauncey's *Gay New York*, a gay social world can be created from all these parties and events, not only in a formal setting. Yes, you are not going to find lots of pretty boys here if you are looking for those gym-bodied Chelsea boys, but people here are interesting too in their own ways. Gay men display a strong will to create an affirming society. The Jell-O wrestling definitely leaves a mark in my head, and, yes, Pieces had a little fun this particular evening, as the patrons enjoyed the almost comical, sexually charged environment. Yes, Auggie left the place in a hurry, but he had an extra $100 in his pocket (I doubt that covered his tab). Though it triggered a fight with his blond boyfriend, I am sure he also had some fun rolling around in Jell-O and showing off his body.

Being reaffirmed by the crowd is more than a random complement. The cheer of the crowd definitely did its work. However, I still don't think Pieces is a particularly perverse place, but I don't see what is wrong for being a little "out of control" or "out of line." We are all sexual beings, and PDA is sort of cute at times. This evening definitely starts my spring in a rather good beat, but it will be better if I can hook up with Danny or Ricky. Dreams never quit, I guess!

chapter 10
The Future of the Soft City

L et's return to how we saw the Soft City at the beginning of our adventure, as a category born out of a desire to link all the disparate sex practices we were seeing. We came up with a working definition, and it remains so now, even after we have explored all the different sex situations the city has to offer. The Soft City is a process of imagining. The Soft City is an intellectual fantasy. This future world is meant to stay connected by unbounded imagination, pleasure, and desire.

Thirty-five years ago, when I first began working with this material, I envisioned this book as an interactive text and considered the role technology might play in it. In her book *Sex Media* (2018), the sociologist Feona Attwood points to the new role technology plays.

> Technology and space have also been reconfigured for sex in other ways. While buying and watching porn films was once carried out in designated shops and cinemas within urban sex zones, this kind of consumption has moved into people's homes through video, cable TV and the Internet. The Internet has become an important new space for sex in other ways—seen as a "sexual playground" by some and a "perilous vortex of danger" by others.[1]

But this is all changing, for the future is now. Look at what the Queer theorist Jose Esteban Muñoz proposes:

> Futurity can be a problem. Heterosexual culture depends on a notion of the future: as the song goes, "the children are our future." But that is not the

case for different cultures of sexual dissidence. Rather than invest in a deferred future, the queer citizen-subject labors to live in a present that is calibrated, through the protocols of state power, to sacrifice our liveness for what Lauren Berlant has called the "dead citizenship" of heterosexuality. This dead citizenship is formatted, in part, through the sacrifice of the present for a fantasmatic future. On oil dance floors, sites of public sex, various theatrical stages, music festivals, and arenas both subterranean and aboveground, queers live, labor, and enact queer worlds in the present.[2]

The Soft City offers the reader some purchase on this type of unknown world. In this book, the subject is the Soft City, built, fed, performed, and even defended by the individuals who need or wish to dwell in or return to the Soft City, whether driven by desire, greed, or necessity. The idea of the Soft City also alludes to a pleasant or welcoming core that rests beneath the "hard city" of violence and crime—or simply of work and responsibility. The Soft City is a place that opens at night, receiving anyone (at least anyone with the material means) who wants to have a good time—anyone that, because of the features of their preferences, is confined to these "perverse spaces" where they can unleash

10.1 Public sex drag march, c. 1999.

their most varied sexual appetites and then go on with their normal life as a daylight citizen.

This book has explored public sex in New York City and is based on ethnographic notes taken over the course of several decades. The notes look not only at sex in New York City but at how it has evolved over time. This book is impressionistic, not systematic and formal; because of its exploratory character, it has more of the personality of a personal narrative and the feel of reportage, with individual observations gathered over time replacing a systematic treatise.

What the field notes presented in this book attest to is an astoundingly diverse set of social worlds, all of which commingling on this small urban island. The notes presented here cover three distinct periods of research involving sex and sexuality in the city: 1979 through 1989, 1995 through 1997, and 2000 through 2018. I wanted to allow individuals to tell their own unique stories and to prevent these stories from becoming aggregated, synthesized, and absorbed. I tried to do this for two reasons: first, to demonstrate how the participant-observer strategy can be delicately utilized in field research, and second, because over time I have been able to enter into the experiences of the people glimpsed in these scenes, to enter sympathetically, understandingly, while trying to keep alive the larger implications of those experiences. However, there are indeed some conclusions I have reached with the amount of ethnographic data amassed.

The concepts I sketch here provide tools to help us analyze what we must take as empirical records. These reflections constitute an effective way to understand the Soft City and provide ample empirical support and strong elaboration. As we increasingly see across these vignettes and notes, taken as they are across time, the Soft City is continually threatened by the widening gaps between the haves, the have-nots, and the somewhats; the suburban privatization of leisure and consumption; and the corporate standardization of urban nightlife. All threaten the viability of the city center for nighttime entertainment; all encroach upon the Soft City, which can only move deeper into hiding as an act of preservation, to protect the lives it has nurtured.

In this postscript, one can still detect traces of what I consciously call a "collage ethnography." Instead of a single observation spatially and temporarily bounded, the book offers a "collage" of participant observations, executed by all sorts of people at many different times. This book is part of a larger series that builds a biography of the least-known sides of New York City. In this contribution, I bleed some components of my own biography into the work. I have had the privilege to read some other issues of this large collection, and this pattern appears in the other works as well. Although I personally find this method fascinating, this could be a point of criticism for some social science audiences that insist on a split, fixated relation between the subject and the scientist.

Such a critique is common to many ethnographic works.[3] However, this does not necessarily have to be a problem; for example, in my book *The Con Men*, the presence of the ethnographer itself and alone should be enough warranty, especially in situations that can go unrecorded or undocumented by any other means. In this book, then, I envision the Soft City as a useful analytic category. Note that if you try getting a drag queen to express some kind of solidarity with a teenage prostitute/sex worker by telling her that they are both part of the same "Soft City," you might run into some difficulty. In this respect, the Soft City must remain merely an analytic category, the invention of analysts, not entirely unlike the categories used by former mayor Rudy Giuliani or the conservative Pat Robertson. After all, both would see what we are describing here as a Soft City, too, albeit for different ideological reasons.

Once, the teen prostitute and the drag queen might not have seen sisterhood as possible, but now they are both sex workers, and that could indicate a change. It is my sense that assuming the existence of Soft City would have to take into account the differences within it and the necessary objectifying attitude from which such an object could be imagined to exist.

One key issue brought out in this book through this method is how various areas of the city's nightlife nurtured and continue to nurture sexual life as we know it. This question is still relevant today, as people continue to ask, for example: What parts of the city would survive if places like Times Square were changed, developed, or destroyed? Times Square was once the heart and soul of the city's sex life, involving after-hours clubs, street prostitution, bawdy bars, and houses of assignation. It was the commercialized vice district nonpareil that drove both tourism and entertainment for all New Yorkers. The neighborhood, however, has changed. Disneyfication is all the rage, as the area designated as the West Village reveals.

When these studies began, I asked a few basic questions. What is the Soft City, and how is it possible? Can this world be evoked via the field note? Now I have a different question in mind: Is it possible for cities to have a vibrant nightlife in their centers, or must the contemporary urban commercial center go dark and lifeless after business hours, as is the case in so many cities throughout North America?

Acknowledgments

This book is dedicated to Natalia Williams.

The propositions, theories, and suppositions expounded in this book are not presented in terms of absolutes but are really working hypotheses that invite the challenge of future investigation. My debt lies, therefore, first to the contacts, informants, and apprentice ethnographers (my former students) who encouraged me. By their interest, hard work, intelligence, and bettering their instruction, they have continued to teach (me) and instruct me. I have exploited their observations, ideas, insights, and field experiences in this book, no doubt in more than I know.

Hakim Hasan has been a steadfast behind-the-scenes confidant and mentor, and his expert knowledge much appreciated. Executive Editor Eric Schwartz and Lowell Frye at Columbia University Press are to be appreciated and thanked for making this book possible. Eric saw the notes and instantly offered to publish, and without his strong initial enthusiasm and heartfelt sincerity, this book would probably not exist. He took risk in taking it on, and I am wildly thankful for his diligence and fortitude in sticking with this project. Thomas Gerry, my data mentor and factotum, helped this book be the best it could be by using his gallant wordsmith tools, indefatigable charm, and belief in the possibility of this work.

The scholars, contacts, collaborators, colleagues, sponsors, and guides in this book are: Adam, Adrian, Alex, Alys, Amir, Amy, Anahi, Andrade X, Andras, Anette, Angela, Anna, Ariana, Ariel, Bar, Barbara, Barton, Bettine, Bev, Beverly, Bichat, Bonnie, Boocita, Brendan, Brian, Bridgette, Carol, Catherine, Cesar, Charles, Chen-Chia, Cheryl, Chia-Huei, Chin-Yu, Dana, Daniel, David, Dawn, Dennis, Desiree, Donna, Dory, Elizabeth, Enid, Eric, Erica, Erika, Evan, Florian, Gerard, Giancarlo, Guyatri, Hakan, Harlan, Harrison, Hanan, Hay Ding, Heather, Hui-ling,

James, Jana, Jeffrey, Jennifer, Jessica, Jhon, Jo, John, Jonathan, Joseph, Josette, Julia, Julie, Julius, Jussara, Karen, Kat, Katherine, Kevin, Leanne, Lorraine, Marcos, Marga, Maria, Matthew, Megan, Michael, Michelle, Miguel, Molly, Nancy, Natalia, Panagiotis, Patricia, Paoyi, Pearl, Raphael, Rana, Reginald, Robbie, Robert, Ryan, Sam, Samantha, Sandra, Sanja, Santiago, Sara, Sarah, Sari, Sergio, Shelly, Sheila, Siobhan, Silva, Sterling, Susan, Tamara, Tara, Trevor, Trudy, Valerie, Vanessa, Victor, Viola, Wendy, Zaynah.

Ana Cardenas Tomazic was extremely important in reading, critiquing, and providing key ideas in the making of this book. Santiago Mandirola and Robert Proverb, whose assistance is invaluable, did key analytic work in the transitions of chapters. Others who assisted, including personal contacts and or access to key people: James Abro, Michelle Buchanan, Ryan Buck, Iris Caballero, Mitchell Duneier, Natalia Filippova, Nancy Geist, Yang Hai, William Kornblum, Lenny (Hellfire owner), Jhonathan Mendez de Leon, Harvey Molotch, Catherine Murphy, Barbara Nitke, Julie Oakes, Josette Rodriquez, Candida Royalle, Rick Savage, Harrison Schutz, Joel Simundich, Nadine Strossen, Harte Weiner, Elizabeth Ziff. Much thanks to all the students in the "Living Book: From Research to Manuscript" class: Popy Begum, Roy Cohen, Mark Fang, Miranda Gilbert, Evan Howard, Laura Martin, and Lucille Perez. All assisted in caring ways, offered intellectual ideas, and provided engaging conversations. The photographs by the brilliant photo artist Efrain Gonzalez and writer Luc Sante are owed special thanks and appreciation.

Also special appreciation to S. G. for her artistic creations and interstitial excavations; she provided an overall vision for all the materials in this collection. Even though many people helped make this book possible, I am especially appreciative to the anonymous reviews whose assistance was especially valuable. I take sole responsibility for its shortcomings.

appendix
Methodological Ethics

Seminar of Engagement: a pedagogical model that engages students in the field by way of the classroom. It involves multiple epistemologies of doing, where students, as they present the questions, experience the problematic in the seminar. How students know what they know is by the give and take in the seminar after their experience in the field. This approach treats every adventure as a deliberate inauguration of a discussion continued by scholars, students, and observers as writers and theorists interested in the subjects brokered here.

While it is not wholly accepted in the university to use personal quests or autobiographical adventures in scholarly work, we must not forget that in our current information age, truth, however problematic the notion, still largely exists in the form of personal testimony. And while the knowledge gained is "personal," it is still evidence. One need only reflect on the continuous flow of testimonies of victims, be they from popular culture, political forums, civil-administrative entities (courts), or state violence ranging from war, poverty, and institutional racism to rape, torture, and prison brutality. All extend a private dimension for all to hear and bear witness. Of the many ways of knowing that are currently available at the New School, say, library work, lectures, and the reading of texts, none is more underutilized than outside experiential learning.

This pedagogical model was particularly appropriate for discussing issues that necessitated experience, including sex and race; youthful inspiration; female gaze-ing; male gaze-ing, the Blatino (black and Latino) body; fetishism linked to desire, objectification, and the commodity of capital; urban underground worlds and definitions of the situation; ethnography; phenomenological, "autopsical" views, which is to see with "one's own eyes"; perverted spaces of which sex is a part; engagement with sex and drugs; toxicomania and crack-cocaine culture; sex in after-hours clubs; freak-house master blaster and double master blaster acts; lesbian strolls; Times Square studies; voyeurism; anecdotal sex live visits; fluffer life; and sex supermarkets.

FIELD RESEARCH AND FIELD NOTES

I present my own notes as the main basis of the book as anchor, and I set my notes as the grounded essence because they are done over time and are not just one-night impressionistic accounts, as the apprentices' notes tend to be. But, I might add, not all my contacts were one-night-stand-type notes either. Many of these individuals, sex enthusiasts, sex addicts, sex scholars, and doctoral candidates spent years researching the sex scene in New York, spawned out of an interest in their own predilections, and they have produced valuable scholarship that stands alone as solid ethnographic/anthropological or narrative renderings of the New York night scene.

SEX AND THE CITY COURSE

I wanted to make sure my contacts or those they observed were not harmed during fieldwork, so training took on various stages. Students were given detailed information regarding what to do in the diverse settings in which they found themselves. Students came to the class eager and interested in wanting to learn about human sexuality as social practice. The class is an open forum, where reflection, inquiry, and excitement can be realized with scholarly intent; it is seen as a judgment-free environment.

The events were considered "border-crossing experiences," since all participants faced and interrogated their prejudices, shifted their positions, raised questions for which there were no easy answers, and ventured out to explore the bold reality of city life. Participants, auditors, visitors, and doctoral scholars all were told how to navigate the social erotic worlds they visited, what to look out for, and how to be safe. For example, let people know where you are; inform friends, partners, or family of your location; don't leave drinks unattended in the setting; don't take drugs offered by strangers (or at all); and avoid going into deprivation tanks, coffins, or other enclosures, even with safe words. Researchers must have a feeling of "psychological safety," and that means not worrying that something bad will happen to you. Last but not least, don't create enemies while in the field.

Everyone is given a debriefing session after these encounters to offer a space to talk. These discussions were held so the contacts could understand their boundaries, safety, and limits and to help avoid any danger associated with their experiences. I stressed that danger is not where you find it but where it finds you. Over several decades, my Sex and the City class has never had anyone harmed while taking the course.

Several microstudies were also conducted while my Sex and the City course took place; these microstudies involved more advanced scholarship done by individuals who chose to do dissertation- or masters-related research after taking the course and realizing the research possibilities available to investigate the sexual terrain they were exploring.[1] Many MA/PhD candidates who took the class have become professionals, deans, and chairs of sociology departments; one is now a college president. The work it took to get to those positions involves years of dedication, hard work, diligence, and scholarly effort. At the time of the work, no IRB approval was required.

At the same time, I used the notes to look for themes related to desire, and from there was able to conclude that desire plays a major part in the construction of the Soft City. Without desire, the Soft City could not function. What is desire? How does desire function within the Soft City? Why would the Soft City not exist without it? What notes do I have that I could use to buttress this argument? Take, for example, the following excerpt from my early fieldwork in a location in Times Square.

> I had been curious about this kind of place, but in spite of my desires, I never got the opportunity to actually visit a sex emporium before conducting this research. So when I suggested to contacts we visit Show World Center, I felt excited. This excitement and curiosity mixed with desire that causes other people (students alike) to want to visit places like this. But as so many people come to this place I wonder when this desire becomes a craving, an obsession, an addiction.

I cross a threshold when I am in the field, finding myself constructing a distinct version of myself, both as a heuristic device, that is, to make the field exist, and to retain an intimate reminder that there is a time for research but personal time as well. But regardless, the field is a place of inquisitive interest, of imagination, and great expectations.

While the most important aspect of this work is by far the notes, the object of the notes are the people themselves, and this book stresses the importance of keeping people as the key focus of the work, as opposed to the reflexivity issues so dominant in the discipline at this time. The goals of *The Soft City* are to share with readers an exploration of the sex lives of New Yorkers and to examine the methodological features of this study.

I originally wanted each chapter to contain my field notes, but on occasion I let the notes take the reader along a different path, with me staying out of the narrative momentarily and remerging in the next scene. Each field note highlights at least one aspect of city sexuality: touch, stirrings, movement, motion, to name only four of those elements. That way, the flow is consistent with the overall text and is different from the notes of the contacts. My notes often set scenes up in a thick rather than thin form, as opposed to the notes of my student contact "flaneurs." My notes are intended to reflect a longer-term view

I have had more than a hundred doctoral scholars/contacts/informants over the years, between 1991 and 2016, and they have produced thousands of pages of field notes and a number of more extended scholarly papers. Most of these papers were used in one way or another: some as reference material, some as scene setters. Some are included verbatim; others are truncated because the events they detail were not completed. In a few cases, the situations were too traumatic to be recorded. The vast majority of the writers/scholars completed their assignments, and we discussed their experiences in various locales, from the street to the classroom.

I tell the story over time by using notes from different periods. This vignette approach is living proof that I could use different voices in the same locations. There is a relationship between the storiettes and science to be identified here, since I see the field notes combined with analysis as a unique approach to the field of sociology. Books that show the real, honest field notes acting as the supporting infrastructure or scaffolding used to build a larger narrative are rare. And the reasons are obvious.[2]

Field notes constitute the basic evidential structure for the gathering of information and making public the basis of the ethnographer's interpretation. They give episodes a temporal beginning and end and are vital to the interpretation and understanding of the analytical construction of the phenomenon under study.

In the field, I conduct interviews, interact with others on the scene, and generally describe in as luxuriant a fashion as possible the goings-on. This attempt to provide as rounded and dynamic a portrait of people as possible, their habits, work, play, in a word, their world, relies heavily on this participant-observation form. I try to describe everyday behavior and rituals and, in the process, look to reveal hidden structures of power. As this technique requires me to build close relationships with those being studied, it is necessarily slow: days, sometimes weeks may pass before I can begin to conduct an interview. These interviews are often "open"; that is, I have key questions in mind but am willing to let the informant's responses lead into unanticipated areas, as these can help me gain a new understanding of the situation under study.

But I want to avoid the term "informant," since the meaning is more akin to law enforcement and, as used in the field these days, has a "negative" connotation. It has lost the neutral meaning it once held and is now viewed despairingly as "snitching." The snitch is a dreaded character who "turns state" when arrested and will inform on friends, family, lovers, and the like to save themselves. In the field, the street worker sees the informer/informant as someone who has not only betrayed themselves but the community at large. I prefer to the term "contact" over "informant"—perhaps a contextual change, although here I used both interchangeably.

The approach I took and taught my apprentices to employ was "stream-of-consciousness note taking." This approach involves asking them to record their notes after each visit. Several arranged field trips per week were set up in order to write their notes in such a way as to give the "raw" material the upper edge in their writing and to not block primal responses by thinking too much about what they put on the page.

My approach involves careful observation of people in their own social settings, and systematic recording of their actions and speech in their field notes is essential. This can include simple quantitative measures, such as noting the sex and the age and ethnicity of participants. For example, in observing women being spanked at clubs, I've noticed ironically how this has proven to be a rare situation over time, since more men than women are spanked and more men are placed in positions of subservience. Similarly, most men are white males; few men of color frequent the places I've seen. But I also record far more subtle information in my field notes, for example, about language, gestures, facial expressions, and styles of clothing, and I try to watch with care to capture exceptional episodes that can be particularly illuminating.

Clearly, detailed and descriptive field notes are essential in this approach, especially as the observer makes every attempt to record accurately the speech and other behaviors of those observed. In this work and in these locations, irony abounds: instead of finding it difficult to get information about patrons, I found people were willing to talk and engaged with ease.

But none of this means that many of my apprentices weren't nervous entering these establishments. This is a curious situation: being nervous is a *good* reaction, since it puts the person on high alert. As apprentices, nervousness is a way of acknowledging one's vulnerability. It is a natural reaction to a situation of unease. But I instructed people how to deal with nervousness, and one way was by writing about their feelings during the debriefing sessions.

Keep in mind people are not allowed to touch, grab, or in any way accost people once they are in a venue. There are specific rules at every venue, and everyone is expected to adhere. For example, in one of the well-known sex clubs the owner had house rules flyers and pamphlets placed at the entrance as well as bouncers informing all participants of the dos and don'ts. Bouncers were there to enforce the rules; transgressors were immediately escorted out. No touching, grabbing, or other aggressive acts without permission. That is why you will hear people ask: Can I touch? Will you spank me? Can I massage your feet? These were the rules in most or all Soft City venues.

Although I used no tape recordings of events, I did have the eyes and ears of the contacts to count on. This offered some interesting sidebars, in part because no two people see the events in quite the same way. Instead of this being a problem, it was, in fact, wonderful: I was able to have multiple individuals gazing at a scene that would normally have only one, my own. Instead of being in one room, I had the view of multiple rooms. In that way, the idea of "collage ethnography" becomes a kaleidoscopic experience.

Contacts were not required to have perfect grammar or punctuation, and in the second draft of their notes, they could then develop ideas and construct more elaborate theories. I developed a method many years ago that fits the various situations. In dangerous settings I probably would have only one chance of witnessing, I would jot down a key word or phrase immediately after each visit and reconstruct conversations or a scene from those notes the next day. There were some exceptions, when I'd take sketchy notes of some private conversations with people I had gotten to know over time. Field notes usually require at least one day or more of writing for each hour of field observations. The notes in this volume come from hundreds of hours of field work producing hundreds of pages of field notes, including drawings, flyers, sketches, diagrams, photographs, and video records, exhibiting the diversity of the Soft City.

In her classic study *Liquor License* (1978), Sherri Cavan notes that bars in San Francisco can be typed according to the kind of activities found in them: the marketplace bar, the home-territory bar, the convenience bar, and the night spot. These bars offer different services for their patrons. Cavan uses the term "social trouble" to identify dangerous activities in particular ethnographic settings where the expectations established by the settings are the same.

In certain spaces in the Soft City, patrons are expected to get drunk, dance, touch, kiss, fondle, and feel as if the space is an open region. Patrons can interact with one another with the confidence that each person is there to interact. People can approach strangers without the slightest hesitation. In these settings, a certain privilege is afforded strangers, one that is not normally allowed elsewhere. For example, I went to the Blue Angel on several occasions before the actual course event, as I had done for most if not all the events and clubs visited in the course, in order to determine whether it would serve the purpose for a field experience. I reminded contacts/informants based on my experiences that it would be a place where they would find a different kind of topless performance—though, of course, what they would see with their collective eye would be based on their own group collective experience.

The topless bar is the first setting that I recommended because I wanted the observed events to gradually increase in intensity from the most common types of adult entertainment to those that might be less common. I also felt the overall quality of the field notes recorded would be enhanced by this strategy, and, by right, they should also reflect the intensity of that experience.

From 1995 to 2008, students were asked to do the following: state name, date, and location on all field notes; provide the address of the strategic research site (SRS); provide description of activity at the site; record what activity student engaged in at the site and the amount of money spent; provide a physical description of site; give the ethnicity, age, and description of those present at the site; and record both eavesdropped conversations as well as casual interviews. The contacts/informants used a specific surreptitious approach to interviewing: only ask questions after being approached by people at the venue. The strategy was to find out as much as possible about how patrons came to attend such places. This lends itself to the "scenes and impressions" idea, whereby this work, particularly of the last ten years or so, is viewed more through scenes and impressions than by way of systematic field research, especially by the students. This approach would suggest that students are the gatherers of impressionistic accounts and the professor as the individual conducting more thorough systematic data collection and analysis. This interview protocol made sense, since, in many instances, besides me, a handful of student/scholars were the only consistent visitors to the sites.

Another issue concerns the distinction between patrons and voyeurs in these places. Since most students did not spend much time talking to or interviewing people, they were there mostly as voyeurs. But were they more interested in their own reactions and experiences or about the scenes and impressions discovered there?

Anette, a writer states:

> I started to watch out for girls' places, formative places because of the mean-
> ing they produce. I remembered the many hours spent in my best friend's
> bathroom, putting on and removing makeup, spending days transforming my
> (and my friend's) persona, looking for something that would fit "me"—and my
> best friend. Bathrooms are the epitome of privacy, the family's core safety
> zone; they do not have the kind of publicity suggested by a guy's formative
> places like record stores or even street corners, which are at least potentially
> open to strangers and new encounters.[3]

This quick observation is about a public space with which we are all familiar. The familiar quality of this observation gives us a sense of time and place in the Soft City.[4]

I proceed primarily by looking at the modern city via a number of different characters who have, more or less explicitly and extensively, been used as prototypical figures: the flaneur, the street sex worker, the poetess, the photographer, the detective, the ragpicker, the journalist, the urban sociologist. As a narrator, I reflect on my own reactions, opinions, and feelings as well as those of my apprentices as we make our forays into the city.

Now we move to the different scenes in the Soft City. I'm reminded of Miguel de Cervantes's Man of Glass, in his *Exemplary Novels*, where the character saw himself as somewhat fragile—vulnerable in life—and in this book's narratives we start to see vestiges of our own self-images and what each of us consider ourselves to be. This is where a more programmatic account of the trajectory of the argument and the structure of the book as a whole will begin to appear.

Glossary

Blatino: Black and Latino person

Bottle gang: street alcoholics

Bottom: a passive partner in sex; one who submits during masochistic acts

Boy pussy: man-to-man sex or male sex with boys

Cisgender: someone who identifies with the sex they were assigned at birth

Date: to take out a prostitute for sexual purposes

Drag queen: man who dresses as a woman

411: Information

Hustler: male prostitute or sex worker, usually one who has sex with men

In the life: prostitution; living as gay person within a circle of friends; living as a transvestite

Into leather: having a fetish for wearing or having sex with those wearing leather

John: trick; person who pays for sex

Kink: Socially proscribed sex act

Lipstick lesbian: Lesbians who look more feminine

New Olympics: Competition beyond fetishisms of identity

Play: engaging in S/M

Post-Op: transexual who has undergone surgery

Pre-Op: transexual who has not undergone surgery but has started hormone treatments

S&M: part of a family of terms including B&D (bondage and discipline), D&S (dominance and submission), and kink

Scene: to publicly organize sadomasochism (verb)

Top: one who dominates or is the active partner in a sex act

Toy: implement used in sadomasochistic play

Trade: prostitutes and hustlers (current use "sex worker")

Trick: customer of prostitute

TS: transexual; a person who has undergone sex reassignment

Tunnel trick: customer of a prostitute traversing the Lincoln Tunnel

TV: drag queen, or transie, transvestite

Twink: young, pretty boy

Twonks: as opposed to twinks; attractive gay men

Vanilla: someone not part of the "scene" (antiquated)

Work: engage in S&M as "working on" someone or "working with" (archaic)

Notes

INTRODUCTION

1. See the appendix.
2. The Meatpacking District is now landmarked and is between Horatio Street to the south, West Sixteenth Street to the north, the West Side Highway to the west, and Eighth Avenue/Hudson Streets to the east.
3. See Langan and Durose (2004). The peak for violent crimes was reached in 1990 (above 170,000, including more than 2,200 homicides); in 2007, by contrast, the number of homicides fell below 500 for the first time since 1963.
4. "The draconian rule of mayor Rudolph Giuliani saw the institution of a policy that rezoned the vast majority of public sex out of the city. New laws closed down most adult bookstores, bars, movie theaters, peep shows, and performance spaces that featured sexually oriented performance—not only female strippers at straight bars but go-go boys at queer clubs. The crackdown on public sex was part of Giuliani's notorious 'quality of life' campaign, now carried on under the mayorship of Michael Bloomberg. The assimilationist homosexuals who backed Giuliani and back Bloomberg are a sexual proletariat that has been swept into the conservative populism so powerfully characterizing this moment, dominated as it is by neoliberalism and, more specifically, gay pragmatism" Muñoz (2009, 53–55).
5. Zoning laws were fought in court; more details can be found in Liepe-Levinson (2002).
6. Raban (1974).

1. SOFT CITY ENCOUNTERS

1. Goffman (1963, 9).
2. I'm reminded of the sociologist Everett Hughes's dictum when he wrote about the dialectic between observation and participation, stating that the two notions are never really resolved.

3. Passion for feet is not a new phenomenon. The Chinese have had a long fascination with tiny feet (reportedly two inches wide and four inches long) and practiced foot binding from the Sung Dynasty (960 BCE) until 1911, when the new Chinese Republic legally abolished the custom. This particular form of body modification/fetish began as an effort to emulate cherished imperial concubines, who were required to dance with their feet bound in silk. Foot binding first became increasingly widespread among aristocratic women. However, it became much more severe as time progressed, yet by the twelfth century, it was common among the peasants as well as the wealthy. The sight of a woman moving as "gracefully as a lotus floating on a pond" is believed to have had an erotic effect on men.
4. McBride (2005, 88).

2. TOPLESS AND BOTTOMLESS BARS

1. Hakim (2011, 10).
2. Deedra's notes remind me of the paintings by the artist Lucien Freud, who uses mirrors to extract an image. Her descriptions reflect on her personal image, using a mirror as one of her props. She said during the debriefing sessions she wanted to become a stripper. I think Lucien Freud's work is analogous to the method I am building here. "'Like the artless shots in Bunuel which are necessary to set up the rest,' [Freud] suggested. There his characters sit, 'slightly costumey,' four on a bed, the light falling evenly on them, the scent of the verbena mingling, we may deduce, with the whiff of paint. They include a daughter and two girlfriends from different times. 'I didn't want to make too much about the unity, the fact that people are sitting next to each other, know each other very well, not at all, or slightly. I'm interested in all that aspect of things: the people and to what degree they are affected'" (Feaver, 2012).
3. Cook (2005).

3. GENDER PLAY

1. Bettcher (2014).
2. For those interested in transgender studies, here are a few noted sources: Whitley (2015), Labuski and Keo-Meier (2015), Koyama (2020), Adair (2015).
3. At this time, I was on a deadline to complete an article on transvestites for Japanese *Playboy*. But this was not my first encounter with transgender or transsexual individuals, as I previously mention. Come to think of it, I had met several transgendered persons in the process of gender reassignment while visiting and conducting interviews with recent gender-assigned males transitioning at a place called Passage 144 in Leuven, Belgium.
4. Kornblum (1989).
5. Butler (1990, viii).
6. See Viladrich (2013).
7. See Adair (2015).

8. Goffman (1959).
9. Lofland and Lofland (1995).
10. "My idea of portraiture came from dissatisfaction with portraits that resembled people. I would wish my portraits to be of the people, not like them. Not having a look of the sitter, being them as far as I am concerned the paint is the person. I want it to work for me just as flesh does" (Feaver 2012).

4. PEEP SHOWS

1. According to websites such as Cruising for Sex (https://www.cruisingforsex.com), another popular time to visit is during the evening rush hours. The Eighth Avenue houses are especially convenient for commuters because they are adjacent to the Port Authority Bus Terminal, which covers the block bounded by Eighth and Ninth Avenues and Fortieth and Forty-Second Streets. Indeed, the presence of the bus terminal may be the reason these sex-related businesses are clustered in this area.
2. But I need not refer to this as an industry. As Grant (2018, 49) states: "There is no one sex industry. Escorting, street hustling, hostessing, stripping, performing sex for videos and webcams—the range of labor makes speaking of just one feel inadequate. To collapse all commercial sex that way would result in something so flat and shallow that it would only reinforce the insistence that all sex for sale results from the same phenomenon—violence, deviance, or desperation."
3. "These Boots Are Made for Walkin'" was a 1966 hit written by Lee Hazlewood and recorded by Nancy Sinatra.

5. ESCORTS AND CLIENTS

1. Leonard (1985).
2. Although there is only limited empirical reference to these concepts, it is supported by the field notes in chapter 1 on foot modeling.
3. Katherine Zapert, field note interview, personal communication.
4. "Pennsylvania: Judge Criticized in Rape Case," *New York Times*, November 1, 2007. Philadelphia municipal judge Teresa Carr Deni ruled that the rape of a sex worker was not actually rape but rather "theft of services."
5. Katherine Zapert, research notes.
6. Hakim (2011).
7. See Cressey (1932, 196-233).
8. Mears (2011).
9. Madam X and Nana visit, Youth Culture class, personal interview, 2017.
10. In a report in the National Criminal Justice Reference Service, *Navigating Force and Choice: Experiences in the New York City Sex Trade and the Criminal Justice System's Response* (2017).

11. Electronic surveillance is used to keep police at bay, and the girls all carry electronic pagers or similar texting devices to keep watch on the girls. I have only limited knowledge of the ages of the girls answering these calls. All of this relates to the issue of the outcalls pertaining to backpage.com, the online classifieds site where the girls were branded as "escorts." Much of the online-sex ad revenues, reportedly about 75 to 80 percent of it (according to a Senate report), comes from two sources: Backpage.com and Cracker.com, both of which are headquartered in the Netherlands. As of April 2018, Backpage.com has been closed down by the FBI, IRS, and U.S. Postal Inspection Service. I recently learned it is back in business under a different name.

12. Zola (1928, 106).

6. SMELL, TOUCH, AND PARTICIPATION

1. Daynes and Williams (2018, 62).
2. "In elementary schools in what we might call mainstream America, students learn (at the beginning of the twenty-first century) that hearing, touch, taste, smell, and sight are senses, but they do not learn to categorize *balance* as a sensation or a sense. Yet balance is clearly treated as a sense in contemporary textbooks from such disciplines as biology, psychology, and medicine.... A sense of balance even has a corresponding 'organ'—the vestibular organ, or the labyrinth of the inner ear—as the other five senses (seeing, hearing, touching, tasting, smelling) have theirs" (Geurts 2002, 3–4).
3. Largey and Watson (1972, 1021–34).
4. Grazian (2008, 163).
5. Steele (1997, 96).
6. Steele (1997, 5).
7. Foucault (1990, 154).
8. Ernest Becker, quoted in Steele (1997, 107).
9. Steele (1997, 91, 100).
10. Steele (1997, 106).
11. Steele (1997, 58).
12. Steele (1997, 63).

7. SADOMASOCHISM AND BONDAGE

1. Wagner-Pacifici (2017).
2. Cornell (1995, 134).

8. ORGIES AND SWINGER EVENTS

1. Van Gennep (1960, 11).
2. Wolff (1950, 345–73).

3. Wolff (1950, 364).
4. Frapper-Mazur (1996, 1–2).
5. Parsons (1951, 389–90).
6. Martin and George (2006, 165).

9. LESBIAN AND GAY SPACES

1. Lipstick lesbians are women who do not fit the stereotype of "butch" or "dyke." They express more typically feminine gender attributes.
2. Daynes and Williams (2018, 171).
3. Goffman (1959, 59).
4. McBride (2005, 102).
5. McBride (2005, 203–4).

10. THE FUTURE OF THE SOFT CITY

1. Attwood (2018, 106).
2. Muñoz (2009, 49).
3. Just to mention an example, Duneier (2002) questions the verifiability of Wacquant's work *Body and Soul*, given that the gym where his ethnographic work takes place no longer exists.

APPENDIX: METHODOLOGICAL ETHICS

1. Several of these studies stand out: Rodriquez (2007), Brooks (2001), Buchanan (2003). All of these studies have an ethnographic component.
2. See the recent attacks on the sociologist Alice Goffman (2014).
3. Baldauf (1999).
4. All of these studies have an ethnographic signature, such as ethnographic quota sampling, which is a process in which a category is devised, and then a number of cases are chosen from that category to represent the group. An example would be a study on street crime in which five representatives—dealers, pickpockets, hustlers, pimps, and con men, say—would be chosen to be interviewed. Each student discussed the methods used with the class and the professor.

Bibliography

Abbot, S. A. 2000. "Motivations for Pursuing an Acting Career in Pornography." In *Sex for Sale: Prostitution, Pornography, and the Sex Industry*, ed. R. Weitzer. New York: Routledge.

Adair, Cassius. 2015. "Bathrooms and Beyond: Expanding a Pedagogy of Access in Trans/Disability Studies." *Trans Gender Quarterly* 2, no. 3: 464-68.

Allison, Anne. 1994. *Nightwork: Sexuality, Pleasure, and Corporate Masculinity in a Tokyo Hostess Club*. Chicago: University of Chicago Press.

Amadiume, Ifi. 1987. *Male Daughters, Female Husbands*. London: Zed.

Anderson, Elijah. 2002. "What Kind of Combat Sport Is Sociology?" *American Journal of Sociology* 107, no. 6: 1551-76.

Aronoff, Joel, et al. 1970. *Psychology Today: An Introduction*. Del Mar, CA: CRM Books.

Attwood, Fiona. 2016. *Sex Media*. London: Polity.

Baldauf, Anette. 1999. "Shopping: A Comparative Analysis of Two Shopping Streets in Vienna and New York." Dissertation proposal.

Barlow, H. B., and J. D. Mollon, eds. 1982. *The Senses*. Cambridge: Cambridge University Press.

Bauman, Zymunt. 1998. "On Postmodern Uses of Sex." *Theory, Culture, & Society* 15, nos. 3/4: 19-35.

Bederman, Gail, and Catherine R. Stimpson. 1996. *Manliness and Civilization: A Cultural History of Gender and Race in the United States, 1880-1917*. Women in Culture and Society. Chicago: University of Chicago Press.

Bernstein, Elizabeth. 1999. "What's Wrong with Prostitution? What's Right with Sex-Work? Comparing Markets in Female Sexual Labor." *Hastings Women's Law Journal* 10, no. 1: 91-119.

Bettcher, Talia Mae. 2014. "Trapped in the Wrong Theory: Rethinking Trans Oppression and Resistance." *Signs* 39, no. 2 (Winter): 383-406.

Bienvenu, Robert V., II. 1998. "The Development of Sadomasochism as a Cultural Style in the Twentieth-Century United States." PhD diss., Indiana University, Indiana University Dissertation Services #982557.

Blumberg, Joan. 1997. *The Body Project: An Intimate History of American Girls*. New York: Vintage.

Brame, Gloria, William Brame, and Jon Jacobs. 1993. *Different Loving: The World of Sexual Dominance and Submission*. New York: Villard.

Brewer, Gwen, ed. 1997. *Prostitution: On Whores, Hustlers, and Johns*. Amherst, NY: Prometheus.

Brook, Kerwin. 1998. "Peep Show Pimps: San Francisco Strip Clubs May Be Pushing Dancers Into Prostitution." *San Francisco Bay Guardian*, February 4, 18–21.

Brooks, Siobhan. 2001. "Exotic Dancing and Unionizing." In *Feminism and Antiracism: International Struggles for Justice*, ed. France Winddance Twine and Kathleen M. Blee. New York: New York University Press.

Buchanan, Michele. 2003. "Leather Is Thicker Thank Blood: Identity Formation Among Organized SM Practitioners in New York City." PhD diss.

Butler, Judith. 1990. *Gender Trouble: Feminism and the Subversion of Identity*. New York: Routledge.

——. 1993. *Bodies That Matter: On the Discursive Limits of Sex*. New York: Routledge.

Califia, Pat. 1994. *Public Sex: The Culture of Radical Sex*. San Francisco: Cleis.

——. 1996. *Policing Public Sex: Queer Politics and the Future of Aids Activism*. Boston: South End.

Chancer, Lynn. 1992. *Sadomasochism and Everyday Life*. New Brunswick, NJ: Rutgers University Press.

——. 1998. *Reconcilable Differences: Confronting Beauty, Pornography, and the Future of Feminism*. Berkeley: University of California Press.

Chauncey, George. 1994. *Gay New York: Gender, Urban Culture, and the Making of the Gay Male Underworld, 1890–1940*. New York: Basic Books.

Collins, Patricia. 1990. *Black Feminist Thought: Knowledge, Consciousness, and the Politics of Empowerment*. Boston: Unwin Hyman.

Colomina, Beatriz. 1992. *Sexuality and Space*. Princeton, NJ: Princeton Architectural Press.

Cook, Jennifer. 2005. "Shaken from Her Pedestal: A Decade of New York City's Sex Industry Siege." *New York City Law Review* 121.

Cornell, Drucilla. 1995. *The Imaginary Domain: Abortion, Pornography, and Sexual Harassment*. New York. Routledge.

——. 2000. *Oxford Readings in Feminism: Feminism and Pornography*. New York: Oxford University Press.

Cressey, Paul. 1932. *The Taxi-Dance Hall*. Chicago: University of Chicago Press.

Davis, Kingsley. 1937. "The Sociology of Prostitution." *American Sociological Review* 2:744–55.

Davis, Murray. 1985. *Smut*. Chicago: University of Chicago Press.

Daynes, Sarah, and Terry Williams. 2018. *On Ethnography*. London: Polity.

Delany, Samuel. 1999. *Times Square Red, Times Square Blue*. New York: New York University Press.

Dejean, Joan E., and Catherine R. Stimpson. 1989. *Fictions of Sappho, 1546–1937*. Women in Culture and Society. Chicago: University of Chicago Press.

D'Emilio, John. 2002. *The World Turned: Essays on Gay History, Politics, and Culture*. Durham, NC: Duke University Press.

Douglas, M. 1996. *Purity and Danger: An Analysis of the Concepts of Pollution and Tattoo*. New York: Routledge.

Doy, Gen. 2000. *Black Visual Culture: Modernity and Postmodernity*. London: I. B. Tauris.

Duneier, Mitch. 2002. "What Kind of Combat Sport Is Sociology?" *American Journal of Sociology* 107, no. 6: 1551–76.

Economist. 2000. "Sex, News, and Statistics: Where Entertainment on the Web Scores." *Economist*, October 7.

Elias, James, Veronica Diehl Elias, Vern L. Bullough, et al., eds. 1999. *Porn 101: Eroticism, Pornography, and the First Amendment*. New York: Prometheus.

Faust, Beatrice. 1980. *Women, Sex, and Pornography*. New York: Macmillan.

Fausto-Sterling, Anne. 2000. *Sexing the Body: Gender Politics and the Construction of Sexuality*. New York: Basic Books.

Featherstone, Tony. 1991. "The Body in Consumer Culture." In *The Body: Social Processes and Cultural Theory*, ed. Mike Hepworth, Tony Featherstone, and Bryan S. Turner. London: Sage.

Feaver, William. 2012. "Lucian Freud: Reflections of the Artist." *Guardian*, February 2.

Feinburg, Leslie. 1993. *Stone Butch Blues*. Ithaca, NY: Firebrand.

Fisher, Seymour. 1973. *The Female Orgasm*. New York: Basic Books.

Flowers, Amy. 1998. *The Fantasy Factory: An Insider's View of the Phone Sex Industry*. Philadelphia: University of Pennsylvania Press.

Foucault, Michel. 1979. *Discipline and Punish*. New York: Vintage.

——. 1980. *The History of Sexuality*. Vol. 1: *An Introduction*. New York: Vintage.

——. 1990. *The History of Sexuality: An Introduction*. New York: Vintage.

Frank, Arthur. 1990. "Bringing Bodies Back In: A Decade in Review." *Theory, Culture, and Society* 7, no. 1: 131–62.

Frapper-Mazur, Lucien. 1996. *Writing the Orgy: Power and Parody in Sade*. Philadelphia: University of Pennsylvania Press.

Geurts, Kathryn. 2002. *Culture and the Senses: Bodily Ways of Knowing in an African Community*. Berkeley: University of California Press.

Goffman, Alice. 2014. *On the Run*. University of Chicago Press.

Goffman, Erving. 1959. *Presentation of Self in Everyday Life*. New York: Doubleday.

——. 1963. *Behavior in Public Places*. New York: Free Press.

Gold, Penny Schine. 1987. *The Lady and the Virgin: Image, Attitude, and Experience in Twelfth-Century France*. Reprint ed. Women in Culture and Society. Chicago: University of Chicago Press.

Grant, Melissa. 2018. *Playing the Whore: The Work of Sex Work*. New York: Person.

Grazian, David. 2008. *On the Make: The Hustle of Urban Life*. Chicago: University of Chicago Press.

Greenwald, Herald. 1958. *The Elegant Prostitute: A Social and Analytic Study*. New York: Ballantine.

Grosz, E. A. 1995. *Space, Time, and Perversion*. New York: Routledge.

Grosz, E. A., and Elspeth Probyn, eds. 1995. *Sexy Bodies: The Strange Carnalities of Feminism*. New York: Routledge.

Haeri, Shahla. 1989. *Law of Desire*. Syracuse, NY: Syracuse University Press.

Hakim, Catherine. 2011. *Erotic Capital: The Power of Attraction in the Boardroom and the Bedroom*. New York: Basic Books.

Halberstam, Judith. 1997. "Techno-Homo: On Bathrooms, Butches, and Sex with Furniture." In *Processed Lives: Gender and Technology in Everyday Life*, ed. Jennifer Terry and Melodie Calvert. London: Routledge.

——. 1998. *Female Masculinity*. Chapel Hill, NC: Duke University Press.

Hart, Lynda. 1988. *Between the Body and the Flesh: Performing Sadomasochism*. Between Men– Between Women. New York: Columbia University Press.

Hochschild, Arlie Russell. 1983. *The Managed Heart: Commodification of Human Feeling*. Berkeley: University of California Press.

Hoigard, Cecilie, and Liv Finstad. 1986. *Backstreets: Prostitution, Money, and Love*. University Park: Pennsylvania State University Press.

Holzman, Harold, and Sharon Pines. 1982. "Buying Sex: The Phenomenology of Being a John." *Deviant Behavior* 4:89–116.

hooks, bell. 1990. *Yearning: Race, Gender, and Cultural Politics*. Boston: South End.

—. 1992. *Black Looks: Race and Representation*. Boston: South End.

—. 1993. "Consumed by Images." *Artforum* 31, no. 6: 5iVBORw0KGgoAAAANSUhEUgAA AAgAAAAFCAYAAAB4ka1VAAAAAXNSR0IArs4c6QAAABFJREFUCB1jZGBg+A /Egx0AAKGpAQHsAqN1AAAAAElFTkSuQmCC6.

Humphreys, Laud. 1970. *Tearoom Trade: Impersonal Sex in Public Places*. New York: Aldine de Gruyter.

Hunt, Lynn. 1993. *The Invention of Pornography: Obscenity and the Origins of Modernity, 1500–1800*. New York: Zone.

Irigaray, Luce. 1985. *The Sex Which Is Not One*. Ithaca, NY: Cornell University Press.

Janus, Samuel S., and Cynthia L. Janus. 1994. *The Janus Report on Sexual Behavior*. New York: Wiley.

Jenness, Valerie. 1993. *Making It Work: The Prostitutes' Rights Movement in Perspective*. New York: Aldine de Gruyter.

Juffer, Jane. 1998. *At Home with Pornography: Women, Sex, and Everyday Life*. New York: New York University Press.

Junker, Buford H. 1960. *FieldWork: The Place of FieldWork in the Social Sciences*. Chicago. University of Chicago Press.

Kempadoo, Kamala, and Jo Doezema, eds. 1998. *Global Sex-Workers: Rights, Resistance, and Redefinition*. New York: Routledge.

Kendrick, Walter. 1987. *The Secret Museum: Pornography in Modern Culture*. New York: Penguin.

Kimmel, Michael. 2000. "Fuel for Fantasy: The Ideological Construction of Male Lust." In *Male Lust: Power, Pleasure, and Transformation*, ed. Kerwin Kay et al., 267–73. New York: Haworth.

Kinsey, A. C. 1948. *Male Sexual Behavior*. W. B. Saunders Co.

Kinsey, A. C., W. B. Pomeroy, C. E. Martin, and P. H. Gebhard. 1958. *Sexual Behavior in the Human Female*. W. B. Saunders.

Kippen, Cameron. 2004. "The History of Foot Wear: Foot and Shoe Fetishism." Curtin Health Sciences, Department of Podiatry. December.

Kornblum, William. 1989. "Forty-Second Street at the Crossroads." City University of New York Research Paper.

—. 1992. "The Bright Light Zone: West Forty-Second Street." City University of New York Urban Series Natural Areas.

Koyama, Emi. 2020. "Whose Feminism Is It Anyway? The Unspoken Racism of the Trans Inclusion Debate." *Sociological Review* 68, no. 4: 735-44.

Kroker, Arthur, and M. L. Kroker. 1988. *Body Invader: Sexuality and the Post Modern Condition*. London: Oxford University Press.

Labuski, C., and C. Keo-Meier. 2015. "The (Mis)Measure of Trans." *Transgender Studies Quarterly* 2, no. 1: 13-33.

Lane, Frederick S. 2000. *Obscene Profits: The Entrepreneurs of Pornography in the Cyber Age*. New York: Routledge.

Langan, Patrick A., and Matthew R. Durose. 2004. "The Remarkable Drop in Crime in New York City." *Geography*.

Largey, Gale Peter, and Rodney David Watson. 1972. "The Sociology of Odors." *American Journal of Sociology* 77, no. 6: 1021-34.

Laumann, Edward O., John H. Gagnon, Robert T. Michael, and Stuart Michaels. 1994. *The Social Organization of Sexuality: Sexual Practices on the United States*. Chicago: University of Chicago Press.

Lefebvre, Henri. 1991. *The Production of Space*. London: Blackwell.

—. 1999. *Writings on Cities*. London: Blackwell.

Leidner, Robin. 1993. *Fast Food, Fast Talk: Service Work and the Routinization of Everyday Life*. Berkeley: University of California Press.

Leonard, Arthur S. 1985. "Employment Discrimination Against Persons with AIDS." *University of Dayton Law Review*, 681-703.

Lever, Janet, and Deanne Dolnick. 2000. "Clients and Call Girls: Seeking Sex and Intimacy." In *Sex for Sale: Prostitution, Pornography, and the Sex Industry*, 85-103, ed. Ronald Weitzer. New York: Routledge.

Liepe-Levinson, Katherine. 2002. *Strip Show: Performance of Gender and Desire*. New York: Routledge.

Lofland, John, and Lyn Lofland. 1995. *Analyzing Social Settings*. Davis: University of California at Davis/Wadsworth.

Loiselle, Dawnelle. 1998. *Footbinding: Lotus Petals*. Towson University Women's Studies.

Mackinnon, Catharine. 1995. "Mackinnon: Pornography Is Oppression." *Ethical Spectacle*, November. http://www.spectacle.org/1195/mack.html.

Mapplethorpe, Robert. 1986. *Black Book*. New York: St. Martin's.

Martin, Joe, and Matt George. 2006. "Theories of Sexual Stratification: Toward an Analytics of the Sexual Field and a Theory of Sexual Capital." *Sociological Theory* 24, no. 2.

Marx, Karl. 1978 [1844]. "The Economic and Philosophic Manuscripts of 1844." In *The Marx-Engels Reader*, ed. Robert C. Tucker, 66-126. New York: Norton.

Masters, William H., et al. 1995. *Heterosexuality*. Reprint ed. New York: Harper Perennial.

McBride, A. Dwight. 2005. *Why I Hate Abercrombie & Fitch*. New York: New York University Press.

Mears, Ashley. 2011. *Pricing Beauty: The Making of a Fashion Model*. Berkeley: University of California Press.

Merritt, Natacha. 2000. *Natacha Merritt Digital Diaries*. TASCHEN America Inc.

Miller, James. 1993. *The Passion of Michel Foucault*. New York: Simon and Schuster.

Muñoz, Jose Esteban. 2009. *Cruising Utopia: The Then and There of Queer Futurity*. New York: New York University Press.

Nagle, Jill. 1997. *Whores and Other Feminists*. New York: Routledge.

New York Times Magazine. "What's Really on the Minds of Americans." *New York Times Magazine*, May 7, 2000.

Noyes, John K. 1997. *The Mastery of Submission: Inventions of Masochism*. Cornell Studies in the History of Psychiatry. Ithaca, NY: Cornell University Press.

Parsons, Talcott. 1951. *The Social System*. New York: Free Press.

Pateman, Carole. 1988. *The Sexual Contract*. Stanford, CA: Stanford University Press.

Pheterson, Gail. 1993. "The Whore Stigma: Female Dishonor and Male Unworthiness." *Social Text* 37:39-65.

Pinkerton, S. 1995. *Sexual Nature and Sexual Culture*. Chicago: University of Chicago Press.

Plummer, Ken. 1995. *Telling Sexual Stories: Power, Change, and Social Worlds*. New York: Routledge.

Prasad, Monica. 1999. "The Morality of Market Exchange: Love, Money, and Contractual Justice." *Sociological Perspectives* 42, no. 2: 181-215.

Raban, Jonathan. 1974. *The Soft City*. London: Harvill.

Rechy, John. 1963. *City of Night*. New York: Grove.

Rodriguez, Josette. 2007. "Fag Hag Study." PhD diss.

Sade, Marquis de. 1987. *The 120 Days of Sodom and Other Writings*. Trans. Pierre Klossowski. Reissue ed. New York: Grove.

Sassen, Saskia. 1991. *The Global City*. Princeton, NJ: Princeton University Press.

Simmel, Georg. 1971 [1907]. "Prostitution." In *On Individuality and Social Forms*, ed. Donald N. Levine, 121-26. Chicago: University of Chicago Press.

Small, Mario. 2009. "How Many Cases Do I Need? On Science and the Logic of Case Selection in Field-Based Research." *Ethnography* 10, no. 1: 5-38.

Snitow, Ann. 1983. *Powers of Desire*. New York: Monthly Review.

Steele, Valerie. 1997. *Fetish: Fashion, Sex, and Power*. Reprint ed. London: Oxford University Press.

Sterk, Claire. 1999. *Tricking and Tripping: Prostitution in the Era in AIDS*. Social Change Press.

Stevens, Maurice. 2002. "Subject to Countermemory: Disavowal and Black Manhood in Spike Lee's *Malcolm X*." *Signs: Journal of Women in Culture and Society* 28, no. 1.

Strossen, Nadine. 1995. *Defending Pornography: Free Speech, Sex, and the Fight for Women's Rights*. New York: Scribner.

Sullivan, Elroy, and William Simon. 1998. "The Client: A Social, Psychological, and Behavioral Look at the Unseen Patron of Prostitution." In *Theater, Aristocracy, Pornography: The Orgy Calculus*, ed. James Elias et al. PAJ.

Thompson, Beverly Y. 2015. *Covered in Ink: Tattoos: Women and Politics of the Body*. New York: New York University Press.

Thompson, Beverly Y., and Miss Couple. "Consent and Ethics Within Sex Work and Research: An Academic and Practitioners Perspective." *Sexualities*, December 16, 2020, 1-7.

Thompson, Sharon, ed. *Powers of Desire: The Politics of Sexuality*. New York: Monthly Review.

Trub, Valerie. 1996. "The Psychomorphology of the Clitoris." *GLQ* 2:81–113.

Van Gennep, Arnold. 1960. *Rites of Passage*. Chicago: University of Chicago Press.

Viladrich, Anahi. 2013. *More Than Two to Tango: Argentine Tango Immigrants in New York City*. Tuscon: University of Arizona Press.

Wagner-Pacifici, Robin. 2007. *What Is an Event?* Chicago: University of Chicago Press.

Walkowitz, Judith R., and Catherine R. Stimpson. 1992. *City of Dreadful Delight: Narratives of Sexual Danger in Late Victorian London*. Women in Culture and Society. Chicago: University of Chicago Press.

Weber, Max. 1958. *The City*. New York: Free Press.

Weeks, Jeffrey. 1997. "Inverts, Perverts, and Mary-Annes." In *The Subcultures Reader*, ed. Ken Gelder and Sarah Thornton, 268–81. London: Routledge.

Weitzer, Ron. 2000a. "Why We Need More Research on Sex-Work." In *Sex for Sale: Prostitution, Pornography, and the Sex Industry*, ed. Ron Weitzer, 1–17. New York: Routledge.

Whitley, Cameron. 2015. "Trans-Subjectivity: Exploring Research Positionality in the Field." *Qualitative Sociological Review* 11, no. 4: 67–80.

Williams, Linda. 1989. *Hardcore: Power, Pleasure, and the Frenzy of the Visible*. Berkeley: University of California Press.

Williams, Terry, and Trevor Milton. 2015. *The Con Men: Hustling in New York City*. New York: Columbia University Press.

Willis, Paul. 2001. *The Ethnographic Imagination*. London: Polity.

Wolff, Kurt H. 1950. *The Sociology of Georg Simmel*. New York: Free Press.

Zola, Emile. 1928. *The Works of Emile Zola*. New York: Walter J. Black Co.

Index

customers: clients, 93, 95, 96, 98–102,
104–106, *108*, 108–113, 117–130; at Club
Edelweiss, 62–64, 66–67, 69, 70–73; at
Club Glamour, 73–75; creeps, 99, 106,
108, 141–142, 153; as dancers, 47–48,
49–50; dress codes for, 55; at Frisco Club,
89; at Gray Gardens, 77–78; Hogs &
Heifers, 46–50; at Kinematics, 83–84,
90–92; objectification of, 89–90; patrons,
168, 183–184, 186–188, 192–195, 198–200,
209–220, 222, 225–229, 241–247; Roxy
Theater, 86–87; strip club, 41, 43–45,
52–53; of topless dancers, 30, 31–32, 33
cutting and piercing workshop, Paddle Club,
191–193

dancers: at Blue Angel, 37–46; customers as,
47–48, 49–50; dress codes for, 53; lap, 39,
40, 51, 52, 54, 146; masturbating, 40, 41;
at Private Eyes Club, 53–54; Stiletto,
51–53; topless, 29–34
dancing: in front of mirrors, 64, 211, 212;
A Touch of Class, 211–215; without
touching, 138
dead citizenship, of heterosexuality, 261
degradation ceremonies, 167
Delany, Samuel, 50
Dell, Michelle, 10, 46
DeMars, Venus, 59
demographics, escorts, 113
Department of Buildings, NYC, 6
Department of City Planning study (1994), 6
Desclos, Anne, 177
desensitization, 187
desire, 110; action and, 132–133; fulfillment,
32; heterosexual, 223, 239; mutual
interaction, 14; positionality and, 26; sex
and, 86
desperation, 140, 142, 190, 279n2
deviant behaviors, 94–95, 97, 116, 224
dildos, 83, 91, 101, 183, 186, 189, 232

discrimination, racial, 71
Disneyfication, of Times Square, 4, 7, 264
dissonance anxiety, odors and, 133, 134
Divine (actor, drag queen), 69
Divine Gusty Winds, Urge MC, 244–247
DJs, 44–45, 53, 74, 211, 212, 220, 254
dominatrix: in corsets, 144, 206; Hellfire
Club, 186, 188–189; at Parasoul Club
fetish party, 144–146; Pyramid Club, 204;
at TES "Anal & Vaginal Fisting" meeting,
176–177, 181
DomSubFriends, cutting and piercing
workshop, 191–193
drag: gender and, 69; public sex march, 261;
queens, 65, 69, 184, 241, 244–246, 253, 263
dress codes, 53, 55. *See also* clothing
drivers, escort agencies, 100, 101, 111
drugs, 67, 94, 101, 106, 111, 115, 119, 133.
See also alcohol
dykes, 38, 224–228, 281n1

economy: champagne sales, 30–31; erotic
capital, 27, 35, 95, 113; escort agency
business costs, 93; escorts and, 113; fees,
20, 36, 42, 51, 53, 80, 89, 143, 169, 179, 187,
192, 209, 228, 230; money, 29, 30, 32, 33,
40, 43, 44, 93, 95, 97, 100, 101, 108, 110,
111–112, 113, 117, 118, 119, 122, 123, 152, 241,
255, 256, 280n11; pimps and hos, 20;
sexical labor, 95; sex market, 61–62, 152,
153, 159; underground, 152
education level, escorts, 113
electronic surveillance, 280n11
emotional labor, 96, 109, 119
emotions: body and, 113; shame, 2, 19, 25–26,
167, 199; smells and, 131; swinger events
and, 208; women and, 229
enemas, fisting and, 176
entrepreneurial spirit, 29
erotic capital, 27, 35, 95, 113
erotic gratifications, 222–223

escort agencies: bookers, 100, 105, 106,
110-111; call-girl operations and, 100,
104-105, 113, 116; clients, 93, 95, 96,
98-101, 102, 104-106, *108*, 108-112, 113,
117-130; with culture and race, 95;
drivers, 100, 101, 111; fuck the agency, 97,
100, 101; ledger of professional clients,
108; ledger of professional workers, *107*;
with money and business costs, 93;
orientation, 103, 111; owners, 93, 95, 96,
101-106, 110-114, 116-121; security, 93, 113
escorts (girls): acting, 113, 120; with age and
beauty hierarchy, 95, 96, 105; black
books, 103, 105; bookers and, 110-111;
boyfriends of, 93, 95, 101, 126; clothing,
101, 102; cocaine, 106; with creeps, 99,
106, 108; demographics and education
level, 113; with emotional labor, 96, 109,
119; families of, 97-98, 104, 114-115; fuck
the agency, 97, 100, 101; hierarchy, 109,
111-112; in-calls, 121-130; ledger of
professional, *107*; Madam X as, 101, 103,
109-110, 114, 116; money and, 97, 101, 110,
111-112, 113, 117, 118, 119, 122, 123; as
pimps, 93; rules for, 104, 105, 106;
security checks for, 98-99, 117-118; sex
and, 104, 105, 109, 111-113, 118-120,
122-130; S&M and, 113, 119; voice sex, 112
exploitation, of women, 33, 34, 38, 53

fabrics, clothing, 153
Fabric Factory, foot fetish worship, *132*
fag hags, 243
families, 121; of cross-dressers, 72; of escorts,
97-98, 104, 114-115
fantasies, 133; clothing and, 154-155; of
dominatrix, 188; of escort agency clients,
99, 101; gender as illusion and, 72; S&M,
194; Soft City as, 260; tickling, 18; topless
bars and, 33
fantasy bank, 190, 213

fashion, 159, 162, 163. *See also* clothing
fast sex, 93, 115
FBI, 122, 280n11
fear: of genitals, 162; knife play to build up,
196
fees: admission, 20, 36, 42, 51, 53, 80, 143,
169, 179, 187, 192, 209, 228, 230; peep
show, 89
feet. *See* foot
female identity, bathrooms and, 66-67
feminism, S&M, bondage and, 181
feminists, 33, 42
femmes du monde, 116
fetish: fashion and, 159, 162; gear, 152-158;
latex, 91; leather, 91, 153, 161; as magical
charm, 160; Marxist use of, 159, 160;
parties, *15*, 16-18, 142-151, 198;
pornography, 83; psychoanalysis and, 159,
160, 162; shoes, 160-162
Fetish (Steele), 159
fetishism, 159, 160
films, 24, 63, 69, 80, 90-91, 110, 260
fistees, as receptacles, 177
fisting. *See* "Anal & Vaginal Fisting" meeting,
TES
Flesh Theatre party, 145
foot: binding, 278n3; fetishism, 14, 16-18,
109-110, *132*, 146-151; models, 16, 279n2;
odors, 150
Foucault, Michel, 160
freedom, freelancing and, 96-97
Freud, Lucien, 78, 278n2 (chap. 2), 279n10
Freud, Sigmund, 162
Frisco Club, Times Square, 88-90
front region, 76
frontstage behaviors, 56, 239
fuck the agency, escorts, 97, 100, 101
futurity, heterosexual culture and, 260-261

gay marketplace, race in, 18-19
Gay New York (Chauncey), 259

sexuality: attraction and, 149; with people as surfaces, 78; space and, 239

sexual labor, beauty and, 95

sexually transmitted diseases (STDs), 94, 122

sexual proletariat, 277n4

sex-video bookstores, 4

sex work: as career identity, 94; industry, 29, 33–34, 55, 100, 279n2; power and, 18; stigma of, 98

sex workers, 27, 33, 97; with emotional labor, 96, 109, 119; with hierarchy and systemic racism, 94; with rape as "theft of services," 98, 279n4; sisterhood, 34. *See also* escorts; prostitutes

Sexy New York City guide, 227

shame, 2, 19, 25–26, 167, 199

shaming degradation, 167

shit, 109, 176

shoes: fetish, 160–162; high heels, 158, 162, 163, 201, 204, 205–206

shopping, in sex stores: experience, 153–156; money spent, 152

Show World Center (SWC), 13, 23, 27, 28, 59, 80, 85

silence, 19, 86, 183, 213, 219, 234, 240

silicone implants, 60

Simmel, Georg, 202

Sinatra, Nancy, 88, 279n3

sisterhood, sex workers, 34

60–40 rule, 6

slaves, 90, 159, 163, 166–168; dominatrix and, 176–177, 181; masters fisting, 169, 171–176, 180–181; submissives, 191–193, 196, 204

slut shaming, 167

S&M, 12–14, 24, 90, 113, 119, 194, 198

S&M, bondage and: BDSM, 94, 157, 159, 160, 164, 182; cutting and piercing workshop, 191–193; feminism and, 181; Gene Frankel Theater, 167–170, 178–180; Hellfire Club, 182–190; mirrors, 186, 187; real-life

"event," 166–167; TES "Anal & Vaginal Fisting" meeting, 167–181

smells: alcohol, 256; Body Shop, 133–134; emotions and, 131; fabrics, 153; foot fetishism, 150; leather fetish, 153, 161; odors, 131, 133, 134, 150; pheromones, 150, 207; setting defined by, 131, 133; sex, 134, 202, 207, 208; touch and, 131, 133, 139; Truth Club, 137–138; The Vault, 198

social function, of topless bars, 33

socialization, psychoanalysis and, 222

social production of value, modeling and, 113–114

social worlds, 9, 197, 232, 234, 259, 262

sociology, 1, 50, 151

Soft City, 5, 7; future of, 260–264; Hard City and, 8, 233, 261; as invisible and "soft," 8, 13–14, 93; as nomadic, 8, 61, 142, 191; sex market, 61–62, 152, 153, 159; urban ceremonials in, 197–198

Soho Hotel, 10

sounds: fabrics, 153; fisting, 172–174, 175; A Touch of Class, 201–202; at The Vault, 25, 199. *See also* music

South America, 62, 64, 65, 118

spaces: gay, 224, 230–238, 240–248, 251; lesbian, 59, 224–229; perverse, 249, 256–257; power, knowledge and, 239; private, 4, 6; public, 4, 6, 7, 277n4; sexuality and, 239; technology, sex and, 260; zoning ordinance and performance, 277n4

spanking, 144–145, 146, 184–185, 188, 194

speed culture, 115

spiritual connections, 150

spitting, Hellfire Club, 141–142

Splash, 241, 251

spoiled identity, 98

Spring Fling, at Pieces, 249, 259

STDs (sexually transmitted diseases), 94, 122

Steele, Valerie, 159

Stiletto (strip club), 51–53, 54, 55

Stonewall Inn, 4